100 Documentary Films

100 DOCUMENTARY FILMS

BFI screen guides

Barry Keith Grant & Jim Hillier

A BFI book published by Palgrave Macmillan

First published in 2009 by
PALGRAVE MACMILLAN

on behalf of the

BRITISH FILM INSTITUTE
21 Stephen Street, London W1T 1LN
www.bfi.org.uk

There's more to discover about film and television through the BFI. Our world-renowned archive, cinemas, festivals, films, publications and learning resources are here to inspire you.

Palgrave Macmillan in the UK is an imprint of Macmillan Publishers Limited, registered in England, company number 785998, of Houndmills, Basingstoke, Hampshire RG21 6XS. Palgrave Macmillan in the US is a division of St Martin's Press LLC, 175 Fifth Avenue, New York, NY 10010. Palgrave Macmillan is the global academic imprint of the above companies and has companies and representatives throughout the world. Palgrave® and Macmillan® are registered trademarks in the United States, the United Kingdom, Europe and other countries.

Series cover design: Paul Wright
Cover image: *Bowling for Columbine* (Michael Moore, 2002, © Iconolatory Productions Inc/© Babelsberger Filmproduktion GmbH)
Series design: Ketchup/couch
Set by Cambrian Typesetters, Camberley, Surrey
Printed in China

This book is printed on paper suitable for recycling and made from fully managed and sustained forest sources. Logging, pulping and manufacturing processes are expected to conform to the environmental regulations of the country of origin.

British Library Cataloguing-in-Publication Data
A catalogue record for this book is available from the British Library

ISBN 978–1–84457–264–9 (pbk)
ISBN 978–1–84457–265–6 (hbk)

Contents

Acknowledgments ix
Introduction 1

À propos de Nice, Jean Vigo, 1930 7
The Act of Seeing with One's Own Eyes, Stan Brakhage, 1971 10
The Atomic Café, Jane Loader, Kevin Rafferty, Pierce Rafferty,
      1982 12
The Battle of Chile/La batalla de Chile, Patricio Guzmán,
      1975–9 14
*Berlin: Symphony of a Great City/Berlin: Die Sinfonie der
      Großstadt*, Walter Ruttmann, 1927 16
Bowling for Columbine, Michael Moore, 2002 19
A British Picture: Portrait of an Enfant Terrible, Ken Russell,
      1989 21
British Sounds, Jean-Luc Godard, Jean-Henri Roger, 1969 23
Bus 174, José Padilha, 2002 25
Cane Toads: An Unnatural History, Mark Lewis, 1988 27
Le Chagrin et la pitié/The Sorrow and the Pity, Marcel Ophüls,
      1969 29
Chronique d'un été/Chronicle of a Summer, Jean Rouch,
      Edgar Morin, 1961 32
Close-Up, Abbas Kiarostami, 1990 35
Coal Face, Alberto Cavalcanti, 1935 37
Crisis: Behind a Presidential Commitment, Robert Drew, 1963 39
Daughter Rite, Michelle Citron, 1980 42
David Holzman's Diary, Jim McBride, 1967 44

Dead Birds, Robert Gardner, 1965 46

A Diary for Timothy, Humphrey Jennings, 1945 48

Dont Look Back, D. A. Pennebaker, 1967 51

The Emperor's Naked Army Marches On, Hara Kazuo, 1987 54

Être et avoir, Nicolas Philibert, 2002 56

The Fall of the Romanov Dynasty, Esfir Shub, 1927 59

Farrebique, Georges Rouquier, 1946 61

Fast, Cheap and Out of Control, Errol Morris, 1997 64

For Freedom, Hossein Torabi, 1979 66

Forgotten Silver, Peter Jackson, Costa Botes, 1995 68

Les Glâneurs et la glâneuse/The Gleaners and I, Agnès Varda,
    2000 70

Grey Gardens, Albert and David Maysles, Ellen Hovde,
    Muffie Meyer, 1975 73

Grizzly Man, Werner Herzog, 2005 75

Handsworth Songs, John Akomfrah, 1986 78

A Happy Mother's Day, Richard Leacock, Joyce Chopra, 1963 80

Harlan County USA, Barbara Kopple, 1976 82

Harvest of Shame, David Lowe, 1960 85

Heidi Fleiss: Hollywood Madam, Nick Broomfield, 1995 87

Hoop Dreams, Steve James, 1994 89

The Hour of the Furnaces/La hora de los hornos, Octavio Getino,
    Fernando Ezequiel Solanas, 1968 92

Housing Problems, Edgar Anstey, Arthur Elton, 1935 94

Las Hurdes/Land without Bread, Luis Buñuel, 1933 97

I for India, Sandhya Suri, 2005 100

In the Year of the Pig, Emile de Antonio, 1968 102

Jazz, Ken Burns, 2001 105

Kon-Tiki, Thor Heyerdahl, 1950 107

Koyaanisqatsi: Life Out of Balance, Godfrey Reggio, 1982 110

Lessons in Darkness/Lektionen in Finsternis, Werner Herzog,
    1992 112

Let There Be Light, John Huston, 1946 114

The Life and Times of Rosie the Riveter, Connie Field, 1980 116

Lonely Boy, Wolf Koenig, Roman Kroitor, 1962 118

Lost Lost Lost, Jonas Mekas, 1976 121

Lumière Programme, Louis and Auguste Lumière, 1895 123

Les Maîtres fous, Jean Rouch, 1955 126

Manhatta, Charles Sheeler, Paul Strand, 1921 128

Man of Aran, Robert Flaherty, 1934 130

Man with a Movie Camera, Dziga Vertov, 1929 133

March of the Penguins/La Marche de l'empereur, Luc Jacquet,

    2005 136

A Married Couple, Allan King, 1969 138

Minamata, Tsuchimoto Noriaki, 1971 140

My Winnipeg, Guy Maddin, 2007 143

Nanook of the North, Robert Flaherty, 1922 145

Native Land, Leo Hurwitz, Paul Strand, 1942 147

Necrology, Standish Lawder, 1971 149

New Earth/Nieuwe gronden, Joris Ivens, 1934 151

News from Home, Chantal Akerman, 1976 154

North Sea, Harry Watt, 1938 158

Nuit et brouillard/Night and Fog, Alain Resnais, 1955 161

Not a Love Story: A Film about Pornography, Bonnie Sherr Klein,

    1981 163

One Man's War/La Guerre d'un seul homme, Edgardo

    Cozarinsky, 1982 165

Paris Is Burning, Jennie Livingston, 1990 167

People on Sunday/Menschen am Sonntag, Robert Siodmak,

    Edgar G. Ulmer, 1930 169

The Plow that Broke the Plains, Pare Lorentz, 1936 171

Portrait of Jason, Shirley Clarke, 1967 174

Primary, Robert Drew, 1960 177

Primate, Frederick Wiseman, 1974 179

Les Racquetteurs/The Snowshoers, Michel Brault, Gilles Groulx,

    1958 181

Roger and Me, Michael Moore, 1989 183

Salesman, Albert and David Maysles, Charlotte Zwerin, 1968 185

Le Sang des bêtes, Georges Franju, 1949 .187

Sans soleil/Sunless, Chris Marker, 1983 190

79 Primaveras/79 Springs, Santiago Alvarez, 1969 194

Shipyard, Paul Rotha, 1935 196

Shoah, Claude Lanzmann, 1985 199

El sol del membrillo/The Quince Tree Sun/The Dream of Light,
    Victor Erice, 1992 202

The Spanish Earth, Joris Ivens, 1937 204

Surname Viet Given Name Nam, Trinh T. Minh-ha, 1989 206

Talking Heads, Krzysztof Kieślowski, 1980 208

The Thin Blue Line, Errol Morris, 1988 211

This Is Spinal Tap, Rob Reiner, 1984 214

Time Indefinite, Ross McElwee, 1993 216

Titicut Follies, Frederick Wiseman, 1967 218

Tongues Untied, Marlon Riggs, 1990 220

Triumph of the Will/Triumph des Willens, Leni Riefenstahl, 1935 222

Truth or Dare, Alek Keshishian, 1991 225

Turksib, Victor A. Turin, 1929 227

Very Nice, Very Nice, Arthur Lipsett, 1961 .230

Waiting for Fidel, Michael Rubbo, 1974 232

The War Game, Peter Watkins, 1965 234

We Are the Lambeth Boys, Karel Reisz, 1958 236

When the Levees Broke, Spike Lee, 2006 .239

Why We Fight 1: Prelude to War, Frank Capra, 1943 241

Woodstock, Michael Wadleigh, 1970 243

Zidane: A 21st Century Portrait, Douglas Gordon, Philippe
    Parreno, 2006 245

References 248

Select Bibliography 250

Index 253

Acknowledgments

Barry Keith Grant would like to thank Rob Macmorine, technician in the Department of Communications, Popular Culture and Film, Brock University for his expertise and assistance, and Genevieve and Gabrielle Grant for their lively and thoughtful discussions about the dozens of documentary films we watched during the writing of this book. For logistical help, stimulus and encouragement, Jim Hillier would like to thank John Archer (Hopscotch Films), Chris Bacon (University of Reading), Jonathan Bignell (University of Reading), Paul Henley (University of Manchester), Aaron, Martha and Fiona Morey, Alastair Phillips (University of Warwick), Mike Stevenson (University of Reading) and Rosie Thomas (University of Westminster). Both would like to thank Rebecca Barden and Sophia Contento at BFI Publishing/Palgrave for their support.

Introduction

Twenty-five years ago it would have been difficult to predict the present high profile, prestige and level of production of documentary films made for theatrical cinema distribution and exhibition. During particular historical periods, such as the 1930s and the 1960s, documentary cinema proved particularly influential, but, historically, documentary film-making has often been associated more with television than with theatrical distribution and attracted limited critical attention. Over those last twenty-five years, however, documentary films intended for both theatrical and television release have become once again both commercially popular and the subject of intense critical scrutiny. Documentary film in various guises (some new, like so-called 'reality television') has remained a staple of television programming, and even been given a new lease of life through the proliferation of cable and digital channels, while documentaries made for theatrical exhibition have enjoyed commercial success unparalleled since the 1930s.

Those years have also been marked by a veritable explosion of critical writing about the documentary form, as our Select Bibliography makes clear, most notably perhaps in the 2005 publication of the three-volume *Encyclopedia of Documentary Film*, edited by Ian Aitken, a great resource for anyone interested in documentary cinema. Overall, documentary film has regained the very important place it occupied in both production and critical writing at various times in the past. This importance has been reflected also in the growth of higher education courses devoted to documentary cinema. Such popularity and critical interest speaks to what Bill Nichols calls our common 'epistephelia', our desire to know the world and how others perceive and make sense of it, and documentary film's particular relationship to the real world. This book tries to build upon this renewed vigour in documentary production and critical study by looking at 100 examples of documentary (or documentary-related) films from the last 110 years that we consider significant or influential, or both.

Of course, these developments should not really surprise us, because documentary or non-fiction film constitutes a major part of film history. Despite often being regarded as secondary to fiction cinema, the realm of non-fiction played an equally, if not more important, role in cinema's origins (though 'non-fiction' embraces a wider range of film-making than documentary – newsreel, for example). It represents the other 'half' – often submerged and even invisible – of cinema history. In historical, statistical terms, many more documentary/non-fiction films have been made than fiction films. Aesthetically and ethically, documentary/non-fiction cinema has always provided an important point of reference for fiction cinema, and the two have often overlapped and blurred the boundaries between them.

Our aim in this Introduction is not to try to define 'documentary film'. Many critics and theorists writing about documentary film have been beached on the rocky shores of an attempted encompassing definition of this distinctive form of non-fiction cinema. Such definitions always seem problematic or insufficient, always overwhelmed by the astonishing diversity of documentary film-making practice. This is especially true of debates about the supposed 'purity' of documentary and questions about the 'staged' and the 'unstaged'. John Grierson happily refers to arrangements, rearrangements and interpretations, and nobody really objected to reconstruction and dramatisation as valid and necessary documentary strategies until the late 1950s. It is true, certainly, that technical developments from the late 1950s *seemed* to make possible greater 'truth' or authenticity, the ability simply to observe and record. And this no doubt explains in part the emergence of what became known, variously, as 'documentary drama', 'docudrama' or 'drama documentary' forms in the 1960s, terms that were not considered necessary or appropriate for earlier documentaries featuring sometimes extensive dramatic reconstruction. There were then, of course, decisive further developments such as the late-1960s/1970s fashion for radical deconstruction and the 1980s/1990s preference for the 'post-modern', where the 'truth' being represented was often that there *is* no truth. Our entries try to chart such aesthetic and ethical developments, as well as some of the technological changes in cameras, sound recording, film stocks, video and digital recording, and so on, that prompted or accompanied them.

As scholars who have watched, enjoyed, lived with, pondered, taught and written about documentary film for decades, we certainly were aware of the enormous diversity of documentary production and the occasionally tenuous relationship between some supposed 'reality' and its representation in individual documentary films. Yet while researching and writing this book, we renewed our appreciation for the richness and diversity of the form, an appreciation that we hope comes across in the text.

It has proved extraordinarily difficult to choose just 100 films for inclusion. In part, this is because the equivalent of *100 Documentary Films* is not *100 Westerns* or *100 Bollywood Films* but '100 Fiction Films'. Looked at like that, it sometimes seemed absurd to try to select just 100 titles, and there were several hundred equally worthy documentary films waiting in line. To some small degree, we were influenced by other volumes in the '100' series: both Jason Wood's *100 American Independent Films* and Patrick Russell's *100 British Documentaries* include films that we seriously considered. In a few cases, we have written our own entries on the same titles, hoping to provide different insights, but both of those other volumes contain very useful accounts of documentary titles that we do not cover.

What *do* our choices represent? Certainly, we do not intend them to represent the 100 'best' (though no doubt some of the films would or could figure on some 'best documentaries ever made' list). We approached the task with the aim of being comprehensive rather than canonical, while recognising that many canonical films have been groundbreaking or influential. Across our entries we try to sketch out a history of documentary film-making and its changing aesthetics, technology, means of distribution, fashions. Over half of the films are North American, and a dozen or so more were also made in the English language. This might be considered disproportionate, but it reflects both the cultures in which the authors live and work and the greater difficulties encountered by documentary films – as compared with fiction films – in finding distribution via cinemas, television or video: the global reach of many documentary films often remains significantly more constrained to domestic markets, or those defined by language, than is the case with fiction films. Nevertheless, we are acutely aware of the low level of representation in the book of, for example, African and Asian documentary film-making. At the same time, it is certainly true that over the last fifty years English-language documentary films – no doubt in part due to the international power of their cinema and television distributors – have been very important in shaping debates about the changing forms and functions of documentary.

Availability has been a crucial issue for the selection of titles, for several reasons. In most cases, we needed to re-see films, so availability was vital. Then, too, there seemed to us limited point in talking about 100 documentary films that no reader – or very few readers – would be able to see. At the same time, making availability an absolute criterion would mean accepting the priorities of an often random market, so that while a number of the films discussed here are not readily accessible, we considered them important enough to include nevertheless. Perhaps their inclusion here can help to encourage availability. Given the overwhelming choice at hand and the shortage of space to write about them, it may seem perverse that several of our entries are fictions ('mockumentaries', for example) or films that significantly blur the boundaries between documentary and fiction, but it is our view that such films – which represent a powerful tendency in documentary film-making over the last twenty-five years – have used the stylistic strategies of documentary film-making in ways that have been highly productive for discussions about the nature of documentary. Similarly, aware that definitions of documentary have often been rather narrow, we have included a number of films that many might classify more readily as 'avant-garde' or 'experimental'; here again, we hope our entries will encourage rethinking about rigidly narrow definitions and inflexible boundaries.

Other factors came into play in making our choices. We wanted to ensure that there would be adequate representation of most periods, however uneven, though it will be readily apparent that the period 1895–1920 (during which, as Bill Nichols puts it, there was a 'striking absence . . . of any single word for what we now call documentary and no clear frame of reference for either the production or reception of such works') is, to say the least, under-represented (though *100 British Documentaries* discusses several films from this period that could certainly be thought of as documentaries). Similarly, despite our earlier points about the preponderance of English-language films, we wanted to include titles that reflected a broad range of national and ethnic backgrounds and represented a variety of documentary types and formal approaches. Though it was clearly important to include examples of the work of exceptional documentary film-makers or auteurs, we decided, given the limitations of space, that no single film-maker, no matter how important in our view, would be represented by more than two entries.

Ultimately, the list attempts to balance titles that are accepted as having major status within the documentary form, works that open up some of the critical, theoretical and aesthetic issues central to it, and films that, though not necessarily much written about, we find of particular interest and value. Despite the many recent worthy books about documentary film, no work that we knew of offered a substantial number of authoritative, but relatively short, critical commentaries on individual documentary films. We try to place films within their historical and aesthetic contexts and to extend those contexts by frequent cross-references to other films discussed in the volume (as well as to films not included in the book). Wherever possible, to try to provide something of their flavour, we refer to specific images or scenes from the films under discussion.

Following the design format of other volumes in the series, the films are arranged alphabetically, though a chronological ordering might have made more sense in this case. In the case of non-English-language films, we have tried to use as the main entry title the title by which we think, largely intuitively, the film is best known – sometimes in the original language, sometimes in English; to try to avoid confusion, such films are entered under both their original and translated titles in the index. Each entry provides an appraisal followed by brief credits. Film titles in CAPITALS within an entry cross-refer to other entries (though there are also references to other documentary films of related interest that are not included in the volume). Occasionally, entries quote or refer to specific critical sources: we have not provided these with full academic citations, but they can be followed up by referring to the list of References at the end of the book. Finally, for further reading, we provide a Select Bibliography.

À propos de Nice
France, 1930 – 25 mins
Jean Vigo

Jean Vigo made only four films before dying at a young age of tuberculosis, and only one of them is a documentary, but *À propos de Nice* has become regarded as the most lyrical of city symphony films. While this short film about the decadent lifestyle of the leisured class who vacation at the resort town of Nice on the French Riviera is comprised in

large part of documentary footage, it is as much poetic as it is polemical, as much avant-garde experimentalism as it is documentary exposé.

Shot by Boris Kaufman, brother of Mikhail Kaufman, cinematographer on Vertov's MAN WITH A MOVIE CAMERA (1929), Vigo's treatment of Nice clearly borrows from the earlier film, as well as from BERLIN: SYMPHONY OF A GREAT CITY (1927). However, *À propos de Nice* differs noticeably from other city symphony films in a number of respects. While films in this tradition tend to valorise the scale, efficiency and vitality of the cities they show, *À propos de Nice*, even as it focuses on a number of literal celebrations, seems more caustic than commemorative in its appraisal. Like these other films, it emphasises shots of sport and physical activity (tennis, bocce ball, auto racing), but in contrast to them, it presents the energy of Nice as manic and superficial, like the frantic Charleston danced by the row of flappers, an image to which Vigo keeps returning towards the end of the film, this insistent return itself echoing the frenzied determination of the dancers.

À propos de Nice does not adhere to the 'day-in-the-life' approach of *Berlin* and *Man with a Movie Camera*, though it does incorporate scenes, such as the early shots of street sweeping and later shots of dancers in the evening, that might suggest such a structure. Instead, the film is constructed more associatively than chronologically, revealing Vigo's interest in surrealism. It begins boldly, with shots of fireworks in the night sky, functioning both as a fanfare for the film that is beginning and as an opening thematic statement about Nice as a flashy spectacle. Rather than bringing us into the city from the perspective of a train, as *Berlin* does, Vigo introduces Nice in a series of aerial shots taken from an airplane, suggesting that the film's view will be from above it all, detached from the city's party atmosphere. He then shows us a pair of dolls dressed as tourists, swept away by a croupier on a gaming table. Shots of Mediterranean waves breaking on the shore follow, suggesting that this fate awaits every new group of tourists visiting Nice. Images of strollers promenading on the seaside boardwalk, many photographed by Kaufman from a camera hidden in his lap as Vigo pushed him along in a wheelchair, show them to humorous effect, as in the shot of a woman dressed in furs followed by an image of an ostrich craning its neck. In a series of dissolves, one woman appears in a variety of outfits, then finally without any clothes, stripped bare of the surface signifiers of her social class and pretensions. Recurring shots of the giant papier-mâché figures suggest the narcissistic egotism of the people there, while the surprising cutaway of trash in the gutters reminds us of the wastefulness of their lifestyle. Vigo's disdainful view of Nice was doubtless influenced by the anarchist views of his father, who died in jail under suspicious circumstances. BKG

Dir: Jean Vigo, Boris Kaufman; **Scr**: Jean Vigo; **Phot**: Mikhail Kaufman (b/w).

The Act of Seeing with One's Own Eyes
US, 1971 – 32 mins
Stan Brakhage

Stan Brakhage's grand theme was vision, specifically our ability to look at the world in new and open ways, a preoccupation that is central to one of his greatest films, *The Act of Seeing with One's Own Eyes*. In his famous essay 'Metaphors on Vision', Brakhage enjoined the reader to 'Imagine . . . an eye unprejudiced by compositional logic, an eye which does not respond to the name of everything but which must know each object encountered in life through an adventure of perception.' *The Act of Seeing with One's Own Eyes* (the literal meaning of the Latin word 'autopsy') is an attempt to put this call into practice by challenging viewers to look at a normally taboo sight in a way that abandons the sense of abject disgust – a culturally learned response – with which we normally regard the process and so keep hidden from the public view.

Like other experimental film-makers such as Bruce Conner and Standish Lawder (NECROLOGY, 1971), Brakhage often employed documentary material to explore perceptual adventure, as in, for example, *The Wonder Ring* (1955), an Impressionist documentary that chronicles both a ride on the Third Avenue El, Manhattan's only remaining elevated subway line, and the film-maker's interest in the play of light and shadow produced by the moving train and its raised structure on a sunny day. Among Brakhage's most representational works, *The Act of Seeing* at the same time pushes toward metaphysical abstraction.

One of three films made in 1971 and known informally as the Pittsburgh Trilogy (the other two being *Eyes*, about the police department, and *Deus Ex*, about open heart surgery), *The Act of Seeing* is composed of numerous shots of relatively short duration showing various aspects of the autopsy process. As with almost all of Brakhage's work, the film is silent, allowing the viewer's attention to focus exclusively on the images. As it is not about the autopsy process as such, but our perceptions of and attitudes about it, the film does not present the process in a linear fashion, making explicit the various steps, though in a general sense it does bring us forwards from the beginning to the end of the procedure. Brakhage was not allowed to show the faces of the deceased (most of which have been, in any case, peeled away so that their skulls can be opened), and this restriction becomes a means for the film to address more the wider theme of our cultural attitude towards death. Early on, we see hands with pens and rulers prod and examine bodies, but then Brakhage seeks to move us beyond measurement and science, beyond such 'compositional logic'. The opening shots of one examination discreetly frame the body so that the genitalia remain out of view, but soon enough this taboo is violated and the camera shows all the body parts, even looking within torsos and heads.

Brakhage manipulates the camera's lens aperture and depth of field, transforming the normally abject sight of the interior of the human body into a wondrous drama of colours and textures. At times, the images go dark momentarily, Brakhage closing and reopening the lens aperture as if flinching from the sights he is filming, but the camera remains steadfast, just as the sight of a brain being lifted from its skull begins out of focus but soon sharpens. Towards the end of the film, a body is wheeled out of the autopsy room as the camera focuses on the doors closing behind it; in this film, in contrast, Brakhage succeeds in opening for us the doors of perception. BKG

Dir/Phot/Ed: Stan Brakhage (colour).

The Atomic Café
US, 1982 – 92 mins
Jane Loader, Kevin Rafferty, Pierce Rafferty

A masterfully crafted compilation documentary, *The Atomic Café* is about the dawn of the atomic age, the Cold War that followed and their impact on American culture and politics. Eschewing a voiceover narration and composed entirely of footage and audio clips from the 1940s and 1950s, including public-service announcements, newsreels, television news, advertisements, radio broadcasts and military training films, the film is structured as a historical narrative that shows how post-war America responded to the new reality of the Bomb. The film's array of visuals, gathered over a research period of five years by Pierce Rafferty and his assistants from almost two dozen sources including Fox Movietone News, the Library of Congress, Los Alamos Scientific Laboratories and the BBC, is matched on the soundtrack by a collage of contemporaneous pop music tunes that use the atomic bomb as a metaphor for love and desire ('I can't stand this cold, cold war with you'), revealing how thoroughly post-war consciousness was preoccupied with nuclear weaponry.

The archival material presented in the film is infused simultaneously with a frightening paranoia and camp humour, as with Burt the Turtle, the cartoon figurehead of the 'Duck and Cover' campaign that had schoolchildren across the US hiding under their desks in preparation for a nuclear attack. But Burt's duck-and-cover exercise, *The Atomic Café* suggests, is more a case of a collective burying of heads in the sand than a plausible defensive measure. (The film's final words are spoken by a reassuring father to his children in their fallout shelter: 'Nothing to do now but wait for the authorities and relax.') The title refers to a roadside diner, which we see briefly at one point, with its kitsch sign featuring a nuclear explosion at the top that bespeaks the curious admixture of anxiety, commercialisation and trivialisation of potential atomic devastation that the film argues characterised American society.

Reminiscent of Peter Watkins's *The War Game* (1965), politicians, priests and other authorities of the day appear as talking heads offering Cold War opinions as they struggle to reconcile morality to mass destruction.

It is easy to laugh at some of the archival material in *The Atomic Café*, such as the clip of the two earnest girl scouts who, following the dictum of being prepared, have canned a wide variety of foods for a possible stay in a fallout shelter. The humour arises partly from the girls' blissful ignorance of the magnitude of atomic destruction, though this same lack of knowledge seems horrifying in the army footage of soldiers witnessing a nuclear test without protective gear and then emerging from their foxholes and walking towards ground zero (many of them would later develop leukaemia and other illnesses). And certainly there is nothing at all funny about the shots of the radiation burns and poisoning suffered by *hibakusha*, the victims of the Hiroshima and Nagasaki atomic bombings, shown early on. The film's combination of the serious and the silly is well modulated to prevent viewers from watching it with the kind of passive placidity that seems to inform the many stereotypical nuclear families of the era we see in the film gathered around their television sets and radios. One of the film's directors, Kevin Rafferty, who has produced and directed several other documentaries, including *Feed* (1992), a comic look at the 1992 New Hampshire primaries, was a cinematographer on Michael Moore's ROGER AND ME (1989) and an acknowledged influence on Moore, who similarly combines comic and disturbing elements in his documentaries. BKG

Dir/Prod: Jane Loader, Kevin Rafferty, Pierce Rafferty; **Ed**: Jane Loader, Kevin Rafferty; **Sound**: Marge Crimmins, Lee Dichter; **Prod Co**: Archives Project, Inc.

The Battle of Chile (*La batalla de Chile*)
Venezuela/France/Cuba, 1975–9 – 265 mins
Patricio Guzmán

Patricio Guzmán, a 'privileged witness' of Chile's 'peaceful path to socialism', had already devoted several documentaries to the subject before the 1973 events that ended in the military *coup d'état* and Salvador Allende's death. *The Battle of Chile* (or 'The Battle *for* Chile'), one of the most important political films of its era, documents those events.

Part 1 ('The Insurrection of the Bourgeoisie', 1975, 96 mins) begins with dramatic footage of the 11 September bombing of the Moneda presidential palace, then flashes back to Allende's Popular Unity February election victory, attempts by the right (with CIA support) to orchestrate a slide into paralysis (strikes by transportation owners and copper miners, and street demonstrations designed to destabilise the government) and attempts to counter them (workers' occupations of factories, government strategies to distribute food and pro-government demonstrations). It ends with the notorious footage of army officers, during a premature, failed coup on 29 June, firing directly at Argentinian reporter Leonardo Henricksen, whose camera, still running, topples sideways as he dies.

Part 2 ('The Coup d'État', 1977, 88 mins) begins with the Henricksen footage and follows events from June to September, when the right began to engineer a military coup, ending with the Moneda bombing, the televised press conference by Pinochet and other military chiefs, suspects being rounded up and Allende's final message about history belonging to the people, accompanied by the sound of gunfire and sirens.

Part 3 ('Popular Power', or 'The Power of the People', 1979, 79 mins) is more reflective (achieved partly by introducing music), forgoing the dramatic chronology of Parts 1 and 2, and makes no reference to the coup. Employing unused earlier footage, it examines unresolved political issues relevant to Allende's 'failure', such as factory and land expropriations and arming the people.

Though in the tradition of political Latin American film-making of LA HORA DE LOS HORNOS (1968), *The Battle of Chile* is not montage-based; *La hora de los hornos* was an agitprop polemic for change, while *The Battle of Chile* documents change in progress. It is not a compilation film like IN THE YEAR OF THE PIG (1968): though the Moneda bombing and Henricksen's death were borrowed news footage, almost all the rest was shot by Guzmán's team, in observational but interventionist cinéma vérité style. Like the Iranian film-makers of FOR FREEDOM (1979), Guzmán's team needed to respond to unfolding events, but planned the filming with a much clearer sense of the nature of the struggles and edited with greater hindsight. Similarly, hindsight very much informs our reading of the coup leaders' promises to respect the law and constitution that end Part 2, and a sequence showing senior officers talking together at an assassinated general's funeral strongly suggests plotting. The sympathies of the film's authoritative voiceover are clear: Henricksen's 'last shot', for example, 'doesn't only record his own death – he also records, two months before the final *putsch*, the true face of a sector of the Chilean armed forces', but 'the battle for Chile is not over'.

Guzmán, held for two weeks in Santiago's National Stadium before escaping into exile, dedicated the film to chief cameraman Jorge Müller Silva, one of the many 'disappeared', whose footage was smuggled out of Chile. In Paris to thank Chris Marker for supplying film stock, Guzmán made contacts that enabled him to use Cuba's ICAIC facilities to assemble the film. Since his return to Chile, Guzmán has made several other films about Allende and Pinochet, and has used *The Battle of Chile* to educate young people about the period. JH

Dir/Prod/Scr: Patricio Guzmán; **Phot**: Jorge Müller Silva (b/w); **Ed**: Pedro Chaskel; **Music** (Part 3): J. A. Quintano; **Prod Co**: Equipe Terco Año/Instituto Cubano de Arte e Industrias Cinematográficos/Chris Marker.

Berlin: Symphony of a Great City
(Berlin: Die Sinfonie der Großstadt)
Germany, 1927 – 65 mins
Walter Ruttmann

Berlin: Symphony of a Great City offers an extended montage that chronicles the 'day in the life' of this major German city. Along with both MANHATTA (1921) and Alberto Cavalcanti's *Rien que les heures* (1926), about Paris, it was one of the most important and influential works in the cycle of city symphony films popular during the 1920s and early 1930s. Director Walter Ruttmann began making abstract experimental films in the 1920s and then moved into documentary.

In the opening sequence, the camera approaches Berlin by train, the passing view becoming increasingly urban. Ruttmann uses the train to suggest the industrial modernisation of Berlin as well as to establish an editing rhythm that carries the film forwards like a locomotive along the tracks. The rhythm of the montage, along with the frequent movement of automobile traffic, as well as trains, streetcars and airplanes, adds to the kinetic sense of the big city as marked by constant flow and motion, recalling Piet Mondrian's abstract expressionist painting *Broadway Boogie Woogie* (1943). Once the train arrives in Berlin, the film slows to a more leisurely pace: it's daybreak, and as night becomes morning, shops open for business. As in Dziga Vertov's MAN WITH A MOVIE CAMERA (1929), sports activities feature prominently, similarly suggesting that the inhabitants of the city are as vigorous and vital as the metropolis itself. The film takes us through the day, concluding with scenes of Berlin's active nightlife, and includes shots of people playing hockey, skiing and sledding, as well as boxing matches and dance contests. Shots during the day of a wedding and a hearse suggest that the city is the lifeblood of its people, encompassing and accommodating every aspect of its citizens' lives.

At lunchtime workers break for a meal, as do the various animals in the zoo. The juxtaposition of humans and other animals is often amusing, as when the film cuts from shots of telephone conversations

and switchboard operators plugging in lines to a chattering monkey. However, at least two such instances of ironic editing suggest something more serious. In one, a shot of a policeman directing traffic followed by two rows of identical bobble-head toys nodding in unison implies conformity and sheepish obeisance on the part of citizens. The second matches a shot of workers entering a factory and cattle being corralled.

The image of a wealthy diner matched with a lion gnawing on a bone might suggest a Marxist view of class struggle in the manner of Eisenstein, as do the images of hungry children in rags, but some have argued that Ruttmann shows the city as a soulless urban space that is indifferent to the lives of individual people. At one point, a woman commits suicide by jumping from a bridge. The river swallows her up, and we see only a pool of water closing over her, a visual pattern echoed elsewhere in the film in shots of revolving doors, roller-coasters and swirling leaves. John Grierson admired *Berlin*, but thought it sacrificed social analysis for formalism, while Siegfried Kracauer considered its emphasis on formal editing patterns implied a fascist aesthetic, anticipating the rise of Nazism in Germany. Indeed, Ruttmann chose to remain in Germany after Hitler took power, directing several pro-Nazi documentaries and working as an assistant to Leni Riefenstahl on TRIUMPH OF THE WILL (1935). BKG

Dir: Walter Ruttmann; **Prod**: Karl Freund; **Scr**: Walter Ruttmann, Karl Freund, from an idea by Carl Mayer; **Phot**: Reimar Kuntze, Robert Baberske, Laszlo Schaffer, Karl Freund (b/w); **Ed**: Walter Ruttmann; **Music**: Edmund Meisel; **Prod Co**: Deutsche Vereins-Film/Les Productions Fox Europa.

Bowling for Columbine
US, 2002 – 120 mins
Michael Moore

Taking as his touchstone the April 1999 massacre at Columbine High School in Littleton, Colorado, by two disaffected students, Eric Harris and Dylan Klebold, Michael Moore's *Bowling for Columbine* explores the US's obsession with guns and violence, relating the school tragedy to larger issues of a culture that promotes paranoia and fear. As in his other films ROGER AND ME (1989), *Fahrenheit 9/11* (1994) and *Sicko* (2007), as well as his short-lived television series *TV Nation* (1994), Moore inserts himself in his work as a vérité catalyst; but unlike the self-effacing Ross McElwee (see TIME INDEFINITE, 1993) and considerably more aggressively than Nick Broomfield (see HEIDI FLEISS: HOLLYWOOD MADAM, 1995), Moore, with his folksy and dumpy baseball cap-wearing persona, not only investigates but also prods and provokes his profilmic subjects. As it happens, Moore is a card-carrying member of the politically powerful National Rifle Association, and here his familiarity with firearms allows him to meet and interview a Michigan militia group and actor Charlton Heston, at the time president of the NRA.

Employing a more eclectic approach than either McElwee or Broomfield, *Bowling for Columbine* incorporates animation, archival footage and pop songs along with its vérité interviews. As in Moore's other documentaries, the film also mixes tones, combining humour with seriousness, shifting abruptly and uncomfortably from one to the other in a manner that is ultimately disturbing. For example, during an interview James Nichols, brother of Terry Nichols, one of the men convicted in the bombing of a federal building in Oklahoma City, the deadliest act of domestic terrorism in US history, in a tense moment shows Moore the loaded .44 Magnum he keeps under his pillow and then observes that not everyone should be allowed to bear arms, including weapons-grade plutonium, because 'there's wackos out there'. One sequence entitled 'A Brief History of America' manages to be both funny and frightening at the same time, presenting the history of the nation in terms of white Americans' fear of the Other, its cartoonish caricatures also an accurate analysis of the nation's propensity for racial violence.

Much criticism was levelled against Moore for staging events, as when he apparently receives a rifle as a gift immediately after opening an account at the North County Bank in Texas: in reality he had to wait several days until an identity check had been completed (as, in fact, we hear one of the bank employees explain to Moore). The film's most emotionally powerful scene, in which Moore confronts Heston and pushes him to apologise to the people in Flint, Michigan, for his insensitivity in appearing at a NRA rally there just after a six-year-old girl had been shot and killed by a classmate, was also its most controversial: granted a spontaneous interview at the actor's home after ringing his doorbell, Moore proceeds to ambush Heston, already suffering from the early stages of Alzheimer's, and to shamelessly tug at viewers' heartstrings by placing a photo of the little girl in the actor's front yard before shuffling away, his head lowered as if burdened with the pain of her tragic death.

Despite such criticism, Moore does manage a small victory in getting retail giant K-Mart, which sold the bullets used by Harris and Klebold at Columbine, to agree to discontinue stocking ammunition in its stores. When *Bowling for Columbine* won the Academy Award for Best Documentary (having already won a special jury prize at the Cannes Film Festival), Moore gave an acceptance speech that was, contrary to etiquette, overtly political, eliciting some boos from the audience. BKG

Dir/Scr: Michael Moore; **Prod**: Kathleen Glynn, Jim Czarnecki, Michael Moore, Charles Bishop, Michael Donovan; **Phot**: Brian Danitz, Michael McDonough (colour); **Ed**: Kurt Engfehr; **Music**: Jeff Gibbs; **Sound**: Francisco Latorre, James Demer; **Prod Co**: Dog Eat Dog Films/Salter Street Films/Iconolatry Productions.

A British Picture: Portrait of an Enfant Terrible
UK, 1989 – 50 mins
Ken Russell

Made to accompany the publication of his autobiography in the same year, similarly entitled *A British Picture*, director Ken Russell, known for his wildly unconventional and outlandish biographical films about musicians and other artists, here at last turns the camera on himself, looking back at his own career. In Russell's idiosyncratic personal documentary, his witty narration recounts the highlights of his early life, including being enamoured of movies, causing a scandal by directing a drag musical at school and discovering the joys of classical music. Employed as a film director for the BBC, Russell takes the viewer on a quick tour through some of his films (and later music videos), bringing us right up to date, as the film ends with a telephone call from his producer, Melvyn Bragg, inviting him to make this film about himself. Along with home movies and clips from his films, Russell also includes some more conventional documentary material, such as the footage of worshippers at Lourdes that accompanies the director's account of his earlier fascination with Catholicism.

Russell is very selective about what he chooses to include in his life story, mentioning, for example, nothing about *The Boyfriend* (1971), *Lisztomania* (1975) or *Valentino* (1977), and next to nothing about his first wife, Shirley Russell, who provided the marvellous costumes for a number of his films. He describes his career in terms of the films' provocation of scandal, and as a continual struggle for financing. Ironically, for a film-maker who has so often been described as vulgar, excessive and puerile, and whose work features a fondness for bold, startling images of eroticism, physical revulsion and violence enhanced by shock editing effects, Russell presents his own life with the most spartan of means (in the first shot following the credits, his birth is visualised as simply a rocking cradle). Family members portray various people, the film's new material looking very much like one of the home movies that

Russell says he enjoys making but that don't pay the bills. *A British Picture* is itself evidence of Russell's difficulties securing funding, for its deliberately modest special effects look surprisingly similar to those in his first amateur film effort, *Peepshow* (1956), a clip of which is included.

Although producers have shied away from him because of his scandalous and excessive approach, Russell revels in his role as British cinema's *enfant terrible*. He is happy to repeat his once shocking description of *The Music Lovers* (1970), a film about Tchaikovsky and his disastrous marriage to Nina Milyukova, as 'the story of a love affair between a homosexual and a nymphomaniac'. Until the end of *A British Picture*, Russell is portrayed by his young son, with the director's own voice lip-synched on the soundtrack, as a literal innocent child among men, wrongly stigmatised as outrageous. As an *enfant terrible*, the boy Russell suddenly sports a shocking rainbow-coloured wig that he wears until the end, at which point Russell appears as himself. Accompanied by a clip of the conclusion of *The Rainbow* (1989), Russell suggests that at this point he, like that film's protagonist Ursula Brangwen, has attained a new maturity, and tosses away the wig. In the way he uses clips of his own films to comment on his life, as when he refers to the domestic tensions at home during his divorce from Shirley with the memorable shot of the lake house exploding in flames in *Mahler* (1974), Russell provides further proof that he is one of the greatest auteurs in the history of British cinema. BKG

Dir/Scr: Ken Russell; **Prod**: Renaldo Vasconcellos; **Phot**: Dick Bush (colour); **Ed**: Xavier Russell; **Art Dir**: Michael Buchanan; **Sound**: Richard King, John Murphy; **Prod Co**: London Weekend Television/RM Arts/Sitting Ducks Production.

British Sounds (US title: See You at Mao)
UK, 1969 – 52 mins
Dziga Vertov Group (Jean-Luc Godard, Jean-Henri Roger)

If the early 1960s marked the high point of direct cinema's 'simply observers' ethic and claims that new technology at last allowed unfettered access to 'the real' (as in, say, PRIMARY, 1960, CRISIS, 1963), the late 1960s and early 1970s saw emerge, amid an explosion of radical politics, an insistence on the ideological implications of film form and the very impossibility of 'capturing the real' – ideas that have informed much documentary film-making since. As British Sounds puts it, 'Photography is not the reflection of reality. It is the reality of that reflection.' Jean-Luc Godard was at the centre of this rigorously political, experimental phase, most obviously with Le Gai savoir (1968), One Plus One (Sympathy for the Devil, 1968), Tout va bien and Letter to Jane (both 1972), as well as his work with (and doubtless dominant voice in) the Dziga Vertov Group collective (Pravda, Vent d'est, Lotte in Italia, all 1969, Vladimir et Rosa, 1971).

Shot on 16mm by one of Britain's pre-eminent documentary cameramen, British Sounds is as determined an assault on the assumptions and conventions of documentary film form as Godard's 'fictions' of the 1960s/1970s were on those of the fiction feature form. Meanings could only be made by a distanced, active spectator working with radically deconstructed elements of sound and image rather than synthesised wholes. As the film's opening image and title suggest – a union flag with the crudely written 'Images' in 'British Images' crossed out and replaced by 'Sounds' – Godard at this juncture wanted to emphasise complexity of sound and simplicity of image, though in practice the major task for the spectator revolves around making sense of the relationships between sound and image.

British Sounds goes in search of British equivalents of the radical movements in France in 1968. It begins with a 10-minute continuous parallel tracking shot along a sports car assembly line (the British Motor

Corporation plant's MG cars) accompanied by loud factory noise (whose source is never revealed), 'interrupted' by a male voice quoting from *The Communist Manifesto*. The tracking shot is broken several times by crudely drawn calendars and an adult male voice 'coaching' a child about Britain's long history of radical struggle (the Peasants' Revolt, the Levellers, etc., which is continued into the film's second section) and the words are spoken imperfectly and several times have to be restarted. Similarly, the second sequence, billed as a discussion about the relation between man and woman, features three straightforward static shots of a naked young woman (walking from room to room and in medium close-up talking on the telephone, then framed in the abdomen/pubic area). Over the images, a middle-class woman talks, quietly, about sexism and double standards, interrupted by dubious male sloganeering ('Miniskirt and counter-revolution', 'Sexual perversion and Stalinism'). Here, as problematically as in his fictions, Godard too readily equates 'woman' with 'sexuality'. Though the film's later sequences (including Dagenham car workers discussing work conditions and the need for real socialism, and Essex University students making – rather pathetic – radical songs and posters) are less striking, the whole seeks to underpin its contention that 'Television and films do not record moments of reality, but simply dialectics, areas of contradiction': the challenge for the spectator was to begin to work with them. Unsurprisingly, this was all too much for the television network that commissioned it, London Weekend Television, which refused to broadcast the film. JH

Dir/Scr: Dziga Vertov Group (Jean-Luc Godard, Jean-Henri Roger); **Prod**: Irving Teitelbaum, Kenith Trodd; **Phot**: Charles Stewart (colour); **Ed**: Elizabeth Kozmian; **Sound**: Frederick Sharp; **Prod Co**: Kestrel Films for London Weekend Television.

Bus 174 (*Ônibus 174*)
Brazil, 2002 – 132 mins
José Padilha

Live coverage of unfolding – or unravelling – events is the province of newsreel rather than documentary, but *Bus 174* knits together newsreel footage and the more analytical, explanatory approach of documentary in a fascinating way. In Rio de Janeiro on 12 June 2000, a twenty-year-old former *favela* street kid, Sandro di Nascimento, boarded Bus 174 waving a gun and took its occupants hostage. For four and a half hours, police kept the bus surrounded and negotiated with Sandro, who threatened to kill hostages if his haphazard demands were not met. Remarkably, almost the whole incident was recorded live, minute-by-minute, by Brazilian TV news teams (as well as by CCTV traffic cameras), and an estimated 35 million people watched as the drama unfolded. This television coverage, which must have been almost incomprehensible to those millions watching, provides the heart of *Bus 174*, but around it the film seeks to understand the deprivation and despair at the life chances on offer that led to such a situation (given fictional form – and, arguably, glamorised – in *City of God*, made in the same year).

Live, real-time coverage like this is always perplexing: *what* is going on, and *why*? While preserving a certain confusion about what was happening on the bus and among the police, Padilha seeks to answer those questions. Mostly through interview material with social workers, relatives and people he grew up with, we learn that Sandro at the age of five witnessed his mother's brutal murder, lived rough on the streets, surviving through petty crime and drugs, and at twelve narrowly escaped death when police gunned down street kids taking refuge in front of the cathedral. Interviews prompt exploration of Sandro's police record, police procedures, prison conditions, etc., building up a picture of Sandro's life and, by extension, the lives of many others just like him. Interwoven into this discourse are interviews with some of the hostages who survived the hijacking, which provide information about what the cameras were unable to see and about the hijacker's confusion during the siege (demonstrating surprising sympathy for their captor), as well as with police officers, who detail the chaotic organisation among those supposedly trying to resolve the crisis. What marks almost all the interviews is a sense of the inability to change anything.

Always, though, Padilha returns us to the dramatic, inescapable reality of the bus, skilfully pacing the television coverage right through to the heart-stopping denouement. It is extraordinary that the police allowed such access to cameras and reporters, but what we see is both frightening and fascinating. Several times Sandro yells out of the window that what the cameras are watching is not an action movie. His unpredictable behaviour and impotent rage make the utter impossibility of a way out increasingly clear. Padilha sees Sandro's traumatic experience of the notorious Candeleira cathedral massacre not as just a coincidence, but as the start of a vicious trajectory that is completed by the bus hijack and its outcome: desperate to be somebody but always invisible, Sandro has his moment in front of the cameras before being returned to invisibility, and the cycle begins again with the street kids who close the film. JH

Dir: José Padilha, Felipe Lacerda; **Prod**: José Padilha, Marcos Prado; **Scr**: José Padilha; **Phot**: Marcelo 'Guru' Duarte, Cezar Moraes (colour); **Ed**: Felipe Lacerda; **Music**: Sacha Amback, João Nabuco; **Sound**: Denilson Campos, Aloisio Compasso, Yan Saldanha, Armando Torres, Jr; **Prod Co**: Zazan Produções.

Cane Toads: An Unnatural History
Australia, 1988 – 47 mins
Mark Lewis

Lewis's first, and most popular, film in a series of comical documentaries about the relationship between humans and animals, including *The Wonderful World of Dogs* (1990), *Rat* (1998), *Animalicious* (1999) and *The Natural History of the Chicken* (2000), *Cane Toads* brings welcome whimsy to an unpromising subject: the spread of one particular species of South American toad, the eponymous Cane Toad (*bufo marinus*), in Australia, where it was introduced in 1935 in a failed attempt to protect the sugar cane crop from the greyback cane beetle. Reproductively prolific and containing a poisonous gland that is toxic to other animals that ingest it, the toad's habitat has spread across Queensland and into New South Wales, threatening to destroy the indigenous ecosystem. Originating as a television documentary, *Cane Toads* is neither solemn nor sentimental, as are so many nature documentaries from Arne Sucksdorff to Walt Disney; instead, it provides the necessary exposition about the cane toad, such as its mating and eating habits, and in addition comically uses a variety of fiction film techniques to suggest that the toads are evil creatures enacting a deliberate, malevolent plan to conquer the Australian nation.

In *The Wonderful World of Dogs*, Lewis offers a dog dream sequence, literally depicting canine consciousness; in *Cane Toads*, by contrast, no such subjective sequences appear, but it is largely through the use of editing and *mise en scène* that viewers are encouraged to read the film as suggesting that the toads have a conscious motivation. With a handheld camera low to the ground that seems to sweep and jump through the grass, the film frequently shows us the perspective of the toads, employing conventional shot/reaction-shot editing. Often placed in one of the bottom corners of the frame, the camera shooting up from a very low angle, the toads appear to be watching and waiting with cool calculation. In one humorous scene evoking Hitchcock's

Psycho (1960), we see a resident of Cairns, near where the toads were first released, having a shower as they apparently invade his home and watch him from the windows. Some of the people interviewed describe the cane toads as monsters, an impression that is reinforced by a close-up of a toad catching and devouring a mouse in one gulp. At the end of the film, when we learn just how far the cane toad may spread, one jumps into the frame of a long shot with the Sydney Opera House in the background, as if to suggest that in the future the animals may even colonise the continent's largest city.

With the cane toads now an irrevocable part of the Australian landscape ('they are absolutely everywhere. People are brought up with them,' observes one 'social commentator'), Lewis is interested in how people relate to them, a focus shared with his other animal films. In the case of the toads, attitudes are widely divergent: children regard them as pets, town officials see them as potential for boosting tourism, residents view them as either magnificent animals or repulsive pests. Adding to the film's humour is Lewis's penchant for interviewing eccentric people, whether residents or scientific experts. One man, motivated by revenge, veers back and forth across the road in his car as he attempts to squash as many toads as possible under his tyres; another, a man who engages in the practice of boiling toads and drinking the residue for its hallucinogenic effects, mumbles something from behind thick cigarette smoke that obscures his face, visually expressing his obviously clouded consciousness. BKG

Dir/Scr: Mark Lewis; **Prod**: Tristram Miall; **Phot**: Jim Frazier, Wayne Taylor (colour); **Ed**: Lindsay Frazer; **Music**: Martin Armiger; **Sound**: Rodney Simmons; **Prod Co**: Film Australia.

Le Chagrin et la pitié (full title: Le Chagrin et la pitié: chronique d'une ville française sous l'occupation) (The Sorrow and the Pity: Chronicle of a French City under German Occupation)

France/Switzerland/West Germany, 1969 – 249 mins
Marcel Ophüls

As its full title implies, Le Chagrin et la pitié investigates events and attitudes in Clermont-Ferrand under Maréchal Pétain's Vichy government, then occupied by the Germans (1940–4). The first part, L'Effondrement (The Collapse), deals primarily with the general collapse of French defences, while the second part, Le Choix (The Choice), concentrates more closely on Clermont itself, a medium-size town close to Vichy, outside the original occupied zone, industrially important as Michelin's base and a centre of resistance.

Whereas 'direct cinema' mainly recorded events as they happened without film-maker intervention (see PRIMARY, 1960, CRISIS, 1963), cinéma vérité in France (see CHRONIQUE D'UN ÉTÉ, 1961) emphasised interview, discussion and the film-makers' participation. Employing equipment like that used for Chronique – 16mm Éclair Coutant camera, synched Nagra tape recorder – Ophüls opts for the participatory approach, prompting, questioning, challenging (doubtless an influence on SHOAH, 1985, and Michael Moore's ROGER AND ME, 1989, and BOWLING FOR COLUMBINE, 2002). Ophüls also incorporates newsreels and other materials (though less so for the inevitably 'invisible' activities of the Resistance), picking up on the polemical compilation form pioneered by Esfir Shub in the 1920s (THE FALL OF THE ROMANOV DYNASTY, 1927) that was being 'reinvented' in the 1960s, notably by Emile de Antonio (Point of Order, 1963, IN THE YEAR OF THE PIG, 1968).

What made Le Chagrin et la pitié different from other World War II documentaries was its interest less in precise chronology, causes and effects than in questions about history, memory and morality, the way people remember the past (in contrast with, say, Thames Television's 1974–5 *World at War*, which essayed a more or less authoritative history). In *Le Chagrin et la pitié*, we come away with contradictions, questions and doubts about how people behaved, and why. Ophüls refuses judgments, but the way participants answer questions – struggling, or not, to remember – and the settings in which he questions them shape our responses: the former German captain, cigar-smoking and self-satisfied at his daughter's wedding, can hardly be sympathetic, but most of the interviews with ordinary, robust former Resistance members, often recorded on the move, are more like discussions or reunions, with a strongly communal feeling; Ophüls talks at length, sympathetically, with aristocrat Christian de la Mazière, who fought in the Waffen SS Charlemagne division; eminent figures like Pierre Mendès-France and Anthony Eden tend to be interviewed more formally, in isolation, while evasive former schoolteachers are caught more on the hop.

Jaunty Maurice Chevalier songs begin and close the film but, tellingly, Ophüls ends with two newsreel items: in the first, coming shortly after images of the women accused of collaboration having their heads shaved, Chevalier, in English, rebuts the charge of collaboration by insisting that he only toured Germany to entertain French prisoners; in the second, evoking myths of French resistance and De Gaulle as France's saviour, we see the President stopping to shake hands with the Auvergne Resistance chief.

Le Chagrin et la pitié, begun in the late-1960s spirit of openness, was not, as is often claimed, 'censored' by French television, but nor did the state broadcaster opt to buy and show the film; despite its very considerable theatrical success in France and elsewhere (all the more notable given its running time) and its Academy Award nomination in 1971, the film was not shown on French television until 1981 (attracting 15 million viewers) – ample illustration of the state's continuing complicity in maintaining silence about a difficult and contested period of French history. Ophüls brought the same approach to other controversial subjects, such as Northern Ireland (*A Sense of Loss*, 1972), Germany and the Nuremberg Trials (*The Memory of Justice*, 1975) and Klaus Barbie (*Hotel Terminus*, 1987). JH

Dir: Marcel Ophüls; **Prod**: André Harris, Alain de Sedouy; **Scr**: André Harris, Marcel Ophüls; **Phot**: André Gazut, Jürgen Thieme (b/w); **Ed**: Claude Vajda; **Sound**: Bernard Migy, Wolfgang Schroeter; **Prod Co**: Norddeutscher Rundfunk/Télévision Rencontre/Télévision Suisse-Romande.

Chronique d'un été (Chronicle of a Summer)
France, 1961 – 85 mins
Jean Rouch, Edgar Morin

Jean Rouch had been making anthropological films, mostly in Niger and Mali, since the 1940s (see LES MAÎTRES FOUS, 1955). In the late 1950s, declaring that 'fiction is the only way to penetrate reality', Rouch shot, with handheld cameras and largely silent (apart from a few synch-sound sequences modelled on WE ARE THE LAMBETH BOYS, 1958), two semi-fictional feature-length films in Abidjan, Ivory Coast, exploring the effects of colonialism and segregation. In *Moi, un noir* (*Me, a Black Man*, 1957), three young Niger labourers played characters modelled on themselves; *La Pyramide humaine* (*The Human Pyramid*, 1959), which Jean-Luc Godard declared one of the most important French films since 1945, was a psychodrama with black and white school students. Edgar Morin, sociologist and cinema theorist, used the term cinéma vérité – conscious of its historical association with Dziga Vertov (MAN WITH A MOVIE CAMERA, 1929) – in a 1960 article on Rouch, and persuaded him to examine the 'strange tribe' inhabiting Paris. While Americans Robert Drew, D. A. Pennebaker and others were developing technology to synch live sound with lightweight 16mm cameras (PRIMARY, 1960, CRISIS, 1963, A HAPPY MOTHER'S DAY, 1963), in France André Coutant was developing a 16mm camera for Éclair for synching with a lightweight Nagra tape recorder. Rouch persuaded Coutant to let him use his prototype for *Chronique d'un été*.

The film begins with Rouch and Morin explaining their 'experiment in cinéma vérité' and quickly proceeds to them interacting with a small group of people, largely their existing acquaintances. How do they seek to reveal 'not life as it is, but life as it is provoked . . . A new truth . . . which has nothing to do with normal reality'? Instead of 'simply observing', as Richard Leacock claimed the American direct cinema film-makers did, they interview, probe, set up situations in which people can react; instead of pretending to be 'invisible', they visibly orchestrate events. Leacock was bothered both by this interventionist approach and by the fact that, unlike the direct cinema subjects, 'The only thing that's happening to [Rouch's subjects] is the fact they're being filmed.' One long sequence shows the daily life of Renault car worker Angelo, waking, working, returning home, the mobile camera following him, emphasising his 'ordinary' routine (just like an earlier French film Rouch admired, FARREBIQUE, 1946).

Elsewhere, Rouch and Morin set up a meeting between French and black African students and raise questions about racism. Rouch then

Jean Rouch (centre left) and Edgar Morin (right), in discussion at the Musée de l'Homme, being filmed for the final sequence of *Chronique d'un été*

directly asks the black students about the number on Marceline's arm –
they don't know what it is; Marceline explains that it was her
concentration camp number; the camera pans across to record their
embarrassed reactions. This discussion segues into something very
different, a tracking shot of Marceline as she crosses the Place de la
Concorde recalling, in a stream of consciousness monologue, her
memories of deportation and, walking through Les Halles, her return to
France. These improvised monologues, suggested by Rouch, are far
removed from 'objective observation' of unmediated actuality, but offer,
arguably, real insights into the shadows cast on Marceline's present by
her past. More conventionally 'observed', though controversially intrusive,
is Morin's second 'interview' with Marilou; seen earlier in the depths of
personal despair, she now becomes literally speechless, unable to
articulate her feelings of both happiness and dread, the camera relentlessly
recording the complex play of emotions across her face and hands.

In the final sequence of the film, Rouch and Morin discuss what they
have achieved, sensing failure, but nevertheless feeling that their film
'reintroduces us to life' (echoing Vertov's 'Show us life!'). They conclude
'*Nous sommes dans le bain*', which English subtitles wrongly translate as
'We're in trouble'; rather, they mean something like 'We've made a
start'. Rouch and Morin then go their separate ways – reminding us that
this is also a film about the two film-makers' collaboration and
friendship. JH

Dir: Jean Rouch, Edgar Morin; **Prod**: Anatole Dauman, Philippe Lifschitz; **Phot**: Roger
Morillère, Raoul Coutard, Jean-Jacques Tarbès, Michel Brault (b/w); **Ed**: Jean Ravel,
Néna Baratier, Françoise Colin; **Sound**: Guy Rophe, Michel Fano, Edmond Barthélémy;
Prod Co: Argos-Films.

Close-Up (*Nema-ye nazdik*)
Iran, 1990 – 93 mins
Abbas Kiarostami

Like several other Abbas Kiarostami films (*And Life Goes On*, 1992, *Through the Olive Trees*, 1994), *Close-Up* is an intriguing, partly autobiographical reflection on the power and authenticity of cinema. Like EL SOL DEL MEMBRILLO (1992), though more overtly, it invites us to think about some of the complexities of what constitutes 'fiction' and 'documentary', and work that falls somewhere in between. If films must have labels, then *Close-Up* may be a 'documentary drama', part re-enactment and part apparently 'real' documentary, filming real events as they happen, though such distinctions are not always easy to keep in mind while engaging with its Pirandellian narrative.

Close-Up begins with a journalist and two policemen travelling to a house where a man has been passing himself off to a middle-class family as the film director Mohsen Makhmalbaf, promising to include them in his new film. Doubting the man's authenticity, they call in the journalist, desperate for a scandal story to make his name. The man is arrested and the journalist writes up the story, which attracts the attention of film director Abbas Kiarostami. Kiarostami interviews the man, Hossain Sabzian, in jail and decides to make a film in which everyone, including Kiarostami himself, would play themselves, getting permission to film the court hearing. At the court, a camera is fixed on Sabzian in close-up, both to follow his reactions and so that he can turn to it to clarify his thoughts.

The hearing begins and the film cuts between the court and re-enactments of Sabzian's visits to the house, opening up the heart of the film – the power of cinema to represent society. Sabzian argues that Makhmalbaf's films, like *The Cyclist* (1989), 'portray suffering' and 'speak for people like me', but he also found that the authority of cinema as an institution meant that he had been taken seriously and treated with respect, which gave him self-confidence, though in reality he was poor and unemployed. Eventually, we see the 'reverse angle' – Sabzian's point of view – of the journalist's visit and the arrest; while back in court, the film takes a further Pirandellian – or, given the film's strongly social context, Brechtian – turn: asked by Kiarostami what part he would like to play, Sabzian replies, 'My own', to which Kiarostami responds that he *is* playing his own part. The complaints about him withdrawn, Sabzian now has the chance to become 'a useful member of society'.

The film could come to a satisfying conclusion there, but there is a curious coda whose fictional/documentary status – and meaning – is far from clear. Kiarostami's camera watches as Sabzian is freed from a short sentence to be greeted by the real Mohsen Makhmalbaf (who declares himself 'tired of being me'). Makhmalbaf, wearing a faulty mic that causes live sound to drop in and out, takes Sabzian across the city on the back of his moped, followed by Kiarostami's crew, to deliver a potted plant to the house where the 'fraud' took place. The father declares that Sabzian 'will make us proud of him', and the film ends with a freeze-frame of Sabzian holding the plant. JH

Dir/Scr/Ed: Abbas Kiarostami; **Prod**: Ali Reza Zarrin; **Phot**: Ali Reza Zarrindast (colour); **Sound**: Ahmad Asgari, Mahammad Haghighi; **Principal Cast**: Hossain Sabzian, Abolfazl Ahankhah, Mehrdad Ahankhah, Monoochehr Ahankhah, Mahrokh Ahankhah, Hossain Farazmand, Haj Ali Reza Ahmadi, Mohsen Makhmalbaf; **Prod Co**: Institute for the Intellectual Development of Children and Young Adults.

Coal Face
UK, 1935 – 11 mins
Alberto Cavalcanti

In a rough division of 1930s British documentary between more 'straightforward' films like HOUSING PROBLEMS (1935) and NORTH SEA (1938) and more 'experimental' or poetic films like *Song of Ceylon* (dir. Basil Wright, 1934), *Pett and Pott* (dir. Cavalcanti, 1934) or *Nightmail* (dirs. Harry Watt and Basil Wright, 1936), *Coal Face* belongs among the latter. Though hired by the GPO Film Unit in 1933/4 primarily for his expertise in sound – at that time even more in its infancy than in fiction feature film-making, and with greater technical constraints – Cavalcanti had also established his name as an experimental film-maker in 1920s France, most notably with *Rien que les heures* (1926). Much of the experimentation of *Coal Face* lies in its employment of sound, and though later films like *Night Mail* (which, like *Coal Face*, includes verse by W. H. Auden and music by Benjamin Britten) also use sound creatively, *Coal Face* remains the most determinedly experimental. Indeed, it was presented at The Film Society explicitly as an experiment in sound. (The credits list no director of photography and for the most part, if not entirely, the film was compiled from existing footage.)

    Coal Face is quite difficult to read 'as a whole', but then perhaps it isn't a whole, or at least not a familiar one. At its centre are perhaps two films (neither remotely connected to the work of the GPO). One is a resolutely factual account of the coal industry as Britain's 'basic industry', complete with maps of the main coalfields and statistics on how many miners work them, lists of the main uses and by-products of coal and the processes by which coal is mined, all delivered in a voiceover so dense and deliberately blunt that it is difficult to take in. Overlaid, as it were, on this almost parodied, heavily instructional film is another, altogether more 'aesthetic', film, in both sound and image. Though this second film is there from the start – for example, in the music behind the credits – it emerges most clearly as the miners head underground for the coal face, accompanied by a percussive beat and a male choral recitative listing the variety of miners' jobs ('hewer . . . over-man . . . barrowman'). A similarly 'modernist' effect is achieved as the miners return to the surface by singing voices rising in pitch and a montage of cables, pistons and faces. Part of the problem of 'reading' *Coal Face* is that though these choral and montage sequences, neither strictly necessary to the events being recorded, 'work' as exciting cinema, they verge on being absurdly inappropriate, almost laughable.

In the mining community, a women's choir takes over as the voiceover intones about how the miners' lives and housing are tied to the pit. Here, as elsewhere (such as earlier statistics on the number of miners killed and injured), the voiceover does not flinch from recounting harsh realities, realities wonderfully evoked in the sustained image of the stunted tree bent almost double by the wind. As John Corner observes, the phoney lyricism of a film like Flaherty's *Industrial Britain* (1933) is entirely absent from *Coal Face*, whose formal modernism and relationship to industry and the machine owes a clear debt to its Soviet influences. JH

Dir/Scr: (Alberto) Cavalcanti; **Prod**: John Grierson; **Ed**: William Coldstream; **Music**: Benjamin Britten; **Sound**: Cavalcanti, Stuart Legg, Benjamin Britten, E. A. Pawley (sound recording); **Verse/Commentary**: W. H. Auden, Montagu Slater; **Prod Co**: GPO Film Unit.

Crisis: Behind a Presidential Commitment (ABC Special)
US, 1963 – 52 mins
Robert Drew

Crisis was the last film in the pioneering Drew Associates 'Living Camera' series: subsequently, *Time, Inc.* ended its support and Richard Leacock and D. A. Pennebaker left Drew. Its screening reignited debates about direct cinema aesthetics and ethics. Drew wanted to transform television reportage – typified by presenter-led documentaries like HARVEST OF SHAME (1960) – but it was the only 'Living Camera' film broadcast on a major network, doubtless due largely to its current affairs content (racial segregation and integration) and the presence of Attorney General Robert F. Kennedy and President John F. Kennedy. Their inclusion caused much controversy: a *New York Times* editorial asserted that 'the use of cameras could only denigrate the office of the President' and 'to eavesdrop on executive decisions of serious government matters while they are in progress is highly inappropriate. The White House isn't Macy's Window.' John Kennedy had already been featured in PRIMARY (1960) and it no doubt suited the Kennedys' desire to project change and modernity to be involved in such films.

The film chronicles the crisis caused by Alabama Governor George Wallace's determination to prevent black students registering at the state university. The Attorney General had to ensure that the law was administered, if necessary by force, while the President needed to consider how best to address the nation. Stephen Mamber argued that the Drew films depended on a 'crisis structure', which, in contrast with many earlier documentaries, made these films more like fictional narratives, with 'characters' in conflict, climax and resolution – and here was a perfect example.

Theoretically, direct cinema observed and let spectators decide what to think and feel. The film-makers doubtless had their own views on race; did this affect what and how they shot?

Wallace's ornate governor's mansion feels empty; rather awkwardly, he cuddles a lone child, talks to the film-makers and waves to the leg-ironed black convicts working on the estate. By contrast, Robert Kennedy, already associated with Washington, Abraham Lincoln and President Kennedy, participates in his children's noisy breakfast and is still holding a plate when called to the phone. Whether these very different introductions simply reflect the two men's contrasting lifestyles or whether they result from different sets of shooting and editing choices is impossible to say, but it is clear who would most engage spectator sympathy.

One remarkable sequence demonstrates the hazards of direct cinema film-making: at a critical moment, Leacock is filming Robert Kennedy in his office, telephoning Nicholas Katzenbach, his representative in Alabama; tellingly, Kennedy is interrupted by the unexpected appearance of his children, one of whom chats to Katzenbach; Pennebaker was assigned to film events in Alabama, but it was only much later, at the editing stage, that Leacock discovered whether Pennebaker had filmed Katzenbach's end of the call – footage essential to the sequence – or whether he had chosen that moment to go for coffee or to the bathroom.

Drew's methods were well known by 1963, but his films still enjoyed demonstrating the camera's and sound recording's new mobility: a bravura sequence showing Robert Kennedy leaving his office, being driven to the White House and getting out to greet the President is not strictly necessary in narrative terms, but does seem to announce (again), 'Hey, look what we can do with this equipment!' Like *Primary* and DONT LOOK BACK (1967), *Crisis* incorporates several moments of staged manipulation by traditional media, notably Robert Kennedy's participation in a televised debate and black student Vivian Malone's posing for a *Time* magazine cover – moments that, as intended, contrast sharply with the film-makers' own methods. JH

Exec Prod: Robert Drew; **Prod**: Greg Shuker; **Film-makers**: Greg Shuker, Richard Leacock, James Lipscomb, D. A. Pennebaker, Hope Ryden (b/w); **Ed**: Nicholas Proferes, Eileen Nosworthy; **Narrator**: James Lipscomb; **Prod Co**: ABC News/Drew Associates.

Daughter Rite
US, 1980 – 49 mins
Michelle Citron

The politicisation of culture from the mid- to late 1960s and the growth
of the women's movement encouraged women film-makers to replace
the false stereotypes peddled by the media – not least Hollywood – with
'true' representations of women's lives. The 'direct cinema' technology
and supposedly objective observational methods developed in the early
1960s (see PRIMARY, 1960, CRISIS, A HAPPY MOTHER'S DAY, both
1963) offered the means, and films like Geri Ashur and the New York
Newsreel's *Janie's Janie* (1971) resulted. However, the growing critique of
direct cinema's ability to show the 'truth' and an increasingly
sophisticated appreciation of the complexity of media representations led
to more experimental approaches being tried; *Daughter Rite* –
independently made on a $3,500 budget – is a good example.

 Daughter Rite juxtaposes three different kinds of material: extracts
from colour family home movies, step-printed to slow down, reverse and
repeat them; a young woman's voiceover, reflecting, almost elegiacally, on
herself and on her relations with her recently divorced mother, dedicating
the film 'with love, to my mother, a woman who I am very much like and
not like at all'; and direct sound and image documentary-style footage,
with long takes, zooms, etc., of two sisters in their twenties, talking about
their relationships with their mother and with each other. The relations
between these three components is never made clear by the film itself:
the home movies show a mother and two daughters involved in outings,
domestic activities, special occasions, etc; the mother *may* be the mother
being talked about in the voiceover, and the (unseen) woman behind the
voiceover *may* be one of the sisters in the home movies and/or one of the
sisters in the documentary-type sequences (and *may* be the film-maker
too). Certainly, most viewers *assume* such connections.

 As the film proceeds and we learn more about 'the mother', the
'daughters'/'sisters' and the 'I' of the voiceover, it becomes increasingly

difficult to sustain belief in the 'truth' and cohesiveness of the material, particularly where it should be most transparent and direct, namely the direct cinema-type footage: instead, discrepancies or inconsistencies in the discussions arise and some scenes seem awkwardly played. Only in the end credits, however, do we learn that the sisters are in fact actors discussing issues drawn from interviews with forty different women – at one level undermining our faith in the material but, at another, extending two (fictional) women's experiences to those of a generality of (real) women.

The home-movie footage was shot by the father – absent from, but in control of, the image – and events are generally played *to* and *for* him: for example, the mother parading her daughters in their Sunday best. These revealing and moving images show how girls grew up female in 1950s America and how mothers allowed themselves to 'disappear', replaced by their daughters; the girls tend to look happily towards the father/camera while mother tends to avert her gaze. The home movies, inherited by the film-maker on her parents' separation, were the film's starting point: she found the 'voyeuristic images a fascinating record of domestic life', with little correspondence between the smiling family on film and her childhood memories. Slowing the films down 'revealed another film that had been obscured at the normal speed': the mother's casual hand movement became intrusive, jostling between the sisters became hostile. 'It was in this "other" film that my real family existed, complete in its non-verbal expression of warmth, anger, hostility, frustration and love.' Family home movies have become an increasingly rich source for film-makers rooting their work in their own lives (see, for example, I FOR INDIA, 2005, TIME INDEFINITE, 1993). JH

Dir/Prod/Scr/Phot/Ed/Sound: Michelle Citron (colour); **Narrator**: Jerri Hancock; **Phot/Sound Assistants**: Sharon Bement, Barbara Roos; **Cast**: Penelope Victor, Anne Wilford; **Prod Co**: Iris Films.

David Holzman's Diary
US, 1967 – 74 mins
Jim McBride

An incisive and often very funny parody of the mystique of direct cinema, *David Holzman's Diary* is a scripted 'mockumentary' about an aspiring film-maker (played by actor, writer and producer L. M. Kit Carson) and his attempt to make a documentary film about his own (rather uninteresting) life in New York City. Directed by Jim McBride, a fiction film director whose credits include *Breathless* (1983), the American remake of Jean-Luc Godard's first feature, *À bout de souffle* (1960), it clearly reveals affinities with Godard's aleatory experiments during the early days of the French New Wave and was taken at face value by many viewers when it was first released.

Though *David Holzman's Diary* is not a documentary, it contains some true documentary footage (the tracking shot around the little park, for example) and is self-reflexive about the kind of documentary it pretends to be. Its self-awareness is signalled explicitly by the photos of D. A. Pennebaker and Richard Leacock, two of the most important American direct cinema film-makers at the time, that hang on David's apartment wall; David considers himself a cinephile (at one point he says he has nothing to say 'unless you want to talk about Vincente Minnelli') and certainly would be familiar with the 'fly-on-the-wall' approach of these *au courant* film-makers. David is a loner who describes his film equipment as his friends and who loses his girlfriend because he films her instead of interacting with her. His masturbatory inclinations seem consistent with his solipsistic determination to film his life, even when, as in his encounter with a woman on the street (Sylvia Miles), he chooses film-making over lovemaking, settling for what he refers to as 'the widow thumb and her four daughters'. Just as the protagonist of Alfred Hitchcock's *Rear Window* (1954) spies on people in other apartments because his own life is empty, so David films other people in a voyeuristic fashion. Desperately seeking to invest images with greater meaning than the profilmic events he films, he ponders his own film-making efforts while in the background his radio, in pointed contrast, discusses the pressing political issues of the day, including the war in Vietnam and race riots just across the river in nearby New Jersey.

David's problem is that he is working backwards: he wants to make a film that will capture 'the mystery of things', as he says, and get to the truth of his daily existence. But even direct cinema film-makers, working without a predetermined script, must have an animating vision and must order their footage into an aesthetic whole, even if observational cinema so often seems artless, a random 'bric-a-brac of mere observation', as film historian Lewis Jacobs put it. Thus David's forays with his camera into the world outside lead nowhere, and he literally circles around to where he begins when he films the people in the park ('These faces have the look of casually arranged gargoyles in a stunned and perhaps dying world', he muses portentously about the people sitting on the benches). Nevertheless, the ultimate irony of *David Holzman's Diary* is that David's film, despite the empty life he leads and the failure of his film to seem meaningful to him, says much to us about the meaningfulness of good direct cinema films that, like Ross McElwee's *Sherman's March* (1985) and TIME INDEFINITE (1993), are rooted in autobiography but have things to say.

McBride made a follow-up film, *My Girlfriend's Wedding* (1969), which, as Jonathan Rosenbaum has suggested, was more a personal documentary with fictional elements than the fiction with documentary elements of *David Holzman*. BKG

Dir/Prod/Scr/Ed: Jim McBride; **Phot**: Michael Wadleigh (as Michael Wadley) (b/w); **Principal Cast**: L. M. Kit Carson, Eileen Dietz, Lorenzo Mans, Louise Levine, Fem McBride, Sylvia Miles; **Prod Co**: Paradigm.

Dead Birds
US/Netherlands, 1965 – 85 mins
Robert Gardner

One of the most famous examples of ethnographic film-making (see also
LES MAÎTRES FOUS, 1955), *Dead Birds* documents the culture of the
Dugum Dani tribe of Indonesia (formerly Dutch New Guinea), which at
that time was still uncolonised by European culture and modern
technology. The film was produced as part of a three-year
anthropological expedition sponsored by the Peabody Museum of
Harvard University. In addition to Gardner, who initiated the project, the
expedition included the naturalist writer Peter Matthiesen and
anthropologist Karl Heider, who later wrote the influential book
Ethnographic Film (1976), acting here as assistant cinematographer.
All published subsequent important anthropological work about the Dani
after *Dead Birds*. The film aspires to a comprehensive understanding of
Dani culture, based around ritual warfare and death. Though they had
previously had some limited contact with outsiders, the Dani did not
know what cameras were and so the film-makers were able to capture
them going about their lives unselfconsciously.

As the film explains in the deliberately dispassionate voiceover by
Gardner, the various tribes of the Dani people believe that when a person
is killed, his 'seeds of singing', or soul, cannot be at peace unless the
death is avenged. The belief requires continual warfare among the
various tribes in the Baliem Valley, and many aspects of the people's lives
are shaped by the presence of death and the fear of the ghosts of the
dead, such as the ritual amputation of women's fingers each time a
family member dies. Men spend much of their days in watchtowers built
in trees to guard against retributive attacks by enemies, while women
gather food and do domestic work. Birds, which are central to Dani
culture, are used as a symbolic motif throughout: in a particularly
memorable scene, to accompany Gardner's description of how a young
boy, Wejakhe, has been killed by an enemy sortie, ducks on the Aikhe

River, earlier shown paddling peacefully in the water, now squawk and frantically fly away.

In the tradition established by Robert Flaherty in NANOOK OF THE NORTH (1922), *Dead Birds* is structured around the lives of individuals – in this case, Weyak, a warrior who mans one of the watchtowers, and Pua, a young boy who tends pigs, though there are also scenes involving Weyak's wife and other events as well. Gardner's film, like Flaherty's, has been criticised by later ethnographers and cultural theorists for its colonialist gaze, patronisingly presuming an ability to 'explain' another culture in such a totalising fashion. Weyak and Pua, like all the Dani in the film, say very little; instead, Gardner's voiceover seems omniscient, explaining everything about his subjects' behaviour and actions, and even presuming to know what they are thinking and feeling.

In its conclusion, perhaps inspired by the structural anthropology of Claude Lévi-Strauss, the film reaches for universal relevance by suggesting that the myths and rituals of the Dani, which seem at first glance so different from those of Western society, are not unlike our own. After the big battle, featuring extraordinary footage of several encounters expertly edited, the Dani celebrate by running back and forth across a darkling plain as Gardner intones that men 'will try with measured violence to fashion fate themselves. They kill to save their souls and, perhaps, to ease the burden of what birds will never know and what they, as men, who have forever killed each other, cannot forget' – our common mortality. BKG

Dir/Narrator: Robert Gardner; **Scr**: Peter Matthiesen; **Phot**: Eliot Elisofon, Karl Heider (colour); **Ed**: Robert Gardner, Jestrup Lincoln; **Sound**: Michael Rockefeller; **Prod Co**: Harvard University Film Study Center/Peabody Museum.

A Diary for Timothy
UK, 1945 – 38 mins
Humphrey Jennings

Humphrey Jennings is routinely considered one of the greatest British documentary film-makers, though his reputation rests on a very few films, little more than four hours in combined running time (out of a total output, as director, of about eight hours), made in a relatively short period, 1939–45. Like *Fires Were Started* (1943), *A Diary for Timothy* is what we would now call a 'dramatised documentary', rather than the extended sound-image montage form of *Words for Battle* (1941) or *Listen to Britain* (1942), but *Diary* is the Jennings film that most fully integrates characters and narrative line with passages of sophisticated montage.

Almost all of Jennings's major work deals with wartime Britain. *Diary* is an account of the home front in the final phase of the war in

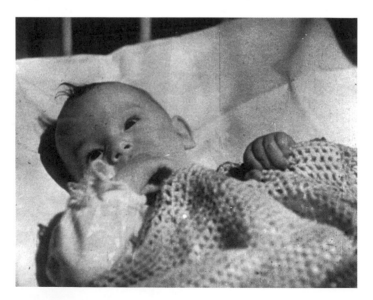

Europe, in the form of a 'diary' written for Timothy Jenkins, born 3 September 1944, as a record of the events of his first nine months. The diary conceit works remarkably well: it is well written (by novelist E. M. Forster, doubtless with much input from Jennings), despite some moments of bathos or cliché, and Michael Redgrave's voice, by turns grave and upbeat, is wonderfully effective. While Tim, resolutely middle class (the Nuffield Rectory, Henley, Oxfordshire), is at the centre of the film – its *raison d'être*, you might say – Jennings juxtaposes him with four other main 'characters' on the home front. Welsh coal miner Goronwy is injured in a pit accident; Londoner Bill is a train-driver; these two working-class figures are supplemented by farmer Alan, reclaiming farm land to increase production, and fighter pilot Peter, undergoing treatment and rehabilitation following an air crash, before returning to flying. The film cuts between these five as fighting in Europe proceeds, the progress of the war charted, and given urgency, by BBC radio newsreaders breaking news and listeners gathered round radios, and the clearing of mines and barbed wire from the beaches.

Jennings achieves remarkable eloquence in the extended 'Rain, too much rain' sequence that traces the dark, grim days following the Arnhem landings: news of the Arnhem survivors drinking water from their capes; brimming street reservoirs; bombed roofs under repair; rain at the pit head; waves crashing on barbed wire; rain on Bill's windscreen; Alan's flooded fields. This montage, linked by commentary and by Myra Hess's National Gallery solo piano performance of Beethoven, ends with Tim's baptism, extending the water motif, but Jennings follows this immediately with Goronwy's accident – 'It's a chancy world'.

Though events proceed towards an increasingly inevitable Allied victory, the film moves towards something darker. Jennings was apprehensive about what post-war British society would be like – a return to the exploitation and inequality of the 1920s and 1930s, or a carrying forward of the greater egalitarianism and national cohesion of the war years (partially articulated, significantly, by Goronwy in conversation with his wife)? *Diary* implies that he was deeply ambivalent about this future. As Tim's face emerges from flames, the commentary wonders what he's going to say, and 'What are you going to *do*?' As the music climaxes, Tim throws his arms out, as if defiant, but Jennings then brings back an anxious violin solo and fades to black. Cut to finish a few moments sooner, the effect would be clearly optimistic; cut as it is, the implications are darker, more doubtful (and even more so in a presumably earlier version with no VE celebrations, in which Tim's face emerges not from the bonfire flames of victory but from the flames of war). JH

Dir/Scr: Humphrey Jennings; **Prod**: Basil Wright; **Phot**: Fred Gamage (b/w); **Ed**: Alan Osbiston; **Music**: Richard Adinsell; **Sound**: Ken Cameron, Jock May; **Commentary**: E. M. Forster, read by Michael Redgrave; **Prod Co**: Crown Film Unit.

Dont Look Back
US, 1967 – 96 mins
D. A. Pennebaker

D. A. Pennebaker's direct cinema account of Bob Dylan's British tour in the spring of 1965 has become one of the iconic films of the 1960s. *Dont Look Back* follows Dylan as he travels to and performs in seven English cities, climaxing with a successful performance at London's Royal Albert Hall. Accompanied on the tour by his manager Albert Grossman, road manager Bob Neuwirth, former Animals' keyboardist Alan Price (who later would compose the score for several films, including Lindsay Anderson's *O Lucky Man!*, 1973), folk singer Joan Baez (whose relationship with Dylan was in the process of ending) and a few others, Dylan is shown alternately in clips performing at the concerts and interacting with assorted journalists, groupies, hangers-on, hotel personnel and local officials backstage and between gigs. The film captures the mercurial Dylan more vividly than any other until perhaps Martin Scorsese's *No Direction Home* (2005). And though *Dont Look Back* features compelling moments of Dylan in performance, it is much more than a conventional rockumentary, for it uses the star, who was enjoying increasing popularity while also becoming a figure of controversy by 'going electric' (the tour took place between the release of his first 'rock' LPs, *Bringing It All Back Home* and the follow-up, *Highway 61 Revisited*), to assert the comparative superiority of direct cinema over other forms of journalism.

Throughout the tour, Dylan frequently reads newspapers and the trade press, bemused by their distorting simplifications and the wish to conveniently label him, whether as folk singer, rock star or, as one news story would have it, anarchist. Hence, Dylan's seemingly mean-spirited mocking of earnest journalists who keep asking him the same questions. His teasing of journalists begins immediately upon his arrival in London at the airport press conference, where he appears with an oversized industrial lightbulb, answering a reporter's question about what his 'real message' is by cryptically saying 'Keep a good head and always carry a lightbulb', and reaches a climax with a lengthy tirade to an unfortunate reporter from *Time* magazine. The press try to generate a sense of drama by referring to Donovan, whose name keeps popping up, as 'the other Dylan', but when they finally meet in a crowded hotel room Dylan's seemingly offhand but riveting performance of the richly poetic 'Love Minus Zero – No Limit' after Donovan's gentle little ditty makes it clear that they are not in the same league.

In the film's famous opening scene, Dylan stands in an alley flipping poster cards containing the lyrics (more or less) to 'Subterranean Homesick Blues' as the song plays on the soundtrack and beat poet Allen

Ginsberg mouths an unheard mantra in the background. The staged, presentational nature of this scene indicates immediately that *Dont Look Back* is aware of Dylan's heightened sense of performance, and will use his complicated persona to demonstrate the mass media's typical inadequacies in representing the whole picture. When the BBC reporter asks him 'how it all began', Pennebaker immediately cuts to older footage of Dylan performing one of his earlier protest songs ('Only a Pawn in Their Game') to a group of black farm workers in a field, suggesting that it says much more than even Dylan's own words alone. In the end, Dylan's question to the hapless science student who comes seeking answers from him, 'Don't you ever just be quiet? Be silent and just watch and don't say one word?', applies not only to his music but to the fundamental observational aesthetic of direct cinema. BKG

Dir/Scr: D. A. Pennebaker; **Prod**: John Court, Albert Grossman; **Phot**: Howard Alk, Jones Alk, Ed Emshwiller, D. A. Pennebaker (b/w); **Ed**: D. A. Pennebaker; **Sound**: Jones Alk; **With**: Bob Dylan, Albert Grossman, Bob Neuwirth, Joan Baez, Alan Price, Donovan, *et al.*; **Prod Co**: Leacock-Pennebaker.

The Emperor's Naked Army Marches On (*Yuki yukite shingun*)
Japan, 1987 – 122 mins
Hara Kazuo

Okuzaki Kenzo was a common soldier in the Japanese Army during
World War II, stationed in New Guinea as the war ended. An anti-war
campaigner, refusing to let Japanese silence about its role in World War II
lie undisturbed, he denounced the Emperor's wartime leadership and
sought the truth about the conduct of the war, serving hard labour jail
sentences for murder and for slingshotting *pachinko* balls at the Emperor
and publishing obscene images of him. *The Emperor's Naked Army
Marches On*, filmed over five years, follows Okuzaki, now in his sixties,
visiting members of his former regiment involved in executing two young
privates to establish exactly what happened and why, and to console the
dead soldiers' souls.

The Emperor's Naked Army Marches On is a challenging and
provocative documentary on several levels. Its protagonist is a complex,
contradictory figure, an anti-Establishment loose cannon obsessively
dedicated to his mission, sometimes likeable and sympathetic, other
times impossible to read. Increasingly, his conviction that he is 'God's
messenger' suggests a deranged personality, without ever confirming it.
Truculently subversive of the courtesy codes of Japanese culture, his
unannounced visits to former comrades and superiors exploit their
hospitality, which he has no hesitation in violating when they refuse to
answer or give answers he does not like, several times physically
attacking them (making Michael Moore's 'ambush' of Charlton Heston in
BOWLING FOR COLUMBINE, 2002, say, look decidedly mild). On these
occasions, their astonished families stand around unsure what to do,
while Okuzaki, adding a farcical edge to proceedings, offers to call the
police himself. On some of his visits, he is accompanied by relatives of
the dead soldiers, but when they abandon the quest, Okuzaki has no
scruples about enlisting acquaintances to impersonate them.

How to describe the film's documentary practice and ethics? Is this US-style 'direct cinema', like PRIMARY (1960), CRISIS (1963) or SALESMAN (1969), where the camera observes events without intervention or interference (except that the presence of the camera and sound recording seems to function as an integral part of Okuzaki's threatening strategy)? Is it rather, then, more cinéma vérité in the manner of Rouch and Morin's CHRONIQUE D'UN ÉTÉ (1961), where the film-makers' presence works as catalyst and provocation, making things happen? Such questions reverberate throughout the film, perhaps most notably when the family of a clearly sick man attacked by Okuzaki appeal to the crew, 'You just film it and do nothing?' Part of the discomfort it causes its spectators – whether more for Western viewers than Japanese is debatable – is precisely that the film itself does not channel our responses and sympathies. As for 'truth', Okuzaki's interrogations build up a sort of *Rashomon* effect as each man gives a slightly, or wildly, different version of events, but his dogged pursuit does clearly establish that in the extreme circumstances of the time, cannibalism was practised. As the film ends, we learn that Okuzaki is back in prison (where, his wife reports with equanimity, he prefers the food), having shot his commanding officer's son, still insisting that 'violence is justified if the end result is good'.

Hara Kazuo thus remains true to his principle that documentaries 'should explore the things that people don't want explored'. His associate producer, Imamura Shohei, better known for his fiction films, was also committed to 'really messy, human films': in the 1970s, he directed several subversive television documentaries about 'official' Japanese history, including *The History of Postwar Japan as Told by a Bar Hostess* (1970) and *In Search of Unreturned Soldiers* (1971). JH

Dir/Phot: Hara Kazuo (colour); **Prod**: Kobayashi Sachiko, Imamura Shohei; **Ed**: Nabeshima Jun; **Sound**: Kuribayashi Toyohiko; **Prod Co**: Imamura Productions/Shisso Production/Zanzou-sha.

Être et avoir (*To Be and to Have*)
France, 2002 – 104 mins
Nicolas Philibert

Être et avoir is an observational documentary about a small rural French school in the Auvergne, with one teacher, Georges Lopez, and thirteen children aged five to eleven bussed in from the surrounding area, occupying a single schoolroom – a type of school that is becoming increasingly rare. It became the most popular documentary in the history of French cinema. The film is a wonderfully observed, understated record of the school's teaching and learning across the academic year, but it also appealed to widespread French nostalgia for a simpler rural life lived closer to nature – a nostalgia shared by many other urbanised national cultures. The film seems to feed that nostalgia – no computers are in view, for example – and though its first images may be of herding cows in driving sleet, its final, almost inevitable, image is a static shot of a harvested wheat field on a sunny summer's day, with the blue Auvergne mountains stretching into the distance.

Natural landscapes marked by the seasons chart the film's progress through the year, an ever-changing but cyclical physical reality against which the children mature and leave school – to be replaced, near the end, by new students – and the teacher edges towards retirement. Though Philibert did not see Lopez as a model teacher, Lopez comes across as wise, patient and sympathetic, and almost a living embodiment of *in loco parentis*, but his life beyond the school remains an enigma. Despite a straight-to-camera interview with Lopez (the only such sequence) in which he reveals how he always wanted to be a teacher and the pleasure he gets from the children, we realise that we *still* know little about him, though his mask slips momentarily when he is close to tears as the children say goodbye and leave – some for good – at year's end.

Commentators have related *Être et avoir* to the cinéma vérité style of CHRONIQUE D'UN ÉTÉ (1961), but in its refusal of commentary (though it makes effective use of music) and its non-participatory, non-judgmental approach, it seems more like Frederick Wiseman's films (see TITICUT FOLLIES, 1967, PRIMATE, 1974) and other North American direct cinema. (Also like Wiseman, Philibert is interested in the ways institutions work; earlier Philibert films include *Le Pays des sourds* [*In the Land of the Deaf*, 1992], about deaf communities, and *La Moindre des choses* [*Every Little Thing*, 1997], about a psychiatric clinic.) However, *Être et avoir* also brings strongly to mind Georges Rouquier's FARREBIQUE (1946). *Farrebique* was a scripted, acted reconstruction, shot with unwieldy equipment, whereas *Être et avoir* was unscripted, shot with lightweight cameras and sound equipment, wide-angle lenses minimising the need to move around and sensitive film stocks making possible shooting with available light; all the indications are that the children got used to the camera's presence; Philibert spent almost a year in the school, editing 60 hours of footage down to under 2. But despite the enormous formal differences, *Farrebique* and *Être et avoir* both draw heavily on the same nostalgia, in part by marking the passing of the seasons.

The film's enormous success in France and abroad prompted Lopez to claim a share of the film's profits (no doubt subtly altering our

response to his 'performance' and Philibert's intentions). He and the children had been paid a low going rate of compensation for their participation, but Lopez argued that his promotional work for the film had contributed to its success. He lost the case, but it is a salutary reminder that the world of fly-on-the-wall documentary is also a world of costs, contracts and bottom lines. JH

Dir/Ed: Nicolas Philibert; **Prod**: Gilles Sandoz, Serge Lalou (assoc. prod); **Phot**: Katell Djian, Laurent Didier, Nicolas Philibert (colour); **Music**: Philippe Hersant; **Sound**: Julien Cloquet; **Prod Co**: Maïa Films/Arte France Cinéma/Les Films d'Ici/Centre National de Documentation Pédagogique/Canal+/Centre National de la Cinématographie/Gimages 4.

The Fall of the Romanov Dynasty (Padenie dinastii Romanovykh)
USSR, 1927 – 90 mins
Esfir Shub

The best-known 1920s Soviet cinema names are probably Eisenstein, Kuleshov, Kozintsev and Trauberg, Pudovkin, Dovzhenko, Dziga Vertov – all, except Vertov, fiction film-makers. But documentaries – not just Vertov's idiosyncratic MAN WITH A MOVIE CAMERA (1929) but other films, like Viktor Turin's TURKSIB (1929) – were accorded enormous importance during this period: Osip Brik argued in *Novyi Lef* in 1928 that the story of the Revolution must be told in documentary rather than fictional form.

Esfir (or Esther) Shub, having for several years recut and retitled foreign films, became an important documentary film-maker with a difference: she can take major credit for developing the historical compilation film. Her films drew on newsreels and other earlier films to chronicle Russian and Soviet history from the early 20th century through to 1927: *The Fall of the Romanov Dynasty*, made to mark the tenth anniversary of the February 1917 Revolution, covered the period 1912–17; *The Great Road* (1927) (made – along with Pudovkin's *The End of St Petersburg*, 1927, and Eisenstein's *October*, 1928 – to mark the tenth anniversary of the October Revolution), the years 1917–27; and *The Russia of Nikolai II and Lev Tolstoy* (1928), the years 1897–1912. The films represented a remarkable feat of archival research, not least because there were no proper archives: 'In the damp cellars of Goskino, in "Kino Moskva", in the Museum of the Revolution lay boxes of negatives and random prints, and no one knew how they had got there.'

Having identified material – at one level, just remarkable footage of varied aspects of Russian life – Shub proceeds to shape it through editing and intertitles. Rhythmically, the film begins slowly, speeding up with the European imperialist rush to war and events in Russia leading up to the tsar's abdication and Kerensky's government, ending with the first, very brief, appearances of Lenin. Many juxtapositions are straightforward, though no less powerful for that: church domes are associated with cannons, and priests with repression; the rich estates of the landowners are contrasted with 'land-short, poverty-stricken villages'.

Shub's intertitles can be largely descriptive, but some cut through film material, such as the ceremony marking the Romanovs' 300th anniversary, very strikingly: 'Emperor and Autocrat of all the Russias, Czar of Poland, Grand Prince of Finland, and so on and so forth, Nicholas the Second . . . and last.' Elsewhere, Shub has a wonderful eye for the telling incident: a provincial governor and his wife stroll through their grounds (cut against peasants toiling with the harvest) and take tea on the lawn, the camera waiting, after they leave, for servants to scurry in and clear up; passing close-ups of noble ladies perspiring after an energetic mazurka, cut against ditch-diggers rolling up their sleeves and wiping their faces; a corpulent nobleman at the anniversary celebrations signalling his irritation to someone in the off-screen crowd who has failed to remove his hat.

It is in the nature of the historical compilation film that the original material was shot for many different purposes and has been selected and arranged to create new meanings. However powerful an argument might be, there must remain in the spectator's mind some level of consciousness that 'meaning' is less inherent in the material than dependent on context. The form remained established but not much practised until the more overtly politicised 1960s, with the work of Emile de Antonio (see IN THE YEAR OF THE PIG, 1968), films like *Mourir à Madrid* (*To Die in Madrid*, dir. Frédéric Rossif, 1963), some of Santiago Alvarez's Cuban films, in more agitprop mode, such as 79 PRIMAVERAS (1969), and later in films like THE ATOMIC CAFÉ (1982). JH

Dir/Scr/Ed: Esfir Shub; **Consultant**: M. Z.Tzeitlin (Museum of the Revolution); **Prod Co**: Sovkino/Museum of the Revolution.

Farrebique (*Farrebique, ou les quatre saisons*)
France, 1946 – 90 mins
Georges Rouquier

Farrebique centres on a farm, Farrebique, and farm family in the Aveyron, South-west France (with dialogue in the Occitan dialect), over the course of a year – hence the full title, *Farrebique, or the Four Seasons*.
Among its admirers were André Bazin and Jean Rouch. The film begins in late autumn and proceeds through winter, spring, summer and harvest time, documenting the seasonal changes in the look of the farm and the jobs to be done; alongside runs the narrative of the farm's inhabitants, Rouquier's relatives – mainly Grandfather and Grandmother, eldest son Roch, his wife Berthe and three children, and Henri, the more outward-looking younger son – working the farm; from time to time, they discuss Grandfather's retirement and Roch taking over the farm, whether to rebuild and enlarge the house, and, with their neighbour Fabre (whose daughter Henri is courting), whether to install electricity; later, Henri has an accident and Grandfather dies.

The farm and its activities are lovingly photographed: Rouquier periodically inserts stop-motion shots of sun and shadow sweeping across the house and landscape, and close-ups of nature; great play is made of the making, baking and cutting of enormous loaves of bread. In mid-winter and spring, Rouquier shifts into lyrical mode, perhaps a little overdone, with wonderful montages of snow dropping from trees or animals and birds in the wintry landscape. Spring elicits a delirious 'poem' about the 'deadness of winter passing away', with accelerated-motion plant growth, microscopic cell imagery, close-ups of sap and pollen, culminating in Berthe giving birth (a sequence doubtless particularly resonant for a France recently emerged from occupation). Here too, the voiceover, otherwise minimal, becomes most insistent.

Farrebique was shot on 35mm with much synch sound; like other documentaries of the era – NORTH SEA (1938), MAN OF ARAN (1934), A DIARY FOR TIMOTHY (1945), *Louisiana Story* (1948), say – it was fully scripted and diverged considerably from 'fact': in reality, Henri was married, and Fabre had no daughter; a third son, not mentioned, was a prisoner-of-war; neither installing electric power nor dividing the property was discussed, though the planned ending – rebuilding the house – had to be changed when money ran out; Henri was not injured in an accident and Grandfather did not die. The special-effects shots were done in a Paris studio. Nevertheless, as its opening title says, the film was 'shot from the first to the last image in the intimacy of a peasant family'; Rouquier claims it as 'real' 'because it was shot in a real Rouergue village

with real peasants as actors. I wanted everything to be real and simple.'
Bazin, in his many-pronged polemic for realism in the cinema, singled out
Rouquier's 'little bit of genius' in rediscovering 'the simple and
elementary joy . . . of recognition' that had marked the reception of the
LUMIÈRE PROGRAMME (1895).

   Farrebique was prepared in 1943–4 under the Vichy regime,
which gave some support in line with its 'Retour à la terre' (Return to the
land) policy, but was shot after the Liberation and took a year to edit.
The film avoids reference to current events, but it no doubt reaffirmed a
mythic *France profonde*, which Bazin characterised here as a 'slightly
ridiculous and nostalgic world which [the spectator] vaguely feels he has
somehow betrayed, the world of the land, of men and animals, which he
dimly remembers from his childhood and from holidays past'.
Farrebique remained sufficiently in the popular imagination to enable
Rouquier, after several other projects, to make a sequel, *Biquefarre*, in
1983, focusing on the changing economics of farming; in the 1950s,
Jacques Demy worked as assistant to Rouquier, who produced Demy's
documentary short debut, *Le Sabotier du Val de Loire*, 1955. JH

Dir/Scr: Georges Rouquier; **Prod**: Jacques Girard, Jacqueline Jacoupy; **Phot**: André A.
Dantan (b/w); **Ed**: Madeleine Gug; **Music**: Henri Sauguet; **Sound**: René Lécuyer;
Prod Co: Les Films Etienne Lallier/Écran Français.

Fast, Cheap and Out of Control
US, 1997 – 82 mins
Errol Morris

Errol Morris's post-modern documentary essays seem pulled between apparently more 'serious' subjects like THE THIN BLUE LINE (1988), *The Fog of War* (2003) and *Standard Operating Procedure* (2008) and seemingly more eccentric subjects like *The Gates of Heaven* (1980) and *Vernon, Florida* (1982) (*A Brief History of Time*, 1991, and *Mr Death*, 1999, perhaps falling somewhere in between). *Fast, Cheap and Out of Control appears* to be about eccentrics, focusing as it does on four figures obsessively involved with their work: Dave Hoover, retired circus lion trainer; George Mendoça, seventy-year-old topiary artist; Ray Mendez, African naked mole rat expert; and Rodney Brooks, MIT robot designer (who provides the film's title). Moving between them, combining straight-to-camera interviews (using Morris's Interrotron system, allowing 'interviews' to work more like face-to-face encounters between film-maker and subject) with sequences of them at work and their working environments, the film – like *Thin Blue Line* and *Mr Death* – fluently incorporates a range of 'miscellaneous' material, including clips from black-and-white B-movie adventure serials, newsreels, 8mm home movies, insect photography, etc. This heady mix is made even more potent by switches in Morris's own footage between colour and monochrome, film and video, slow motion and pixilation, long shot and close-up, with frequently low, tilted and other unusual angles (virtuoso work by Robert Richardson, cinematographer of choice for, among others, Quentin Tarantino, Martin Scorsese, Oliver Stone and John Sayles). One obvious effect is to 'make strange', to make us see and connect in new ways. Is there a consistent rationale behind the variety and mix? This is less clear.

Though each of the subjects is individually fascinating, it is Morris's orchestration of the whole – accumulation, juxtaposition, blend – that impresses, making unexpected links and associations: Brooks's comment that he doesn't 'tell the robot what to do – I switch it on and it does what is in its nature' overlaps with images of circus acrobats; Mendez's comment that people come to look at the mole rats 'and wonder what they're looking at' carries over to stylised images of a circus parade; mole rats and robots are linked by comments about evolution.

Fast, Cheap and Out of Control is brimming with ideas that suggestively and provocatively illuminate and pose questions about each other, but does the film, ultimately, cohere – and does Morris intend that it should, in conventional terms? Is it, rather, an open text, constantly in flux? Critics have interpreted the film so differently that we might conclude that it doesn't cohere, or at least not in the same ways for different viewers. Yet, towards the end, a pervasive sense of loss emerges: the topiary gardener's achievements will disappear when he dies – or before, if the natural forces he battles have their way; the lion tamer, at the end of his career, misses his idol and friend Clyde Beatty, legendary circus animal tamer and 1930s/1940s serial star, whose like will never be seen again; the mole rat expert confesses that his work has nothing to do with science and all to do with seeking self-knowledge; the robot engineer wonders, with evident regret, if the inevitable next evolutionary step, which he is helping to create, will replace humans with robots. But this sense of loss, though real, is counterweighted throughout by the visibly human attributes of vision, ingenuity, energy, curiosity – and, certainly, eccentricity. Morris's affectionate use of clips from the apparently juvenile jungle adventure serials – all legendary lost cities, taboos and Clyde Beatty heroics – is surely intended to resonate in just this way. JH

Dir: Errol Morris; **Prod**: Errol Morris, Lindsay Law (exec. prod), Mark Lipson, Julia Sheehan, Kathy Trustman (co-prods); **Phot**: Robert Richardson (colour & b/w); **Ed**: Shondra Merrill, Karen Schmeer; **Music**: Caleb Sampson; **Prod Des**: Ted Bafaloukos; **Prod Co**: Fourth Floor Productions/American Playhouse.

For Freedom (Baray-e Azadi)
Iran, 1979 – 110 mins
Hossein Torabi

Few film-makers find themselves in the midst of momentous revolutionary events with the opportunity to document them, but such was the case for Hossein Torabi, working at the Ministry of Art and Culture as Shah Pahlevi's regime began to collapse in 1978–9.
For Freedom documents and celebrates the Iranian popular revolution in its various phases, following the familiar progression from neocolonial authoritarian regime and panic-led repression to attempts by an interim moderate government to rescue the regime and the subsequent uncontainable popular uprising and return from exile of a new, revolutionary leader. Here, of course, these phases take place in the less familiar context of a secular monarchy imposed and propped up by Western governments being ousted by a hardline Islamic theocracy headed by Ayatollah Khomeini.

When initial shooting began, no one knew what the outcome might be and this is reflected in a somewhat tentative 'let's film the aftermath of this atrocity or that popular demonstration even though we do not know its significance yet' approach. Though, of course, the film was assembled with hindsight, some of this tentativeness remains in its 'block' structure – extended footage of demonstrations, or preparations for street battles, and so on – rather than an intricately explanatory cause/effect or narrative structure (as in, say, the fictional but often documentary-style *Battle of Algiers*, dir. Gillo Pontecorvo, 1965). There is no linking voiceover commentary (though one was planned) – problematic for a non-Iranian audience, but the film is aimed very clearly at a *national* audience already familiar with at least the broad outline of historical events and figures. What we learn here we learn from the chants and banners of demonstrators, from graffiti, from occasional vox pop interviews, from brief shots of 'decadent' Western film posters, and from press conferences given by Shapour Bakhtiar (who took over when the Shah left for exile) and by Khomeini and his chosen prime minister, Mehdi Bazargan.

Unsurprisingly, given the conditions of its production (very different from, say, TRIUMPH OF THE WILL, 1935, but more like LA BATALLA DE CHILE, 1975), the film is sometimes rough at the edges technically, but it falls within the mobile camera and sound conventions of direct cinema and newsreel (though sound is not always convincingly married to image). In another sense, the film is a montage, with events juxtaposed against each other (occasionally recalling Eisenstein's *October*, 1928, when it cuts between footage of mass grief or popular demonstrations to formal footage of the lavishly decorated Shah greeting his slavishly subservient – and only slightly less lavishly decorated – generals and ministers).

It is difficult to watch the film now without wondering, not so much about the clearly popular nature of the revolution, but about the different aspirations of those taking part, such as the students, aspirations that, as we know, still reverberate through the Iranian polity; or about the ambivalence of the Turkmen, Zoroastrians and other minority groups who ask themselves, at referendum time, what the Islamic revolution will mean for them. Hossein Torabi does not play up these issues, but neither does he play them down – they are 'there'. The film's title comes from its opening: 'Our revolution was everywhere and everybody was present but not even a thousand cameras would have been enough to capture the immensity of the Iranians' movement for freedom.' JH

Dir: Hossein Torabi; **Scr**: Gholamhossein Amir-Khani; **Phot**: Fereydoun Reypoor (*et al.*) (colour); **Ed**: Bahram Raypour, Kazem Raji-Nia; **Music**: Sheida Gharechedaghi; **Sound**: Eshagh Khanzadi, Mohsen Roshan, Parviz Amir-Afshari, Sadegh Alemi; **Prod Co**: Ministry of Culture and Islamic Guidance, Iran.

Forgotten Silver
New Zealand, 1995 – 52 mins
Peter Jackson, Costa Botes

Peter Jackson and Costa Botes's *Forgotten Silver* is at once a comic and convincing 'mockumentary', a faux biography of a supposedly forgotten New Zealand pioneer of early cinema – the hapless but heroic Colin McKenzie, whose long-lost films director Jackson claims in an interview sequence to have discovered in an old chest given to him by a family friend. *Forgotten Silver* pretends to uncover the now forgotten achievements of McKenzie and to restore him to his proper place in film history. Concluding with a sequence from McKenzie's unfinished masterwork, the biblical epic *Salome*, laboriously restored by the New Zealand Film Commission but actually a brilliant parody by Jackson of D. W. Griffith's *Intolerance* (1916), *Forgotten Silver*'s use of documentary rhetoric and techniques is so exact that, when it was first broadcast on television on 29 October 1995, it became New Zealand's most notorious media hoax, comparable to Orson Welles's infamous Halloween 1938 radio broadcast of *War of the Worlds* in the US, with many viewers completely taken in by it.

With numerous in-jokes and references to film history, *Forgotten Silver* incorporates elements of all four documentary modes identified by Bill Nichols and others. As seemingly straightforward exposition, it employs a traditional Voice-of-God narrator and interviews with experts, including producer Harvey Weinstein and celebrity film critic Leonard Maltin, who proclaims with a straight face that McKenzie belongs in the auteurist pantheon and that film history will need to be rewritten. The observational mode is employed in such vérité scenes as when Jackson and crew hack their way through the dense New Zealand brush and 'discover' McKenzie's set for *Salome* buried deep in the wilderness, undisturbed for decades. Here and throughout, Jackson serves the dual role of film-maker and profilmic social actor, as when he discovers the first chest of films in the garden shed belonging to McKenzie's widow.

And the film is playfully reflexive, in that periodic clues invite attentive viewers to question the film's own veracity through witty intertextual referencing (for example, a Soviet culture official is identified as Alexandra Nevsky) and stylistic cues, as when Jackson and his team discover and enter the vault room where McKenzie left all his footage for *Salome*, supposedly sealed for years until this moment, though the camera is already positioned inside when they first open the door.

On one level, *Forgotten Silver*'s satire is aimed specifically at New Zealand culture, its imaginary biography of Colin McKenzie invoking the popular backyard inventor myth. McKenzie is a comic embodiment of the historical character of New Zealand cinema, often characterised by a 'do-it-yourself' approach. Just as McKenzie stole eggs to concoct his own film stock or used a bicycle to power his projector, Peter Jackson worked in his backyard, ingeniously creating his own special effects in his early films with minimal means. Yet *Forgotten Silver*'s wider importance lies in how successfully it encourages viewer acceptance by mocking our general willingness to believe anything told in convincing documentary style. Ironically, the revelation of the film's false status as documentary ultimately served John Grierson's oft-stated goal of increasing social awareness by showing us, in fact, how unaware and gullible we may be in our willingness to mistake style for substance. BKG

Dir/Scr: Peter Jackson, Costa Botes; **Prod**: Sue Rogers; **Phot**: Alun Bollinger, Gerry Vasbenter (b/w & colour); **Ed**: Eric de Beus, Michael Horton; **Music**: David Donaldson, Steve Roche, Janet Roddick; **Prod Co**: New Zealand Film Commission/New Zealand On Air/WingNut Films.

Les Glâneurs et la glâneuse (*The Gleaners and I*)
France, 2000 – 82 mins
Agnès Varda

Agnès Varda was a successful photo-journalist and documentary film-maker (*L'Opéra mouffe* and *Du côté de la côte*, both 1958, for example) before making her first full-length fiction feature, *Cléo de 5 à 7* (1962). Like her New Wave 'Left Bank' colleague Chris Marker (see SANS SOLEIL, 1983), Varda has favoured the 'ciné essay' documentary form (while trying to incorporate 'the *texture* of documentary' in her fictions).

Even so, *Les Glâneurs et la glâneuse*, shot with tiny handheld DV cameras, was a significant new departure. The new technology gave Varda the confidence to film herself, 'get involved as a film-maker' and get closer to her subjects. The film is as much about Varda – her tastes, her sensibility, her endless enthusiasm, her visible ageing – as it is about gleaning. The film's English title misses the nuances of the French, which suggests gleaners, in general, and the – feminine, singular – gleaner: the 'glâneuse' is Varda herself, using her camera to glean the pickings that constitute the film and doing some gleaning herself, taking home, for example, a rejected heart-shaped potato and a clock face with no hands ('my kind of thing – you don't see time passing'). The cheapness and ease of use of the DV camera allowed Varda to follow her impulses without having to worry about the usual logistics of film-making: a sequence about a chef puts her in mind of vineyards and off she goes to film some – though not without a digression on the way about trucks on the highway. Photos of Rembrandt self-portraits from Japan spark off her close-up filming with one hand the lines and liver spots on the other.

Varda explores the origins of 'gleaning': one of her first images is Millet's painting *The Gleaners*, and its final image is Hedouin's *Gleaners*, rescued from the storeroom of the Villefrance-sur-Sâone museum and displayed, buffeted by the wind and held by curators' curiously disembodied hands. But she is as concerned here with more modern

forms of gleaning – people collecting over-sized or irregularly shaped potatoes, food discarded at the end of street markets, apples picked after the harvest or food thrown away by supermarkets. Her film thus becomes in part an essay on the economics of contemporary food production and packaging – no doubt accounting for some of the interest the film has generated.

But as well as a film about art, herself and food economics, *Les Glâneurs* is also a 'road documentary', a reportage on France at the millennium, from the potato-growing north to the wheat-growing Beauce, from wine-growing in Burgundy and the south to west coast oyster collectors. As in her feature *Sans toit ni loi* (*Vagabonde*, 1985), Varda is drawn to the socially marginalised and her encounters range from caravan-dwelling potato gleaners in the north to homeless hippy supermarket bin gleaners in the south, for whom gleaning is a form of resistance. But also here are Michelin-starred chefs, prestigious vineyard owners, legal officials quoting regulations about gleaning and the ownership of abandoned goods, and artists, 'professional' as well as 'amateur', who work with the rich detritus of everyday life.

Varda may like, as she says, 'filming rot, leftovers, waste, mould and trash', but she remains positive, infectiously playful and ever open to 'digressions': a visit to a vineyard owner whose great-grandfather was moving-image pioneer Jules Marey prompts a trip to the Marey museum and some animal locomotion pictures; and when she forgets to switch off the camera, Varda treats us to a 'dance of the lens cap' as she walks along, the camera bobbing up and down beside her. JH

Dir/Prod/Scr: Agnès Varda; **Phot**: Stéphane Krausz, Didier Rouget, Pascal Sautelet, Didier Doussin, Agnès Varda (colour); **Ed**: Agnès Varda, Laurent Pineau; **Music**: Joanna Bruzdowicz; **Sound**: Emmanuel Soland, Nathalie Duval; **Prod Co**: Ciné Tamaris (with Centre National du Cinéma/Canal+/La PROCIREP).

Grey Gardens
US, 1975 – 100 mins
Albert Maysles, David Maysles, Ellen Hovde, Muffie Meyer

In *Gimme Shelter* (1970), the Maysles brothers became more involved with their profilmic subjects than previously, showing the Rolling Stones the footage they had shot of the stabbing to death of a fan at their Altamont Speedway concert and filming their reactions; but with *Grey Gardens*, the Maysles take this aggressive approach even further, continually interacting with Edith Bouvier Beale ('Big Edie') and her daughter Edie ('Little Edie') to the point of prompting much of what these two, clearly psychologically disturbed, women do before the camera and thereby raising significant questions about the ethics of documentary film-making. The aunt and first cousin of Jacqueline Kennedy Onassis (who provided the money for the repairs needed to forestall eviction) live together alone, except for their many cats, in a decaying 28-room mansion in East Hampton, Long Island, where the family has lived for fifty years. They clearly welcome the company of the film-makers and relish their attention and the camera, for which they readily sing, dance and reminisce.

The Maysles's presence is announced at the beginning: after an opening montage of newspaper clippings and photos that provide some basic necessary exposition about the Beales and the fact that they were almost evicted, the Maysles enter their once-stately home as Little Edie happily coos 'It's the Maysles' to her mother. As they film, sometimes they simply ask for further information, such as the identity of someone in an old photo, but often their interaction is more problematic, as when they join the women in an execrable rendition of 'You and the Night and the Music'. Little Edie gives them instructions, feeds and confides in them, appealing to them in arguments with her mother, such as when she whispers about her disagreement with Big Edie over what was appropriate to wear for the film. The Maysles introduce themselves as 'gentlemen callers', evoking Tennessee Williams's *The Glass Menagerie* (1944) and the Southern Gothic.

Little Edie says that it is difficult to keep distinct the line between the past and the present, but Albert's camera occasionally returns to the society portrait of Big Edie leaning up against the wall in her dishevelled bedroom behind the bric-a-brac, emphasising the startling contrast between her appearance then and how she looks now, a difference that the Beales themselves refuse to admit (little Edie even thinks that the young worker, at least half her age, who periodically comes to the house is interested in her sexually). It gradually becomes clear that Big Edie's possessiveness has kept Little Edie from becoming an independent person, and the daughter takes every opportunity to express her anger toward her mother about this denial of her freedom. The Maysles become sounding boards for their broken and unfulfilled dreams to become entertainers. Because the women's hold on reality is so tenuous, the Maysles walk a fine line in the film between examination and exploitation, foregrounding an issue that is always inevitably present in direct cinema (see, for example, TITICUT FOLLIES, 1967).

David Maysles died in 1987, but in 2006, Albert Maysles made available previously unreleased footage for a special two-disc edition for Criterion, including a new feature entitled *The Beales of Grey Gardens*, which also received a limited theatrical release. *Grey Gardens*, having become something of a cult movie, was also adapted into a musical production that premiered in New York City in February 2006; it received good reviews and later that year moved to Broadway, where it won three Tony Awards and ran for nine months. BKG

Dir: Ellen Hovde, Albert Maysles, David Maysles, Muffie Meyer; **Prod/Phot**: Albert Maysles, David Maysles (colour); **Ed**: Susan Frömke (as Susan Froemke), Ellen Hovde, Muffie Meyer; **Sound**: Lee Dichter; **Prod Co**: Portrait Films.

Grizzly Man
US, 2005 – 100 mins
Werner Herzog

Grizzly Man chronicles the life and death of Timothy Treadwell, an American naturalist and environmentalist who was particularly fond of grizzly bears, and lived among them in Alaska's Kitmai National Park for thirteen summers until autumn 2003, when he and his girlfriend Amie Huguenard were killed and eaten by a grizzly at their campsite. Treadwell was also a documentary film-maker who filmed his own adventures and gave school lectures during the winters. Over the years of his filming himself in the wild, Treadwell seemed to have become increasingly obsessed with his persona as an 'eco-warrior'.

Director Werner Herzog combines footage from the more than one hundred hours that Treadwell shot over a five-year period with his own interviews with people who knew him, along with a personal voiceover narration about his own relation to Treadwell and his documentary footage, producing a fascinating film about his, and our, relation to nature – a theme to which Herzog returns in both his fiction films (*Aguirre, The Wrath of God*, 1972, *Fitzcarraldo*, 1982) and his documentaries (LESSONS IN DARKNESS, 1992).

The various interviewees express very different views about Treadwell: helicopter pilot Sam Egli sarcastically refers to him as 'child of the universe who got what he was asking for'; ecologist Marnie Gaede reverently tells Herzog that Treadwell had undergone a religious experience and wanted to merge with the animals; and Sven Aakanson, the native curator of Kodiak's Alutiig museum, criticises Treadwell for having violated nature by crossing the boundary between human and animal. Herzog himself is drawn to Treadwell because he recognises in Treadwell's developing eco-warrior persona and sense of mission as self-appointed bear protector what he calls the madness of the jungle, which Herzog experienced personally during the making of both *Aguirre* and *Fitzcarraldo* (documented in *My Best Fiend*, 1999, about his love–hate

relation with eccentric actor Klaus Kinski, who starred in both films). Herzog saw a similar quality in Dieter Dengler's amazing story of survival as a POW in the jungles of Vietnam and Cambodia, which he documented in *Little Dieter Needs to Fly* (1997), as well as dramatising in a fictionalised version, *Rescue Dawn* (2006).

Over aerial shots of a rugged glacier with jagged spires of ice and gaping fissures, Herzog describes how he sees the Alaskan wilderness as 'a metaphor for the turmoil of Treadwell's soul'. There is the suggestion in Treadwell's own comments that he was driven by a death wish to expiate his troubled past as an alcoholic. He roamed with bears, played with foxes and cried at the apparent death of a bee in the process of pollination, but his fate serves to confirm Herzog's darker view of nature, in comparison to which Treadwell seems a naive hippy. Accompanying a close-up taken by Treadwell of a bear's face, Herzog says he sees nothing of the secret life of bears but only 'the overwhelming indifference of nature'. The audiotape of the fatal attack on Treadwell and his girlfriend that Herzog listens to but withholds from the viewer is so disturbing that he tells Treadwell's former girlfriend Jewel Palovak to destroy it without hearing it. Yet Herzog is not entirely fatalistic, for he perceives how Treadwell's film-making went far beyond nature documentary to become a tool of self-discovery, and at the same time to create documentary images, such as the shot where Treadwell exits the frame while the camera dwells on the waving beauty of grass and bush, that 'themselves develop their own life'. BKG

Dir/Scr/Narrator: Werner Herzog, **Prod**: Eric Nelson; **Phot**: Peter Zeitlinger (colour); **Ed**: Joe Bini; **Music**: Richard Thompson; **Sound**: Ken King, Spencer Palermo, Michael Klinger, D. D. Stenehjem; **Prod Co**: Discovery Docs/Real Big Productions.

Handsworth Songs
UK, 1986 – 61 mins
John Akomfrah

Prompted by the 1982 establishment of Channel 4 Television, with its remit to innovate and represent minority interests, and the technician union's (ACTT) 'Workshop Declaration', several black film-making groups, funded by Channel 4 and the Greater London Council, began making challenging films about the representation of race, gender and class. *Handsworth Songs* was among the most interesting and controversial films produced. Though individuals, many just graduating from art school and/or film school, took specific credits, much work was done collectively. Two major groups were the Black Audio Film Collective (1982–98) and Sankofa Film and Video Collective (1983–92) (which produced Maureen Blackwood's *The Passion of Remembrance*, 1986, Martina Attille's *Dreaming Rivers*, 1988, and Isaac Julien's *Looking for Langston*, 1989, and *Young Soul Rebels*, 1991). Though relatively short-lived, these groups proved lasting influences on British independent film and television production.

The Handsworth area of Birmingham saw serious racial disturbances (following earlier 'race riots' in London) between 9 and 11 September 1985: two Asians died in a burned-out post office, thirty-five people were injured and there was much damage to property. *Handsworth Songs* takes this incident as its starting point for examining the identities of black Britons in relation to complex social and political histories. Refusing both conventional questions and conventional forms, insisting – like 1920s Soviet film-makers – on new forms for new content, its central thrust is towards collage, combining old and new television and film documentary and newsreel footage, still photographs, interviews, multiply voiced, often poetic, commentary obliquely related to the images, music, composed tableaux, etc.

The film's opening, and one of its recurrent, images is a uniformed black man (a bus driver?) perusing an ancient steam engine in a museum, and among the musical motifs are different versions of Parry's setting of Blake's 'Jerusalem' (played in reggae, brass band and choral versions, sometimes blended), with all their eighteenth- and nineteenth- as well as twentieth-century historical implications for British contemporary industrial decline and immigration. A voiceover motif is that 'there are no stories in the riots, only the ghosts of other stories'; one of those 'other stories', dealt with very evocatively, is the *Empire Windrush*'s 1948 journey from Jamaica and the hopes of its new immigrants. Opting for complex, suggestive associations rather than tight exposition and explanation, a central sequence links these 'disparate' elements: a 1977 meeting held by the racist National Front's leader, John Tyndall, and protests about it; newsreel footage of a 1937 Labour Day parade and a Bengali woman demonstrating doll-making; a composed tableau of icons of imperialism; ancient footage of the industrial forging of enormous chains; an old song about the Midlands industrial 'Black Country'; a grim urban landscape – 'derelict epitaphs to the Industrial Revolution' – accompanied by 'Jerusalem'; Margaret Thatcher's speech about fear of 'swamping' by immigrants; the slowed-down reprise of a running Rasta being caught by police. A very striking feature of the film is the way it turns its own cameras away from the supposed 'subject' and on to the serried ranks of press and television news teams.

Salman Rushdie attacked the film for not finding a language or telling Handsworth's stories, but Stuart Hall rightly defended it, arguing that Rushdie had 'missed the struggle which it represents, precisely to find a new language'. JH

Dir: John Akomfrah; **Prod**: Lina Gopaul; **Phot**: Sebastian Shah (b/w & colour); **Music/Sound**: Trevor Mathison; **Prod Co**: Black Audio Film Collective.

A Happy Mother's Day
US, 1963 – 26 mins
Richard Leacock, Joyce Chopra

A Happy Mother's Day, the first film made by Richard Leacock after leaving the Drew Associates (see PRIMARY, 1960, CRISIS, 1963), was shown on European television and won a number of awards at international film festivals, but was never broadcast in its original form on American television. The film chronicles the media frenzy and commercial exploitation that follows the birth of quintuplets (the first to survive in the US and only the third set in the world) to the Fischers, a quiet and unassuming farming family from the small town of Aberdeen, South Dakota. The film was commissioned by the *Saturday Evening Post*, which, unhappy with the result, re-edited it to eliminate any suggestion of crass materialism and commercial opportunism and sold the rights to ABC-TV. With the most egregious footage deleted, the altered film, retitled *Quint City, U.S.A.* and sponsored by Beechnut Baby Foods, instead now seemed to celebrate communal solidarity and care in response to the extraordinary event.

Leacock and Chopra's film cuts to the core of the American heartland, showing how the capitalist machinery ensures that concern for the children's welfare becomes secondary to potential profit. In one scene, the town's Chamber of Commerce (exclusively male) meets to discuss how to deal with the potential influx of tourists, with one member suggesting with a straight face that certain times can be designated for guided tours through the Fischer home. Mrs Fischer protests that she will never allow her children to be put on display, but no one seems to be listening, as planning enthusiastically continues. At one point, even Mr Fischer concedes that it may be necessary to allow the quints to be shown publicly. This disregard for Mrs Fischer is embarrassingly clear when the wife of the head of the Chamber of Commerce takes her clothes shopping for the upcoming banquet and she and the salesman discuss Mrs Fischer's wardrobe choices as if she were not there. For the benefit of the *Post* photographer, Mr Fischer is shot driving his prized antique Model-T Ford in circles in his driveway, suggesting that this traditional family is powerless to resist the contemporary media blitz that produces on his lawn a veritable cornucopia of gifts from companies hoping to jump on the bandwagon for free publicity. In its delivery, Ed McCurdy's droll voiceover commentary, which might in a different context seem reasonably neutral, adds a further sense of brittle irony to the proceedings: when, for example, it literally rains on the parade for the Fischers and they scramble for shelter, McCurdy dryly observes that 'It was a typical day of celebration in Aberdeen, South Dakota, USA' – an appropriate conclusion to this sardonic depiction of all-American materialism.

Of course, the film-makers cannot avoid acknowledging that they, too, are part of the media frenzy they are chronicling with such irony, that their own presence is contributing to the invasion of this introverted family's privacy that we are told is so important to Mr Fischer. As a result, the focus of the film shifts from the quintuplets to Mrs Fischer, whose indignation and fortitude we cannot help but share. Unlike the local businessmen, other photographers and reporters, Leacock and Chopra ask nothing of Mrs Fischer, but instead seem to establish a sympathetic bond with her. The film-makers' empathy with her perspective becomes particularly apparent when, at the banquet, the camera pans away from the execrable singer to the normally stoic Mrs Fischer, who, glancing at the camera, cannot repress the slightest of smirks, as if quietly sharing with the film-makers her opinion of the evening's entertainment, if not the entire affair. BKG

Dir/Phot/Sound: Richard Leacock, Joyce Chopra (b/w); **Prod Co**: Leacock-Pennebaker, Inc., for Curtis Publications.

Harlan County USA
US, 1976 – 102 mins
Barbara Kopple

The main 'action' in *Harlan County USA* concerns a thirteen-month strike
at the Brookside coal mine in Kentucky, precipitated by the miners voting
to join the United Mine Workers of America and the refusal of the owners,
Duke Power, to recognise them. As this partial description suggests, this
Academy Award-winning and theatrically well-distributed film exemplified
the politicisation of American culture in the late 1960s and 1970s.
During this time, Barbara Kopple was involved in the radical *Newsreel*

collectives that reported on events not covered by mainstream media, but also worked with the Maysles brothers. This, Kopple's first feature – in many ways a collective enterprise – was made over a three-year period with small-scale finance from a variety of organisations, including the UMW.

Though its methods derive from 1960s direct cinema (see PRIMARY, 1960, CRISIS, 1963, SALESMAN, 1968) – cameras and sound recording appear more mobile than fifteen years earlier, and faster film stocks enable sequences to be shot in limited light – Kopple and her collaborators are far from 'simply observers' (in Richard Leacock's phrase), albeit closer to those direct cinema films than to late 1960s politically deconstructed films like BRITISH SOUNDS (1969). The film-makers are partial, taking the miners' side both politically, with little time for the views of the mine owners and scabs, and *physically*: when the miners are attacked in a pre-dawn showdown, so are the film-makers; like the pickets, they keep their distance from the owners' gun-toting thugs and scabs. Noticeably, Kopple's off-screen voice is often heard and participants sometimes talk to her – though the film-maker's 'presence' is very different from later films like Michael Moore's ROGER AND ME (1989) and BOWLING FOR COLUMBINE (2002), or Morgan Spurlock's *Super Size Me* (2004).

The film would be much 'tidier', more narratively 'satisfying' – because this is, fundamentally, a narrative – if it remained focused on the local Harlan strike and ended with the winning of the contract. But the film incorporates major 'digressions' – 'Bloody Harlan' in the 1930s, recent major mining accidents, treatment for Black Lung and, at length, power struggles within the UMW – that distract viewers from the 'plot' and 'characters' back in Harlan. Kopple refuses to gloss over complexity: these 'digressions' are considered essential to understanding the complicated, wider national and historical context (hence the *USA* in the film's title) in which the Harlan strike takes place. This is particularly true of the film's 'messy' conclusion – messy because the perpetual struggle of labour against exploitation by capital (encapsulated in the early juxtaposition of men disappearing down the mine on a conveyor belt and

coal coming back out) *is* messy. There are no happy endings: the
narrative satisfaction of the victorious Harlan strike is immediately
undercut by new national strikes and union power struggles, and new
dissatisfactions among miners – generally not those we have followed in
Harlan – and a grudging return to work.

The film is of its time in the attention it pays to Harlan's ordinary,
working-class women and their political discussions and actions (see also
THE LIFE AND TIMES OF ROSIE THE RIVETER, 1980). Kopple traces their
crucial role in the strike, reminiscent of the part women play in Herbert
Biberman's blacklist-made fiction feature *Salt of the Earth* (1953), which
she took down to show in Harlan.

Barbara Kopple's varied and successful film and television career since
Harlan County USA includes another Academy Award for a film about
another strike, *American Dream* (1990), and widely seen films about
Mike Tyson (*Fallen Champ*, 1993), Woody Allen's band (*Wild Man Blues*,
1997), the degeneration of the Woodstock festival (*My Generation*,
2000), the Hamptons (TV mini-series *The Hamptons*, 2002) and the Dixie
Chicks (*Shut up & Sing*, 2006), directing, along the way, episodes of
Homicide: Life on the Street (1997–9). JH

Dir/Prod: Barbara Kopple; **Phot**: Hart Perry, Kevin Keating, Phil Parmet, Flip McCarthy, Tom
Hurwitz (colour & b/w); **Ed**: Nancy Baker, Mary Lampson; **Sound**: Barbara Kopple, Josh
Waletzky; **Prod Co**: Cabin Creek.

Harvest of Shame (aka *CBS Reports: Harvest of Shame*)
US, 1960 – 53 mins
David Lowe (producer)

Edward R. Murrow – now better known as the central character in George Clooney's 2005 film *Good Night and Good Luck* – established himself as a universally respected figure for his radio reporting during World War II (not least the Battle of Britain, 1940–1). In the early 1950s, this reputation helped Murrow and Fred Friendly with CBS Television's weekly *See It Now*, and later *CBS Reports*, to go against the growing political caution. Murrow and Friendly dealt with numerous controversial topics, arousing anxiety and frequent protest among the television and political establishment and commercial sponsors. Celebrated editions of *See It Now* reported from Korea and investigated controversial subjects like McCarthyist blacklisting and segregation. Alcoa withdrew its sponsorship in 1955 and the now one-hour show appeared more intermittently before being replaced by *CBS Reports*.

During the 1950s, network television news divisions exercised increasing influence over television documentary production, and presenter- or reporter-led, on-the-spot reportage shows like Murrow's became the dominant form. *Harvest of Shame*, which looked at the conditions of migrant farm workers, was a fine example of Murrow's style of investigative journalism. It traces the journey of the migrant workers as they make their way northwards from Florida picking beans, corn, tomatoes, etc., interspersed with reporter interviews with both migrant workers, black and white, and crew leaders, as well as the Secretary of Labour (who condemns the workers' exploitation) and, for the classic 'balance', the head of the employers' Farm Bureau Federation (who defends it). Murrow makes his and the programme's critical position very clear: the film begins with a 'shape-up' of black migrant workers shot, as Murrow comments, not in Africa but in the US, quoting a farmer saying 'We used to own our slaves, now we just rent them'; later, Murrow refers to 'forgotten people' working in 'sweatshops of the soil' and 'a 1960 *Grapes of Wrath*'. In a startling juxtaposition, he contrasts the careful packing of agricultural produce and the regulations for the transportation of livestock with the overcrowded and dangerous trucks and buses used to convey the workers. Some of the shots of migrant housing and families self-consciously but vividly recall the work of still photographers like Dorothea Lange and Walker Evans for the Farm Security Administration in the 1930s.

Harvest of Shame pays special attention to migrant workers' children and the obstacles they face in the way of improvement through education. Though one sequence looks at efforts to unionise in California, and new presidential recommendations are referred to at the end, its overall message is very bleak, its subjects caught in a vicious circle of poverty. To press home the plight of 'the humans who harvest the food for the best-fed people in the world', *Harvest of Shame* was broadcast on Thanksgiving Day 1960. Predictably, it sparked storms of protest from vested interests.

By the end of the 1950s and the Eisenhower presidency, both political caution and the dominance of reporter-led documentary were weakening. Meanwhile, Robert Drew was making a concerted effort, technologically and ideologically, to change the face of television reporting with films like PRIMARY (1960) and CRISIS (1963) (though reporter-led documentaries remain an important form, in John Pilger's television work, for example, and, arguably, Michael Moore's films – see ROGER AND ME, 1989, BOWLING FOR COLUMBINE, 2002 – which offer a punchy updating of the form). Perhaps conscious of these developments, Murrow accepted President Kennedy's invitation in 1961 to head the US Information Agency, but the chain-smoking that was integral to his image took its toll and he died of lung cancer in 1965. JH

Prod: David Lowe; **Exec Prod**: Fred W. Friendly; **Dir of Operations**: Palmer Williams; **Phot**: Martin Barnet, Charles Mack (b/w); **Ed**: John Schultz; **Sound**: Larry Giannesci, Robert Huttenloch; **Narrator/Correspondent**: Edward R. Murrow; **Prod Co**: CBS News Productions.

Heidi Fleiss: Hollywood Madam
UK, 1995 – 107 mins
Nick Broomfield

Nick Broomfield has made several of the most distinctive and enjoyable documentaries of the last quarter of a century, and his development as a film-maker mirrors some of the wider aesthetic and political trends in the genre. Earlier films like *Behind the Rent Strike* (1974, co-directed with Joan Churchill) are good examples of polemical film-making in the vérité style; middle-period films like *Soldier Girls* (1981, with Churchill) are more like Frederick Wiseman's observational films (see TITICUT FOLLIES, 1967, PRIMATE, 1974). Since the late 1980s, reacting – like many other film-makers, such as Errol Morris (see THE THIN BLUE LINE, 1988, *Mr Death*, 1999) – against earlier claims about documentary's objectivity and 'capturing the real', Broomfield, a major figure in the new style of performative documentary (see also Ross McElwee's TIME INDEFINITE, 1993), has established an on-screen persona in more self-reflexive, post-modern films tracing the encounter between film-maker, camera and subject (recalling the interventionist cinéma vérité style of Jean Rouch and Edgar Morin in CHRONIQUE D'UN ÉTÉ, 1961).

Broomfield has brought this style to more lurid – and doubtless more commercial – subjects such as serial killers (the Aileen Wuornos films, 1992, 2003) and rock stars (*Kurt and Courtney*, 1998, *Biggie and Tupac*, 2002). Heidi Fleiss was arrested and tried for running a call-girl racket and Broomfield demonstrates a somewhat prurient fascination – whether assumed or real – with the Los Angeles/Hollywood underworld of prostitution, pornography, drugs and crime, through encounters with Fleiss and former associates Ivan Nagy and Madam Alex. From the opening newsreel images of Fleiss's arrest, Broomfield's apparent quest is to discover who is/was the real Heidi and what she did and why. The quest itself is strongly visualised in the travelling view from the windscreen of Broomfield's car, his voiceover explaining the leads that are being followed up. But this is not quite the familiar investigative journalism: bereft of ideas and clues, he comments that 'in desperation, we drove down Sunset Boulevard looking for clues'; later, he concedes that he 'could tell things weren't going so well'.

As this suggests, the tone of the film is often richly comic, self-deprecatory, heavy on irony and understatement, much dependent on the persona developed by Broomfield's polite, ingratiating but persistent, and very English, manner, and his meeting with very different characters: at one point, he questions a thug, over the telephone, sweetly and reasonably, 'I just wanted to ask you if you put the bullet holes in Ivan's ceiling.'

Like other Broomfield films, *Heidi Fleiss* shows the preparatory processes of documentary film-making: researching, interviews and associated cash transactions, a search for structure. In a sense, the film is about this more than anything else. Highlighting issues about directorial 'control', we are invited to consider whether there is really a 'film' to be made here, given the lack of leads and structure. By the end, the film is clearly going nowhere investigatively, and Broomfield is lost. Is this apparent floundering an invitation to ironic reflection on the film-maker's competence – or 'innocent' evidence of Broomfield's defeat and loss of control? Is it a conceit, a carefully engineered descent into confusion? As this is the way that most Broomfield films go, we must assume this is entirely intentional. Either way, he succeeds – entertainingly – in reminding us of the artificial nature of the documentary enterprise and its inherent contradictions. JH

Dir/Prod: Nick Broomfield; **Phot**: Paul Kloss (colour); **Ed**: S. J. Bloom; **Music**: David Bergeaud; **Sound**: Dirk Farner, Mark Rozett; **Prod Co**: Lafayette Film, for BBC Television.

Hoop Dreams
US, 1994 – 170 mins
Steve James

Originally intended to be a 30-minute short for the Public Broadcasting System, *Hoop Dreams* follows two inner-city black American teenagers from Chicago, Arthur Agee and William Gates, for five years, through their entire high school career and into college, as they seek to fulfil their common dream of one day playing basketball for the NBA. The film-makers accumulated 250 hours of footage, which they edited down to just under three hours, providing a deftly constructed portrait of the two boys and their families. Basketball, which has the potential to provide a way for black male youths to escape the ghetto, is the film's ostensible subject, but it uses the sport to explore issues of class and race in American society. Combining direct cinema observation with vérité intervention, and complemented with soulful music by Ben Sidran, *Hoop Dreams* provides a portrait of inner-city life in America with such depth that Roger Ebert named it one of the best films of the 1990s.

As the film begins, Arthur has been scouted as a fourteen-year-old and is about to begin high school, while William is already enrolled and considered a hot prospect. St Joseph's, a racially mixed school in the suburb of Westchester, is known for producing talented players, the most famous of whom is Isiah Thomas, a star point guard for the Detroit Pistons and hall-of-famer generally acknowledged as one of the best to have ever played the game. Thomas's presence looms everywhere: he is invoked by St Joseph's basketball coach Gene Pingatore as the ideal player; Arthur, who idolises him, practises Thomas's spin moves; and a large photo of Thomas in uniform is mounted in the school hallway display case, which the boys must pass regularly and to which the camera periodically returns. At an orientation rally, Thomas himself makes an appearance and Arthur gets the opportunity to attempt to defend (unsuccessfully) against him as he drives to the basket.

While the boys may have fantasies of NBA stardom, the film is awake to the harsh institutional realities that comprise the stuff of which such dreams are made. Both families have personal and economic problems (single parenting, drug addiction, spousal abuse) that repeatedly underscore the difficulties of poverty and racial discrimination. Upon Arthur's eighteenth birthday, his mother is happy just to know he's still alive. Using extracts of recorded interviews with members of the families as voiceover commentary to accompany shots of them, often in close-up, doing other things, it seems as if we are hearing what they are thinking. In this way, we are encouraged to empathise with them, and at times the film-makers themselves become involved with the families, as

Steve James, Peter Gilbert and Fred Marx setting up a sequence for *Hoop Dreams*

when they express interest in an essay that Arthur is attempting to write and prod him to discuss it further.

Basketball is revealed as an astonishingly organised business and a significant part of its social actors' lives. In the end, neither boy makes it to the pros, and William expresses disillusionment with basketball because it was no longer just a game. Earl Smith, the scout who first noticed Arthur, confesses that while he first saw his job as facilitating opportunities for black youth, he now regards the pressures put on them to perform as a form of exploitation, and at the Nike-sponsored summer basketball camp that William attends, director Spike Lee sums it up by telling the boys that it's all about money. The film-makers focused on Agee and Gates once more in *Hoop Dreams Reunion*, televised the following year. BKG

Dir: Steve James; **Prod**: Catherine Allen; **Scr**: Steve James, Frederick Marx; **Phot**: Peter Gilbert (colour); **Ed**: William Haugse, Steve James, Frederick Marx; **Music**: Ben Sidran; **Sound**: Corey Coken, Ric Coken, Bryen Hensley, Margaret M. S. Marvin, Chuck Rapp, Adam Singer, Tom Yore; **Prod Co**: KTCA Minneapolis/Kartemquin Films.

The Hour of the Furnaces (*La hora de los hornos*) (full title: *La hora de los hornos: notas y testimonios sobre el neocolonialismo, la violencia y la liberacion*)

Argentina, 1968 – 260 mins
Octavio Getino, Fernando Ezequiel Solanas

The Hour of the Furnaces – named after the cooking fires sighted by the first Europeans in Latin America, and taken up as a militant slogan in the 1960s ('Now is the hour of the furnaces: let them see nothing but the light of the flames') – had enormous international impact in the late 1960s as a model of revolutionary 'third' cinema. This was a moment when real change in the world order seemed not only possible but imminent, and when cinema seemed in the vanguard. The film is in three parts: the best known, Part 1 – 'Violence and Liberation: Notes on Neo-Colonialism' (in thirteen sections) – analyses Latin American political and economic history, based on the premise, as the film quietly puts it, after the emotionally charged Prologue, that 'Latin America is a continent at war'; Part 2 – 'Act for the Revolution' (in two parts, with a break for live speeches and debate) – examines Argentina in the post-1945 period from a Peronist perspective (as, for the film-makers, Peronism offered the best chance for change); and Part 3 – 'Violence and Liberation' – looks at liberation struggles globally.

The Hour of the Furnaces, and in particular Part 1, is best understood as a montage film. Each of its sections takes a different approach, juxtaposing image and image, and sound and image, in startling and revealing ways, 'making strange', asking us to see things differently. The cross-cutting of cattle being slaughtered with US-style consumer advertising, for example, is brutally effective – all the more so given the importance of Argentina's meat industry; elsewhere, in, say, the juxtaposition of historical images of English-dominated nineteenth-century banking and exploitation with images of the contemporary leisured classes playing golf, the montage dialectics are subtler, and easier to miss. Part 1's celebrated prologue juxtaposes fragmented scenes of violent repression and revolt and brief flashes of light with revolutionary captions, black screens and rhythmic drumming. This search for coherent images of struggle and change is 'answered' by its extraordinary conclusion: for over three minutes, with the drumbeat from the start returning, the screen retains the static image of the face of the dead – but, metamorphosing in the viewer's mind, somehow very 'alive' – Latin American revolutionary Che Guevara.

Solanas and Getino's film owes something to 1920s Soviet montage documentary (MAN WITH A MOVIE CAMERA, 1929, THE FALL OF THE ROMANOV DYNASTY, 1927), but more to the 1960s revolutionary Cuban cinema of Santiago Alvarez and others (79 SPRINGS, 1969). However, the influence of the new 1960s documentary styles of 'direct cinema' (PRIMARY, 1960, CRISIS, 1963) and cinéma vérité (CHRONIQUE D'UN ÉTÉ, 1961) is also clear: in a cinéma vérité-style sequence about the fate of the Indians, for example, the mobile camera is seen as threatening and intrusive.

As Getino later recognised, *The Hour of the Furnaces* makes proper sense only in the context of its time. Its enduring importance is due in part to Solanas and Getino's manifesto, 'Towards a Third Cinema', a hugely influential attempt to define militant cinema, and a useful framework for thinking about their film. In a wide-ranging discussion, they argue for the role of 'documentary' in revolutionary film-making and conclude: 'Our time is one of hypothesis rather than of thesis, a time of works in progress – unfinished, unordered, violent works made with the camera in one hand and a rock in the other.' JH

Dir/Scr: Octavio Getino, Fernando Ezequiel Solanas (b/w); **Prod**: Fernando Ezequiel Solanas; **Prod Co**: Grupo Cine Liberacion (completed with the assistance of Arger Film, Rome).

Housing Problems
UK, 1935 – 15 mins
Edgar Anstey, Arthur Elton

Among the different impulses of mainstream British documentary film-making in the 1930s, *Housing Problems* remains the epitome of the no-nonsense style (by comparison with more experimental projects like COAL FACE, 1935). In its opening sequences, *Housing Problems* gets down to business without superfluous visuals or editing, explaining some of the problems of slum housing and proceeding to first-hand testimonies of the working-class people who live in them. Ameliorative in outlook, and in classic expository mode, *Housing Problems* identifies a problem, amplifies it and shows what is being done to solve it – in this case, new council-built blocks of flats. Many later 'investigative' documentaries follow precisely such a pattern.

Nevertheless, *Housing Problems* is notable in several respects. First, its use of voice – or, more properly, voices – reveals much about the ideological assumptions of 1930s state- and corporation-sponsored documentary: the plummy, upper-class, unidentified voice of an omniscient narrator introduces, and names, Stepney Councillor Lawder, whose distinctly lower-middle-class voice gives some historical background to industrial expansion and the building of slum housing. Solidifying that sense of 'us' and 'them', the narrator returns: 'Now let us hear from some of the people who have to live in the slums', introducing a series of straight-to-camera 'testimonies' by working-class tenants recounting their experiences (slightly clumsily intercut with silent footage of vermin, decayed plaster, etc.). The narrator returns again for the film's central section, which unveils the designs for new apartment blocks followed by further testimonies from the grateful tenants who have moved into them.

The tenants' testimonies feel somewhat stilted and rehearsed – Ruby Grierson confirmed that though their words were their own, they were 'coached'. This should not surprise us, given that they would have been

addressing an enormous battery of cameras, lights and sound-recording
equipment – not the best conditions in which to appear 'natural'.
Though this was the heyday of working-class comedies (starring the likes
of Gracie Fields and George Formby), this would have been a rare
opportunity for many audiences to hear authentic East End working-class
voices telling of authentic hardships. The speakers focus on their often
horrific experiences and frustrations, as victims of the system, rather than
protest in political terms. Only one testimony refers to the rights of the
working man to a proper home, and the film fails to raise issues
(circulating widely in the early 1930s) about property ownership and the

distribution of wealth (contrast the explicitly political Joris Ivens's and Henri Storck's roughly contemporaneous, independently produced *Misère au Borinage*, 1933).

Following Councillor Lawder's optimistic closing comments, Anstey and Elton insert a coda that they thought quite daring, partially breaking with the tone of the rest of the film: a montage of shots of slum dwellers cleaning, playing, etc., accompanied by a non-synch sound montage of comments suggesting that their problems are not their own fault. It is as if the film-makers wanted to end the film by reminding us that the 'problems' – housing and other – remain, and remain to be solved. This still smacks of putting the poor 'under the microscope' but, nevertheless, poverty and exploitation are more evident here than in any other 'official' 1930s British documentary film, and we should probably regard the British Commercial Gas Association's sponsorship as relatively enlightened. Though the new blocks of flats use gas, the film's main impulse seems to be less the promotion of gas than a felt responsibility on the sponsors' (and directors') part to address – however inadequate in the end – the state of the body politic. JH

Dir: Edgar Anstey, Arthur Elton; **Phot**: John Taylor (b/w); **Sound**: York Scarlett; **Prod Co**: British Commercial Gas Association.

Las Hurdes (aka *Las Hurdes – tierra sin pan/Land without Bread*)
Spain, 1933 – 27 mins
Luis Buñuel

Las Hurdes, Luis Buñuel's film about the underdeveloped Las Hurdes area
of western Spain and its inhabitants – and his only documentary – has
perplexed and disturbed spectators in equal measure (like most of his
fictions). Is it an exposé of a poverty-stricken people living almost
medieval lives in the 20th century, or a travelogue fascinated by the
strange customs and lifestyles of a remote community? Part of the puzzle
the film poses, and the disturbance it generates, is that it refuses
classification, adopting the form and style – including grand Brahms
music and matter-of-fact, often ironic, commentary – of the travelogue
to uncover its shocking material. It is perhaps a response to a 1922
documentary (*Las Hurdes, Land of Legend*) that suggested that the
Spanish king would save the backward area – though ten years later,
nothing has changed. Though of its time, the film also seems somehow
timeless, a view of life as nasty, brutish and short, an extreme image of
Buñuel's 'badly made world', as Surreal a vision as *L'Âge d'or* (1930).

Who is responsible? Buñuel damns religion and property: the
relatively prosperous town of La Alberca owns the Hurdanos's land and
the beehives they look after, its citizens practising a strange mix of
Christian and pagan ritual (newly-wed horsemen tearing the heads off
live chickens strung across the street); at the gateway to Las Hurdes, a
largely abandoned monastery lies in lush surroundings, now taken over
by reptile life (lizards, snakes, toads); the new school teaches its poor,
hungry pupils to respect the property of others; the only signs of wealth
in the villages are in the churches; religion is everywhere associated with
death. Much of the film is structured so that the Hurdanos's modest
attempts at self-help are frustrated: they build narrow, terraced fields
near the river, but have to transport the soil for them, and if the rivers
flood, the fields are swept away; because the soil is thin, yields soon

diminish, so compost has to be collected from afar; the areas with the best compost abound with vipers, and although viper bites are not life-threatening, the methods used by the Hurdanos to treat the bites make them worse.

Buñuel paints a bleaker picture than, apparently, he needed to or the conditions merited, and doubts have often been raised about the documentary 'authenticity' and 'honesty' of various scenes. Were goats deliberately heaved over precipices to be filmed? Was the hive-carrying ass deliberately set up to be stung to death by bees? Did the dead infant whose coffin was floated across the river and transported to another

village really die? Such reconstruction or re-enactment – however extreme these examples might be – were surely commonplace documentary practice of the period (see, for example, MAN OF ARAN, 1934, NORTH SEA, 1938, FARREBIQUE, 1946) rather than subterfuge. One moment – fabricated or not – stands out: when the film-makers encounter a sick child in a village street, a crew member comes from behind the camera to inspect her, breaking a documentary taboo; the commentary tells us they could do nothing, and learned several days later that she had died.

Las Hurdes wasn't received well by the republican government of the time, and it was banned in Spain until 1936. The French (and most current) version ends with a later caption suggesting that community action has improved conditions elsewhere in Spain, contributing to the new Popular Front government, and that the Fascist rebellion threatens future progress (linking it to THE SPANISH EARTH, 1937) – but it's a caption that seems strangely at odds with many of the film's implications. JH

Dir/Scr/Ed: Luis Buñuel; **Prod**: Ramón Acín, Luis Buñuel; **Phot**: Eli Lotar (b/w); **Music**: Darius Milhaud (and Brahms, Fourth Symphony); **Sound**: Charles Goldblatt (French version); **Commentary**: Rafael Sánchez Ventura, Pierre Unik; **Prod Co**: Ramón Acín.

I for India
UK/Germany, 2005 – 70 mins
Sandhya Suri

Home movies have proved a valuable source for documentary films about social life in the past – offering different, more domestic perspectives than those of newsreels or documentaries – and even for investigative documentaries like *Capturing the Friedmans* (dir. Andrew Jarecki, US, 2003), as more or less incriminating evidence. Of at least equal interest is the use of home movies in documentary film-making of a more personal or subjective kind (see, for example, DAUGHTER RITE, 1980, TIME INDEFINITE, 1993) in which film-makers reflect upon their own and their family's past.

There is always a curious pleasure in seeing home movies, generally shot somewhat 'innocently', being put to revealingly different purposes – given a kind of second life. In 1965, Yash Pal Suri and his wife left India to come to England – part of a more general pattern of immigration from the former empire – to complete his medical qualifications. He bought two Super 8mm movie cameras, two projectors and two reel-to-reel tape recorders, one set of which he sent back to his family in India. Over many years, Yash documented his new life in England – family trips by train and car, the weather, children's birthday parties, hospital colleagues and the like – with tape-recorded reflections on his experience, and sent them to India. The family in India responded with their own 'cine-letters', documenting family life, weddings, festivals. These home movies, discovered by the daughter/film-maker Sandhya, constitute the essential, fascinating core of *I for India*.

Several themes of great interest emerge. The film provides a living dramatisation of the experience of Indian immigration, and particularly of the Indian diaspora: the father stays on as a hospital doctor, children are born and attend English schools, integrating into the English social system; one daughter marries a white British man (though in a traditional ceremony); later, another daughter, continuing the diasporic theme, emigrates to Australia; another goes to film school and makes this film.

Frustrated by aspects of his life in England (such as people's inability to pronounce his name), and pressured by his family in India, Yash goes back to India but fails to establish a viable medical consultancy and finds difficulty readjusting to a more extended, less nuclear, family lifestyle, finally returning to northern England. This is where the film finds them in the present, a little 'exotic' but otherwise socially accepted in the bourgeois round of camcorder clubs and women's societies. A telling scene, recorded discreetly by Sandhya from inside the house, shows Yash discussing rose pruning and lunch over the garden fence with a middle-class neighbour, the epitome of a certain kind of English lifestyle, though another daughter's emigration to Australia raises again questions about nationality and ethnic identity and notions of 'home' that weave through the film.

Extracts from crudely condescending BBC television films aimed at immigrants provide occasional reminders of historical context, but could also be seen as distractions from the family's story, yet this remains a fascinating document. Coincidentally, almost, the film documents the astonishing shifts in home-movie technology since the 1960s, from silent Super 8mm film and non-sync sound on tape to video and camcorders (and, near the end, a videophone conversation). JH

Dir: Sandhya Suri; **Prod**: Carlo Cresto-Dine, Kai Kuennemann, Thomas Rufus; **Phot**: Sandhya Suri, Lars Lenski, Yash Pal Suri (Super 8mm) (b/w & colour); **Ed**: Cinzia Baldessari; **Sound**: Karl Attein, Alexander Weuffen; **Prod Co**: Fandango/YLE Teema-ZDF/Arte-Zero West GmbH.

In the Year of the Pig
US, 1968 – 101 mins
Emile de Antonio

Point of Order (1964), Emile de Antonio's compilation of footage from the televised Army–McCarthy hearings, was rejected by the New York Film Festival as being 'television and not a film', suggesting that de Antonio's politically controversial films – *Rush to Judgment* (1967) (on the Kennedy assassination), *In the Year of the Pig*, *America Is Hard to See* (1970) (on Eugene McCarthy's 1968 presidential campaign) and *Millhouse: A White Comedy* (1971) (on Nixon) – were inventing new documentary forms. De Antonio's 'compilation films' owed something to the pioneering Soviet efforts of Esfir Shub (see THE FALL OF THE ROMANOV DYNASTY, 1927), and continued the Marxist-inspired US documentary tradition represented by Frontier Films with THE SPANISH EARTH (1937) and NATIVE LAND (1942).

In the Year of the Pig looks at French and American historical involvement in Indo-China. Reacting against the lack of socio-political analysis in the 'simply observers' ethic and methods of US direct cinema (see PRIMARY, 1960, CRISIS, 1963), de Antonio adopted a didactic, essay style, partly to counter increasingly meaningless nightly television news coverage of the Vietnam War. Screen time is shared by old and recent news footage on Vietnam, de Antonio's interviews with journalists, commentators and politicians (mostly American but also French) and archival public pronouncements by politicians and statesmen. De Antonio aimed to produce 'a collage of people, voices, images, ideas to develop a story line or a didactic line, uninterrupted by external narration', its austere visuals focusing attention on content.

The film skilfully juxtaposes and overlaps his sound-image materials, pointing to strategic miscalculations, contradictions and obfuscations in US political and military policy (particularly in relation to Ho Chi Minh's popularity as a nationalist leader) without telling us what to believe or think. Official statements about not bombing civilians or the treatment of prisoners are cut against footage of destruction or suspects being beaten (footage that would be used very differently in 79 SPRINGS, 1969); official accounts of the Gulf of Tonkin incident are contradicted by witness accounts. Often, de Antonio simply lets subjects condemn themselves: Colonel Patton talks about his men's reverence for dead comrades, then smiles broadly and declares them 'a bloody good bunch of killers', while soldiers on leave refer derisively to 'gooks'. Key US policies like 'strategic hamlets' and 'search and destroy' emerge as double-think for brutal but unproductive military actions, and key concepts like the 'domino theory' are exposed.

The alternative, sceptical American voices enable de Antonio to frame the film, only half ironically, with references to American values of independence and liberty. After Daniel Berrigan's comments about 'the war is not working' and 'the last days of the Superman', de Antonio concludes with dramatic newsreel footage of a US military unit, faces marked by exhaustion, distress and incomprehension, struggling to get their injured into a helicopter, followed by a Vietnamese-style rendition of 'The Battle Hymn of the Republic'. Though the film could not know the war's outcome, this final sequence – following on from footage of North Vietnam's defence arrangements and relatively 'normal' life – makes it clear that the war is unwinnable. Given the current US involvement in Iraq, *In the Year of the Pig* remains a potent document.

The film is strikingly more analytical and less focused on the *American* experience than the Academy Award-winning Vietnam documentary *Hearts and Minds* (dir. Peter Davis, 1974). Michael Moore's polemical films – such as ROGER AND ME (1989) and BOWLING FOR COLUMBINE (2002) – build on de Antonio's work, orchestrating a partisan thesis from interview-type material and archive footage. The effect, however, is very different: Moore's approach is more scattered and his grandstanding 'regular, blue-collar guy' persona dominates, while de Antonio is never seen and even his distinctive voice is only heard once – though his 'voice' is clear enough. JH

Dir/Prod: Emile de Antonio; **Phot**: John F. Newman, Jean Jacques Rochut (Paris) (b/w); **Ed**: Lynnzee Klingman, with Hannah Morcinis, Helen Levitt; **Music**: Steve Addiss; **Sound**: Jeffrey Weinstock, Harold Maury (Paris); **Prod Co**: Emile de Antonio Productions/Turin Film Productions.

Jazz
US, 2001 – 10 x 120 mins episodes
Ken Burns

Producer, director and writer Ken Burns has created numerous documentaries on American history and historical figures, many of which have been screened on the PBS network in the US, including *The Civil War* (1990, ten episodes), *Baseball* (1994, nine episodes) and *The War* (2007, six episodes), about World War II. As with much of his other work, the ten episodes of *Jazz* combine well-researched and compelling archival visual material, including both still photographs and film clips, with a voiceover narration, here provided by actor Keith David – and, as might be expected given the subject in this case, an excellent sampling of great jazz recordings on the soundtrack. Using the careers of two jazz giants, trumpeter Louis Armstrong and composer/bandleader/pianist Duke Ellington, as anchors around which to provide the history of this uniquely American art form, *Jazz* tells an engrossing but largely orthodox narrative of the music's birth in New Orleans through to bop and fusion.

Mixed with the archival material are interviews with jazz musicians representing several generations, from Artie Shaw to Dave Brubeck to trumpeter Wynton Marsalis, who also served as Senior Creative Consultant on the project; jazz writers and critics, including Stanley Crouch and Gary Giddens; and family members such as Mercedes Ellington, who reminisces about her famous grandfather. The ten parts are arranged chronologically, with individual two-hour episodes devoted to such developments as bop (episode 7) and swing music, which is the subject of two episodes (5–6). But the final episode, 'A Masterpiece by Midnight', which attempts to cover jazz since 1961, inevitably treats more recent developments superficially and suggests that such styles as fusion, free jazz and acid jazz are hardly worth mentioning. Some jazz enthusiasts were disappointed, because there is little new here in terms of jazz history, but Burns's archival material vividly captures the twisted tale of race relations in the US that informed every aspect of jazz history. If anything, he is excessively careful in this regard, seriously underestimating, as some critics have rightly noted, the contribution of white jazz musicians other than Benny Goodman.

As in his other documentaries, Burns pans and zooms over photographs and other archival material, ultimately coming to rest on a particular face or area to illustrate or complement the narration. This technique has become known in some image software applications as 'The Ken Burns Effect', though it had been used many years earlier in such documentaries as *City of Gold* (dirs. Wolf Koenig and Colin Low, 1957), made for the National Film Board of Canada, about the gold-rush town of Dawson City in the Yukon. But the device is associated with Burns because of the widespread popularity of his films by dint of being broadcast on PBS. Thus the premiere broadcast of the series, beginning on 8 January 2001 and weekly thereafter, was regarded as a significant cultural event in North America, where it was accompanied by the marketing of a series of judiciously selected CD releases, each one spanning the career of a major jazz artist, on two major labels known for their jazz lists, Columbia (which released thirteen CDs) and Verve (which issued eleven). A number of boxed sets and various artists CDs were also released. The documentary series, which was nominated for five Emmy Awards, is supported by an elaborate page on the PBS website (<www.pbs.org/jazz/>) that provides some background information about jazz history, capsule biographies of the jazz artists who are covered in the documentary and even sample bits of classic recordings. BKG

Dir: Ken Burns; **Prod**: Ken Burns, Lynn Novik; **Scr**: Geoffrey C. Ward; **Phot**: Ken Burns, Buddy Squiers (colour); **Ed**: Paul Barnes, Sandra Marie Christie, Lewis Erskine, Erik Ewers, Sarah E. Hill, Craig Mellish, Tricia Reidy, Shannon Robards, Aaron Vega; **Sound**: Mark Roy, Ira Spiegel, Dominick Tavello, John Zecca; **Prod Co**: General Motors Mark of Excellence Productions/BBC Television/Florentine Films/Jazz Film Project/WETA, Washington DC.

Kon-Tiki
Norway/Sweden, 1950 – 77 mins
Thor Heyerdahl

Question: which Norwegian film won an Academy Award? Answer: *Kon-Tiki* – Best Documentary Feature, 1951 In 1947, the Kon-Tiki expedition (named after the Inca sun-god) epitomised daring and perilous adventure as fully as men landing on the moon did almost twenty years later. Expedition leader Thor Heyerdahl, struck by the similarity of ancient statuary in South America and Polynesia, and noting the prevailing westerly winds and Humboldt current, surmised – contrary to previous thinking, which argued the impossibility of long-distance migration by sea – that there must have been some westward migration across the Pacific. Using techniques described by seventeenth-century Spanish explorers, Heyerdahl's team constructed a balsa-wood raft with primitive materials – rope lashings rather than nails and screws – and set sail. Many predicted disaster, but 101 days and 4,500 miles later – their only contact with the outside world a wind-up ham radio, and without having sighted a single ship en route – Kon-Tiki reached land (on the Polynesian island of Raroia) and made contact with nearby inhabitants. Heyerdahl's book sold over 20 million copies worldwide and the subsequent film was seen widely.

Though the Academy probably made its award less for the film than for Heyerdahl's almost mythic heroism, the film itself is a remarkable document. It is, essentially, an amateur film, a celluloid diary, shot silent on a 16mm Bolex camera by a crew who knew little about making movies (filming at the silent speed of 16 fps caused problems when the film was assembled). This was certainly not an expedition organised with a view to being filmed. Perhaps the film is a relative of the genre of exploration-ethnographic films stretching back to *South* (dirs. Frank Hurley, UK, 1919) and *Grass* (dirs. Merian C. Cooper and Ernest B. Schoedsack, US, 1925).

The film's opening caption claims it as 'the authentic film' about the expedition, presented 'in its original form, as filmed by crew members . . .

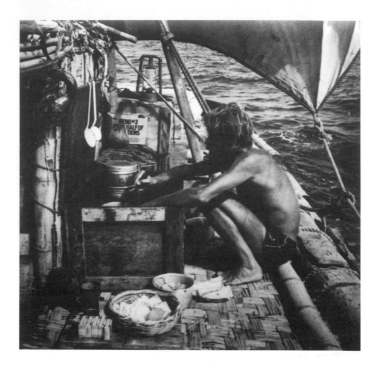

What is shown . . . is what actually took place.' After a formal, lecture-like introduction, and footage of the making and departure of the raft, most of the film is devoted to the voyage itself, and almost all of that footage is taken from and on the raft (a small rubber dinghy allowed a few shots of the raft at sea). Many shots are low-angled, dominated by sky and big seas. One senses that at times they were unsure what to film, so we see mostly the routine of fishing, inspecting the raft, cooking, relaxing, the antics of their stowaway parrot, checking rations, etc. – all very 'ordinary', but all very fascinating too. The post-recorded commentary, like the footage, deals very matter-of-factly with dangerous moments like landing sharks and the presence of whales. Footage inside the cabin or hut on the deck, where they lashed themselves down at night, got spoiled and had to be represented by a few still photos.

What might have been exciting highlights – a storm, or the whales – are either entirely absent or dealt with very briefly, simply because the crew was too busy at such times to pay much attention to filming: during a five-day gale, they were unable to film at all. But as André Bazin noted perceptively (in 'Cinema and Exploration'), the film's snatches of action and partial accounts prove more impressive and moving than anything a more fault-free, better-organised film might have achieved, because its 'imperfections bear witness to its authenticity' and the missing images form 'the negative imprint of the adventure'. JH

Dir/Prod/Scr: Thor Heyerdahl; **Phot**: Knut Haugland, Erik Hasselberg, Thor Heyerdahl, Torstein Raaby, Herman Watzinger (b/w); **Ed**: Olle Nordemar; **Music**: Sune Waldimir; **Graphics**: Gösta Bjurman; **Prod Co**: Artfilm/Syncronfilm.

Koyaanisqatsi: Life Out of Balance
US, 1982 – 86 mins
Godfrey Reggio

The first in a trilogy that includes *Powaqqatsi: Life in Transformation* (1988) and *Naqoyqatsi: Life as War* (2002), all three in collaboration with composer Philip Glass, *Koyaanisqatsi* combines documentary footage with an avant-garde emphasis on montage and formalist *mise en scène* to construct a meditation on the fraught relations between nature, culture and technology. One of the first in a recent cycle of eco-documentaries such as *Baraka* (1992, directed by *Koyaanisqatsi*'s cinematographer, Ron Fricke) and *The 11th Hour* (2007) to rely on such cinematic means to build a vision of the world as a complex and troubled ecosystem, *Koyaanisqatsi* (the title, unexplained until the film's final credits, comes from the Hopi word meaning 'life of moral corruption' or 'life out of balance') eschews dialogue and voiceover narration, relying only on Glass's score to accompany its steady barrage of stunning images, which were shot and edited over a period of seven years.

Koyaanisqatsi evokes earlier city symphony films such as Walter Ruttmann's BERLIN: SYMPHONY OF A GREAT CITY (1927) and Dziga Vertov's MAN WITH A MOVIE CAMERA (1929), but with a new global perspective that reverses the form's traditional celebration of technological progress and the harmony of man and machine. Instead, *Koyaanisqatsi* shows how modern technology is destroying the beauty of the natural world as well as humanity's soul. The film begins with sublime images of natural beauty, including Lake Powell and the iconographic Monument Valley. Gradually, human intervention is revealed with dams and power lines and, finally, a nuclear explosion in the Nevada desert. The film then shifts tone, marked – as are other such transitions in the film – by a corresponding shift in Glass's music, in this case the addition of a choral motif that expresses the human element upon which the next section focuses. It begins with a shot of a man and a child sleeping on a beach as the camera cranes up to destroy our initial perception of this apparently idyllic scene by revealing the industrial squalor surrounding them. This image, which beautifully encapsulates the film's theme of the human relation to nature, suggests the extraordinarily visual richness that informs every shot.

During the film, Glass's music increases in tempo and volume, characterised by repetition that bespeaks modern urban life as seen in images of people in fast motion frantically moving through cities like mindless automatons, the mad pace of office workers compared through editing to factory assembly lines. Occasional slow-motion shots of particular people in the crowds emphasise the alienation of the individual in the contemporary city, reminiscent of Standish Lawder's image of commuters on an escalator in NECROLOGY (1971). Yet the film also acknowledges the seductive lure of our technologised lifestyle: a bird's-eye view of Glen Canyon Dam, for example, confers on its clean cement curve an undeniable aesthetic beauty, and in the film's longest shot (lasting more than 3 minutes) two United Airlines passenger jets are shown taxiing, the heat shimmering off the runway pavement and giving their movement an extraordinary balletic grace. Director Godfrey Reggio had trained for fourteen years to be a monk, and a sense of grace certainly pervades the film, but the montage of buildings being demolished also suggests a world that is collapsing under its own weight – a foreboding underscored by the final image, a long take of an Atlas rocket blasting off, then exploding, its wreckage falling back to earth as singer Albert de Ruiter chants the title word over Glass's music. BKG

Dir/Prod: Godfrey Reggio; **Scr**: Ron Fricke, Michael Hoenig, Godfrey Reggio, Alton Walpole; **Phot**: Ron Fricke (colour); **Ed**: Ron Fricke, Anton Walpole; **Music**: Philip Glass; **Prod Co**: Sante Fe Institute for Regional Education.

Lessons in Darkness (*Lektionen in Finsternis*)
Germany/France/UK, 1992 – 54 mins
Werner Herzog

In *The Wild Blue Yonder* (2005), Werner Herzog mixes elements of science fiction and documentary, using NASA training and mission footage and documentary footage of undersea exploration in the Antarctic combined with a voiceover narration by actor Brad Dourif to construct a fantastic yarn about aliens attempting to colonise a despoiled Earth as humans move out to space. Similarly, in *Lessons of Darkness*, taking his camera to the post-Gulf War oilfields of Kuwait where retreating Iraqi forces had set fire to the wells, Herzog creates another otherworldly vision animated by ecological concern, this one of hellish devastation. With his sci-fi approach to the real, Herzog demonstrates all too clearly how inhuman human beings can be to themselves and their environment – a theme shared with, but approached entirely differently in, GRIZZLY MAN (2005).

The war itself is covered in less than a minute of CNN footage. Then, as we are introduced to the scene, a shot of workers in the blazing inferno signalling to Herzog is accompanied by the film-maker's voiceover narration, which notes that 'The first creature we encountered tried to communicate with us.' Immediately, Herzog makes the place seem strange, and a lengthy, sweeping helicopter shot approaching and passing over Kuwait City, with its unique structures, cannot help but look alien. In this strange and treacherous land, pools of oil hide from sight by reflecting the sky and 'masquerade as water'. Herzog's images are largely absent of people, with slow tracking shots of wreckage in the desert landscape and conflagrations burning with an incandescent beauty. Periodically, a moving vehicle enters the frame, abruptly giving the scene a sense of scale. Large excavation and construction vehicles at work appear strange, like giant insects moving across a prehistoric landscape. Herzog's narration lends the scene a sense of cosmic apocalypse, reinforced by the choice of musical accompaniment, which includes Verdi's Requiem and Siegfried's funeral music from Wagner's Ring cycle.

Just as the smoke from the fires blots out the sun, so Herzog's voice eventually disappears from the film as we are left to contemplate these images, at once so terrible and so beautiful. To maintain his own sanity, Herzog distances himself and us from what he sees, casting it as a sci-fi scenario, for the apocalyptic is beyond human comprehension. In a sense, Herzog's aesthetic strategy is analogous to the way the people he interviews have coped with the experience of war. One woman, clearly traumatised by what she has been through, has lost the ability to speak after seeing her two sons tortured and killed; Herzog explains that she wants to 'tell us something', but she can do so only through gestures accompanied by the occasional appeal to Allah. Another woman tells about her young son, whose head was crushed under a soldier's boot, and who has refused to talk since; as she speaks to the camera, the boy buries his head in his mother's breast to avoid its gaze and engagement with the world.

But if these people are mute in the face of war's horror, Herzog's camera is not. He laments the astonishing destruction of war even as he captures its seductive beauty. After a lengthy sequence showing the successful extinguishing of a well fire and the capping of its gushing oil, the workers expressing a great sense of accomplishment, Herzog ends the film with the inexplicable shots of them rekindling a fire as he hypothesises that they must have gone mad ('Is life without fire unbearable for them? Others, seized by madness, follow suit'). It is a fitting ending that suggests our steadfast participation in warfare despite the knowledge of its barbarity. BKG

Dir/Scr: Werner Herzog; **Prod**: Paul Berriff, Werner Herzog; **Phot**: Paul Berriff, Rainer Klausmann (colour); **Ed**: Rainer Standke; **Sound**: John Pearson; **Prod Co**: Canal+/Première.

Let There Be Light
US, 1946 – 58 mins
John Huston

During World War II, a number of celebrated Hollywood directors made documentary films in support of the war effort for the American military, including William Wyler, John Ford and John Huston, who made three (*Report from the Aleutians*, 1943, *The Battle of San Pietro*, 1945, and *Let There Be Light*). The latter, shot in 1945 at the end of the war, was commissioned to demonstrate the Army's success in rehabilitating soldiers who had been emotionally scarred in battle, though ultimately the film may be seen as an anti-war documentary, just as *The Battle of San Pietro* seems to critique war rather than celebrate a victory in its depiction of a battle over a small Italian village in which 1,100 American soldiers were killed. Filmed at the Mason Army hospital on Long Island, NY, *Let There Be Light* follows a group of soldiers from their stateside return, through an eight-week rehabilitation programme, to their discharge and presumed successful reintegration into civilian life.

The narration is provided by the director's father, actor Walter Huston (also the narrator on Frank Capra's WHY WE FIGHT films made during the war), who brings an appropriate tone of *gravitas* to explain that these men, though physically unharmed, are also among the war-wounded ('modern psychiatry makes no distinction between the ills of the mind and the body'). The elder Huston also informs us that 'No scenes were staged' and that 'The cameras merely recorded what took place in an Army hospital', but the film clearly intends to inspire confidence in the military's ability to rehabilitate soldiers for civilian life with such alacrity. Frequent tracking and pan shots show that modern medicine and the burgeoning post-war government bureaucracy function with admirable Fordist efficiency in the manner of an assembly line. In the final group therapy session, one soldier confidently proclaims that they are 'as good as anyone else', and in a bucolic baseball game all the disturbed soldiers who appeared earlier in the film are now seen as regular guys again, happily participating in the all-American sport.

Despite the film's remarkably upbeat depiction of psychotherapy, the US Army banned it for thirty-four years, until it was finally released for general viewing in 1980 by order of then-Vice-President Walter Mondale. While Huston considered the film to be his most optimistic, the military brass realised that its depiction of acute battle neuroses in American soldiers (the opening title crawl claims that 20 per cent of casualties during the war were of a neuropsychiatric nature) implies that warfare is considerably more horrifying and traumatic than the familiar myths of patriotism and glory in combat reassuringly imply. Yet, if *Let There Be Light* did not fit comfortably within the military's propaganda programme, it doubtlessly may be seen as a personal statement by its director. Certainly, the film draws upon Huston's interest in psychoanalysis, most evident in his biopic *Freud* (1962), and he returned to the theme of war trauma in his adaptation of Stephen Crane's classic Civil War novel, *The Red Badge of Courage* (1951), starring real war hero Audie Murphy. *Let There Be Light* also reveals Huston's continuing interest in existentialism, as we are told that each traumatised soldier must break out of his own prison and face his particular demons. BKG

Dir/Narrator: John Huston; **Scr**: John Huston, Charles Kaufman; **Phot**: Stanley Cortez, John Doran, Lloyd Fromm, Joseph Jackman, George Smith (b/w); **Music**: Dimitri Tiomkin; **Prod Co**: US War Department.

The Life and Times of Rosie the Riveter
US, 1980 – 60 mins
Connie Field

From the late 1960s, the women's movement looked on film as a major
form for exploring the representation of women – not least because film
was one of the principal forms that had *mis*represented them (see, for
example, DAUGHTER RITE, 1980, NOT A LOVE STORY, 1981). *The Life and
Times of Rosie the Riveter* was part of a wider impulse to record the hidden
histories and current realities of women's lives. The basic structure of *Rosie*
involves interviews, in the present, with five women, now in their fifties and
sixties, about their experiences during World War II, when the US labour
force included some 18 million women; these oral testimonies, shot in
colour, are skilfully intercut with official government 'information' films and
March of Time and other newsreels. World War II was a particularly useful
historical moment to explore, because the initial official encouragement to
recruit women, only to push them out again at war's end, offered a
transparent example of the way society viewed women's roles.
Other contemporaneous oral history films like *Union Maids* (dir. Julia
Reichert *et al.*, 1976) and *With Babies and Banners* (dir. Lorraine Gray, 1978)
focus more on trade union issues, though *Rosie* does include material on
both gender and racial discrimination and the crucial role of the unions.
In their exploitation of archive material and their montage forms, these films
owed something to Emile de Antonio's revival of the political compilation
film in the 1960s (see IN THE YEAR OF THE PIG, 1968).

   The five women interviewees are all working class, and three are
African-Americans, very different from the almost exclusively white, more
middle-class women featured in government propaganda films.
Each woman begins by sketching in her background and limited –
particularly for the black women – work opportunities before the war.
Pearl Harbour, the US declaration of war and the mobilisation of males
brought these women, ironically, whole new possibilities in their working
lives, as skilled labour in the defence industries – and new ways of

looking at themselves as confident and economically independent people. Typically, the film contrasts the official picture on some issues, peddled by newsreels as well as government films, with the interviewees telling the 'truth' about their recruitment and training and the ingrained gender and racial prejudice they came up against. For example, government films emphasise safety measures at work or promise easily accessible childcare, but the women recount the dangers they were exposed to and their significant childcare problems. Indeed, an important focus of much feminist debate in the 1970s and 1980s was the 'double day', which saw women working their factory shifts and then being expected to take care of domestic duties as well.

The empowerment and pride in their work the women experience is then, of course, extinguished as victory is celebrated. Government films that employ emotional blackmail to encourage women to return to domestic and maternal duties are juxtaposed with their enormous reluctance to do so. World War II thus proved a false start to new and different lives for women: 'We believed we were the new women', but they quickly realised that the dominant ideology prepared women for whatever roles society was deemed to need. The women's movement of the 1970s and 1980s sought to initiate a *true* start to new and different lives for women, but the confident and humorous, though disappointed, older women featured in the film come across less as martyrs than as pioneers. JH

Dir/Scr: Connie Field; **Prod**: Connie Field, Ellen Geiger, Lorraine Kahn, Jane Scantlebury, Bonnie Bellow; **Phot**: Cathy Zeutlin, Bonnie Friedman, Robert Handley, Emiko Omord (colour); **Ed**: Lucia Massia Phenix, Connie Field; **Sound**: Mark Berger, Jenny Stein; **Prod Co**: Charity Productions.

Lonely Boy
Canada, 1962 – 27 mins
Wolf Koenig, Roman Kroitor

Made by members of Tom Daly's Unit B of the National Film Board of
Canada and examining the career of Paul Anka, the first Canadian singer
to make it in the American entertainment industry, *Lonely Boy* was
significant in the development of cinéma vérité in North America.
The film was made at the height of the teen idol craze, when Anka was
nineteen, four years after his initial success and at that point in his career
when he was consciously seeking to change his image to a more adult
one. It begins by looking at his phenomenal popularity with adolescent
girls, goes on to show his successful engagement at New York's
Copacabana nightclub, and then returns to Anka as a teen idol in an
American amusement park. The NFB's Unit B, responsible for films about
cultural topics, was known for documentaries that took a distanced,
questioning attitude toward their subjects. And while at first glance
Lonely Boy seems a straightforward Canadian success story, a feel-good
celebration of a local boy who makes good, the film in fact is consistently
ironic, examining the shallow nature of pop stardom itself.

Central to its investigation of the pop idol phenomenon, *Lonely Boy*
emphasises Anka's constructed image. He makes his first appearance on
a billboard, his name moving across an electronic marquee, its fleeting
nature providing one of the film's comments on the ephemerality of pop
fame a year before Andy Warhol had his first public show. In the film,
Anka becomes a multiplicity of images, appearing on photo buttons
worn by his fans, on the many photos they carry and affix to their
purses, on the covers of fanzines and on concert programmes.
His manager explains Anka's success in terms of his plastic surgery, which
made him look more like a popular singer. Dressing before a show, Anka
is reflected in a mirror – an image of an image.

An essential component in the marketing of teen idols was an
emphasis on memorabilia, and *Lonely Boy* highlights this as an important

aspect of Anka's popularity. Early on, we see his fans collecting and displaying Anka buttons, postcards and other items. One of them boasts that she has all his records as well as '555 pictures of Paul all over my room, and I have a Paul Anka sweater'. Displaying an astute awareness of how culture conveys ideology, the film shows how such memorabilia construct sexuality and are central to the apparatus of fetishism that interpellates adolescent girls as consumers of popular culture.

This dynamic is nicely suggested by the shot of one teenage girl gazing longingly at the singing Anka through a haze of cigarette smoke, clearly transfixed by his performance.

At the conclusion of his engagement at the Copacabana, Anka presents Jules Podell, the club's owner, with a framed portrait of himself. Anka positions the picture for the camera rather than for Podell, obviously aware of the film-makers' presence, even though earlier he instructs others to pay no attention to the camera and to act as if it isn't

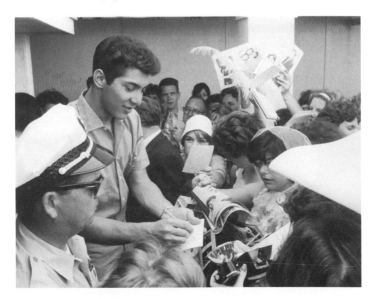

there. When Anka and Podell kiss, the film-makers, seemingly conscious of Paul's performative ability and the insincerity of the moment, ask them to 'do the kiss again, please', which the two do with some awkwardness. The film-makers' intervention here, in which they falsely claim the retake was necessitated by a technical glitch, reveals the extent to which Anka is always on stage, always performing his image. Though the film's title is taken from one of Anka's songs, it also comments on the necessary condition of his fame. The final shot, showing a weary Anka on the road between gigs, exhausted from the demands of manufactured stardom, may be the only moment of genuine expression on his part in the film, in keeping with co-director Roman Kroitor's aim of presenting him as a tragic figure. BKG

Dir: Wolf Koenig, Roman Kroitor; **Prod**: Tom Daly, Roman Kroitor; **Phot**: Wolf Koenig (b/w); **Ed**: John Spotton, Guy L. Coté; **Sound**: Marcel Carrière; **Prod Co**: National Film Board of Canada.

Lost Lost Lost
US, 1976 – 178 mins
Jonas Mekas

Jonas Mekas is probably best known as the founder of the New York Film-Makers' Co-operative, the Anthology Film Archives and the journal *Film Culture* (as well as *Village Voice* film critic) – polemicist-in-chief, since the late 1950s, of the American avant-garde, activities to which his own film-making generally took second place (though he directed *Guns of the Trees* and a highly regarded version of Living Theatre's *The Brig*, both 1964, and other films). As he says in 'The Diary Film', 'I had only bits of time which allowed me to shoot only bits of film. All my personal work became like notes . . .'. Mekas imagined that eventually he 'would make a "real" film'. In the late 1960s, however, he began to realise that the 'bits' he was capturing *were* the 'real' film, the grand opus, and Mekas's work metamorphosed, as David James puts it, from the 'film diary' to the 'diary film'.

A week after landing in New York in 1949 as displaced persons from Lithuania, brothers Jonas and Adolfas Mekas, then in their twenties, bought a wind-up 16mm Bolex camera. Jonas began to document the life around him – streets and parks, weather and seasons, visits to friends, in usually brief, unconnected shots (mostly black and white) – in notes, fragments, bidding himself, as his later, faltering, tentative, accented voiceover recalls, 'to tell a story of a man who never wanted to leave home'.

Lost Lost Lost covers the years 1949–63, its first 90 minutes dominated by Mekas's life of exile in the Williamsburg Lithuanian community, with much footage of Lithuanian friends, marriages, picnics, politics. Mekas's voiceover emphasises the pain and loneliness of the exile's response to a strange new city and the comfort of a known culture· 'I wanted to be the camera historian of exile'. But Mekas also begins to lose touch with the exile community, choosing to look ahead rather than back. In the late 1950s, he moved to Manhattan and begins to refer to New York as 'my city', with much footage devoted to peace demonstrations and friends associated with New York's art scene.

Stylistically, the early years material is marked by short, static or slow pan shots – and throughout, Mekas's crudely typed title cards are as disarmingly simple ('A Picnic', 'A Lithuanian Wedding in Brooklyn', 'Somewhere in Connecticut', 'Roofs of Williamsburg') as his subjects (rainy or snowy streets, waste land, ice in the East River, etc.). By the early 1960s, he starts to adopt a more freewheeling style – reminiscent of Brakhage (see THE ACT OF SEEING WITH ONE'S OWN EYES, 1971) and other avant-garde film-makers whose work Mekas promoted – while beginning to explore what would become his characteristic shorthand pixilation technique. Recognising that his 'direct' shooting methods were also a subjective mode of reflection, Mekas needed to 'liberate the camera . . . I had to throw out academic notions of "normal" exposure, "normal" movement . . . I had to put myself into it, to merge myself with the reality I was filming . . . by means of pacing, lighting, exposures, movements.' The overall result is a superb, fascinating record of both a time and a place – and a place changing over time – and of a film-maker's shifting consciousness and sensibility, his way of seeing, feeling and remembering.

The appropriately titled *Diaries, Notes and Sketches* (aka *Walden*, 1969) continues Mekas's autobiography through the 1960s (though it was assembled and released before *Lost Lost Lost*), recording, among more everyday events, his close encounters with New York arts figures like Andy Warhol, Judith Malina, Norman Mailer, Allen Ginsberg, John Lennon and Yoko Ono. JH

Dir/Prod/Phot/Ed/Music/Sound: Jonas Mekas (b/w & colour).

Lumière Programme
France, 1895 – 7 mins approx
Louis and Auguste Lumière

Many accounts of the evolution of cinema locate its beginnings as an art form and record of reality – as 'documentary' – in the Lumière brothers' first films and its beginnings as an art of illusion in the trick films of Georges Méliès, conveniently forgetting the earlier 'films' of Edison and Dickson that restaged actuality in the studio. It is a problematic proposition, and more interesting to reflect on the ways in which the many contradictions and problems of definition of later documentary film are already apparent in the 'Lumière programme' (first shown Paris, December 1895, and London, February 1896) – no doubt the main reason why it remains endlessly fascinating. Should we even call these static camera, typically 45–60-second scenes – their duration determined by the 50-foot lengths of stock – 'films'? They were known at the time as 'actualities'; remember that for John Grierson, 'actuality' was what needed to be 'interpreted' in order to become 'documentary'.

Questions about whether these scenes are staged or unstaged, played or unplayed, spontaneous or planned, run throughout. In *La Sortie des usines Lumière* (*Employees Leaving the Lumière Factory*), the factory gates are framed centrally and the workers exit the frame left or right rather than towards the camera (though some clearly look), while the photographers in *Neuville-sur-Saône: débarquement du congrès des photographes à Lyon* (*The Photographical Congress Arrives in Lyon*) all look at the camera, some doffing their hats (whether to the camera or its operator Louis Lumière is unclear). In *Repas de bébé* (*Baby's Dinner*), while the parents (Auguste Lumière and his wife) studiously do *not* look at the camera, the baby – less conscious of protocol – does. Both *Partie de cartes* (*Card Game*) and *L'Arroseur arrosé* (*The Waterer Watered*) have some quality of actuality but are clearly taking place only to be filmed, with strong elements of narrative and performance. Surely, these 'scenes', rather than Méliès's trick films, are the first 'fictions'?

Remember, too, that the Lumières liked to show *Démolition d'un mur* (*Demolition of a Wall*) first in forward motion and then, to privilege the trick of illusion as much as the power of record (and to demonstrate the Cinématographe's versatility), in reverse.

Several Lumière scenes are evidently more 'uncontrolled', in Richard Leacock's later phrase, and elicit a consequently more heightened audience response. In *Barque sortant du port* (*Boat Leaving the Port*), the rowers, unable to control the elements, are nearly turned around by a larger wave. In *Arrivée d'un train à la Ciotat* (*Arrival of a Train at La Ciotat*), most people attending the train's arrival, busy finding their carriage or getting on or off, are generally oblivious of the camera.

In *Barque*, the film frame contains all the action, but here it becomes particularly dynamic, as people move in depth towards and away from the camera, changing size within the frame, as well as into and out of the picture, reducing them to a shoulder here, a half body there.

Reputedly, some spectators recoiled in fear at *Arrivée d'un train* as if in thrall to the hyper-reality of the medium – and some found the background leaves fluttering in the breeze more astonishing than the baby being fed in *Repas de bébé*. But Maxim Gorki, in 1896, was struck by almost the opposite qualities of the Lumière films. In 'The Kingdom of Shadows', he describes 'A world without colour and sound. Everything here – the earth, water and air, the trees, the people – everything is made of a monotone grey . . . Not life, but the shadow of life. Not life's movement, but a sort of mute spectre.' JH

Dir/Prod: Louis Lumière, Auguste Lumière; **Phot**: Louis Lumière (b/w); **Prod Co**: Lumière.

Les Maîtres fous (*The Manic Priests/The Mad Masters*)
France, 1955 – 36 mins
Jean Rouch

A major figure in the development of ethnographic documentary film-making (see also DEAD BIRDS, 1965), Jean Rouch made many films in Africa and developed the documentary style of cinéma vérité with sociologist Edgar Morin in CHRONIQUE D'UN ÉTÉ (1961). Going to Africa initially as a civil engineer in 1941, Rouch became fascinated with African cultures and the lingering effects of colonialism on them. Shot in Accra in 1954, then the capital of the colonial Gold Coast (which, as Ghana, achieved independence from the UK three years after the film was made), *Les Maîtres fous* documents the possession ritual of the Hauka – as Rouch's voiceover explains, 'the new gods, the gods of the city, the gods of technology, the gods of power'. During the ritual, the adherents are possessed with the spirits of their colonial 'masters', taking on their roles ('The Governor-General', 'The Admiral', 'Madame Locotoro, the doctor's wife', etc.) and enacting broad caricatures of their behaviour. The Hauka cult was oppressed by both church and state, but the film was shot at the request of Hauka priests, who wanted not only a record of their ceremony but also thought to incorporate it as part of the ritual.

Given the limitations of Rouch's equipment – a camera that allowed for shots of no longer than 25 seconds and an imperfectly synchronous, clockwork tape recorder that, while portable, weighed 40kg and therefore was located, along with the microphone, in one place much of the time and required a post-synched soundtrack – he managed to create an admirably coherent structure for the film. Shot over three days, it follows the lives of cult members, largely seasonal migrant workers from middle Niger who come to Accra looking for 'the great adventure of African cities'. On the first day, shot in the city, we see some of the Hauka initiates working at their quotidian jobs. On day two, they travel by vehicle and then on foot to the rural compound of Mountyeba, the

Hauka high priest. During the ritual, the participants fall under a trance, broadly impersonating the colonial political authorities; the possessed foam at the mouth, speak in tongues, contort their bodies oddly and endure spasms. They sacrifice a chicken as penance and kill, cook and eat a dog in the course of the possession ritual. In the denouement, Rouch shows them back in Accra the following day at their jobs: 'Madame Locotoro' is by day a shop clerk, 'a rather effeminate boy who uses a lot of hair vaseline', and 'The General in real life is just a private'; the Governor, the Engineer and the Truck Driver all work for the Accra Water Works, and are discovered by chance digging a ditch in front of the city's mental hospital. Their broad smiles contrast sharply with their fiery faces and foaming mouths of the day before, a contrast that Rouch heightens by intercutting shots of them in trance.

It has been generally thought that Rouch understood the possession ceremony as a ritualised way of casting off the demons of colonial oppression: the opening titles explicitly tell us that the violent possession ritual of the Hauka is only a reflection of contemporary Western society, and Rouch concludes his narration by wondering whether these people have found 'a panacea against mental disorders', 'a way to absorb our inimical society'. At the time Rouch made *Les Maîtres fous*, the sect, which began in the middle Niger region in 1927, had gained widespread popularity, though it gradually dissipated as the people shed their colonial past. In France, the film became the subject of controversy upon its first screening at the Musée de l'Homme, as some felt that it presented retrograde racist stereotypes of black people. Unsurprisingly, the film was banned in Britain's African colonies, on the grounds of offending the Queen and cruelty to animals. BKG

Dir/Phot: Jean Rouch (b/w); **Prod**: Pierre Braunberger; **Ed**: Suzanne Baron; **Sound**: Damouré Zika, Ibrahima Dia; **Prod Co**: Films de la Pléiade.

Manhatta
US, 1921 – 11 mins
Charles Sheeler, Paul Strand

Is *Manhatta* (aka *Mannahatta/New York the Magnificent*) a hangover from the actuality 'scenics' – short travelogues, often filmed in exotic locations – so popular in early cinema at the end of the 19th century and the start of the 20th, or the first (or one of the first) American avant-garde films? Perhaps it is a bit of both. The title under which it was first shown in 1921 – *New York the Magnificent* – suggests a scenic, but its presentation at London's Film Society in 1927 under the new title *Manhatta* (both the native American name for the island and the title of a poem from Walt Whitman's *Leaves of Grass*, extracted for the film's title cards) suggests something more experimental. It has certainly come to be seen as a precursor to the 'city symphony' films that became a popular European avant-garde form in the 1920s with films like *Rien que les heures* (dir. Alberto Cavalcanti, France, 1926), BERLIN: SYMPHONY OF A GREAT CITY (1927), *Rain* (dir. Joris Ivens, Netherlands, 1929) and MAN WITH A MOVIE CAMERA (1929).

    Manhatta was 'lost' between the late 1920s and early 1950s, which may partly explain why neither Charles Sheeler nor Paul Strand saw it as a significant work in their oeuvres. Strand was best known as a still photographer and Sheeler as a 'Precisionist' painter of modernity and industrial scenes, but Sheeler was also a photographer and freely used still photos as the basis for his paintings (and, in fact, printed still photos from the negative frames of the film). *Manhatta* is a celebration of Lower Manhattan as the epitome of energetic modernity – as it was often seen in the 1920s and later – in a series of still shots, many of them looking down at the city from considerable height. The shots favour skyscrapers, rooftops, bridges, locomotives, tug boats, water, with a painterly emphasis on rising smoke and steam, light and shade on buildings, and with a formality bordering at times on abstraction (as was the case with much of Strand's and Sheeler's photography and Sheeler's painting).

One shot replicates Strand's celebrated 1915 photograph 'Wall Street'. Sheeler's paintings are not very interested in people, and though the shots here do include them – ferry passengers, pedestrians, building workers – they are usually seen, ant-like, in long shot, with little sense of the human cost of urban life.

The film adopts, somewhat loosely but recognisably, the 'day-in-the-life' structure common in later city symphony films, beginning with commuters arriving on the Staten Island Ferry – the closest we get to human beings as individuals – and ending with sunset on the Hudson. The pace and rhythm of the film is generally slow, contemplative, even majestic – very different from the often frenetic *Berlin* or *Man with a Movie Camera* – and slowed down further by the poetic Whitman title cards (though Whitman is not acknowledged), such as 'City of hurried and sparkling waters/City nested in bays'. But the Whitman extracts are important in setting the tone of the film: they emphasise many of the same elements – sunlight, water, crowds – present in the film, and without them, the viewer – certainly the modern viewer – could well read the endless smoke and steam as evidence of pollution rather than of industry, energy and modernity. JH

Dir/Phot: Charles Sheeler, Paul Strand (b/w).

Man of Aran
UK, 1934 – 76 mins
Robert Flaherty

As in his earlier NANOOK OF THE NORTH (1922), Robert Flaherty focuses
in *Man of Aran* on the human ability to survive in the most inhospitable
of environments. John Grierson initially proposed the idea for the film to
Flaherty, who was in England to make *Industrial Britain* (1933), produced
by Grierson for the Empire Marketing Board Film Unit, and Flaherty
negotiated a contract with Michael Balcon and Gaumont British that
allowed him to make a film of his own choosing. *Man of Aran*, shot on a
group of three small and barren islands off the western coast of Ireland,
was the result. Photographed with long lenses allowing him to shoot
from a far distance, Flaherty here distilled his romantic vision of man
against nature into a mythic adventure. While the film was hailed by
many as another great achievement for its director, Grierson and others
attacked Flaherty for imposing his romantic vision on his subjects,
celebrating their fortitude and endurance while failing to address the
economic and social contexts that determined the Aran islanders'
impoverished existence.

As in the earlier *Nanook* and *Moana* (1926), Flaherty depicts the
islands (falsely) as devoid of modern technology. Flaherty intervenes in
the islanders actual lives as he had done with the Inuit people in *Nanook*,
similarly compromising *Man of Aran*'s value as an ethnographic
document but enhancing its considerable picturesque appeal. The method
of farming involving lugging seaweed to the cliff top from rocky
crevasses near the crashing ocean, and the hunting of basking sharks,
which is portrayed as a two-day struggle, had long since been
abandoned by the islanders; indeed, the latter had to be taught to them
anew so that Flaherty could film it. The three members of the idealised
family featured in the film were not in fact a family, but were chosen by
Flaherty for their photogenic quality. But the film's footage of the mother
and son gazing out from the cliffs to the sea, intercut with shots of a

boatload of men fighting to gain shore in a violent storm, is breathtaking, as the boat bobs in and out of view, rising and sinking with monstrous waves in a roiling sea.

Flaherty imparts considerable visual drama to the life of the islanders. There is no voiceover narration, and very few titles, as the film relies primarily on the shots and editing to tell its story. Recalling the compositions of Nanook and his family in the wide expanse of tundra, Flaherty often films the boat near the edges of the frame, emphasising its puny vulnerability in relation to the sea's unforgiving vastness.

Extended montage and frequent pan shots underscore the ocean's relentless rhythms as waves break with ferocious power on the island's jagged, rocky cliffs. Except for one brief shot, Flaherty never shows the entire basking shark, allowing its frightening proportions to be bounded only by the viewer's imagination. The film was shot silent, and while the addition of post-synchronised sound, including snatches of dialogue recorded in a studio, the sound of the sea lashing the fishing boats and roaring winds, may seem crude by today's standards, it adds a stylised soundtrack to match the mythic grandeur of the images.

Once again, Flaherty structures his film as a story of struggle for survival by focusing on a few individuals. As he would do in the later *Elephant Boy* (1937) and *Louisiana Story* (1948), Flaherty uses the boy as our guide into the world of the Aran islanders. We first see him by the water catching a crab, the calm pool of water hardly suggesting the dramatic storm to come. The film's final shot shows the family walking away from the camera, victorious this time in their survival against the elements. The titanic struggle of the Man of Aran (and, from what we see, The Woman and The Boy as well), as the opening title tells us, 'is a fight from which he will have no respite until the end of his indomitable days or until he meets his master – the sea'. BKG

Dir/Scr/Phot: Robert J. Flaherty (b/w); **Prod**: Michael Balcon; **Ed**: John Goldman; **Music**: John Greenwood; **Sound**: H. Hand; **Prod Co**: Gainsborough Pictures.

Man with a Movie Camera (*Chelovek s kino-apparatom*)
USSR, 1929 – 80 mins
Dziga Vertov

Both a documentary and an audacious experimental film, Dziga Vertov's *Man with a Movie Camera* is one of the most famous works of the 'Golden Age' of silent Soviet cinema (see also THE FALL OF THE ROMANOV DYNASTY, 1927, TURKSIB, 1929). Combining numerous optical effects with genuine observational footage, the film is ostensibly structured as a city symphony film, a poetic 'day-in-the-life' form popular in European cine-clubs in the 1920s and 1930s (see also BERLIN: SYMPHONY OF A GREAT CITY, 1972). Actually an amalgam of footage shot in Moscow, Kiev and Odessa, *Man with a Movie Camera* celebrates in lyrical fashion the modern

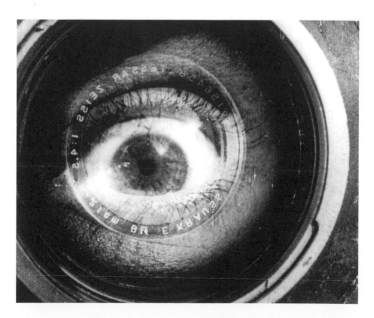

industrialisation and urbanisation of post-Revolutionary Russia. Influenced by the aesthetics of constructivism, the film depicts an imaginary city where, in idealised Soviet fashion, people and machines work together in wondrous harmony.

In support of this view, the film covers an overwhelming range of activities in the daily life of its idealised, imaginary city. Soviet citizens, no less idealised than the city they inhabit, work cheerfully on the assembly lines and enthusiastically engage in collective sport and exercise. Vertov consistently associates human activity with the precision of machinery, emphasising the efficiency of both. Shots of blinking eyes, for example, are juxtaposed to window blinds opening and the camera shutter; thick traffic flows in various directions in the bustling boulevards, like blood coursing through veins, a sign of health in the collective body politic. Obviously set-up sequences combine with those of people genuinely caught unawares, in what would be called 'candid camera shots'.

Reflecting upon its own status as cinematic construction, the various glimpses of the city's activity are loosely connected by recurrent shots of the cameraman of the title (Vertov's brother, Mikhail Kaufman) shooting film or setting up for a shot (which at some subsequent point we see), such as those taken from a moving carriage capturing the motion of a trotting horse. Periodically, shots become freeze-frames, as we are reminded that moving pictures are composed of a series of still images. We also see some of these same images as strips of celluloid in labelled rolls and on the editing table of Yelizaveta Svilova, Vertov's wife and editor, as she edits footage that appears in *Man with a Movie Camera*. One of these scenes is of a magician performing tricks for an appreciative crowd, but Vertov's goal is to demystify the magic of the cinematic illusion by making good Soviet citizens aware of how the film medium works. Towards the end, the camera, through pixilation, even demystifies itself: introducing itself with a bow, it takes itself apart to show us how it functions. In the course of the film, viewers are shown the entire process of film-making, from the cameraman cranking his machine to the projection of the film in a theatre.

Man with a Movie Camera is thus a demonstration of Vertov's theories regarding cinema's documentary capabilities and its duty to abandon the diversions of fiction for the truths of reportage. For Vertov, the camera's 'kino-eye' has the ability to perceive and record reality better than the human eye, capturing life in all of its fullness and complexity. The cameraman and his camera are superimposed over a busy city street, towering over it, able to look anywhere and everywhere, at people being born, getting married and dying; alternately, they are even to be found recording the smallest details of life, as they appear in miniature, filming from within a glass of beer. As Soviet aesthetics hardened into the doctrine of Socialist Realism, Vertov's formalist experimentation fell out of favour, but decades later, in acknowledgment of his rejection of entertainment cinema in favour of documentary, ethnographic film-maker Jean Rouch would call his approach 'cinéma vérité' (after Vertov's newsreel, *Kino Pravda*) and Jean-Luc Godard's radical experiments in collective film-making in the late 1960s and early 1970s (such as BRITISH SOUNDS) were credited to the Dziga Vertov Group. BKG

Dir/Scr/Ed: Dziga Vertov; **Phot**: Mikhail Kaufman (b/w); **Co-ed**: Yelizaveta Svilova; **Prod Co**: VUFKU, Ukraine.

March of the Penguins (*La Marche de l'empereur*)
France, 2005 – 85 mins
Luc Jacquet

March of the Penguins, about the life cycle and mating habits of the Antarctic emperor penguin, is one of the most engaging nature documentaries ever made, a skilfully shot and constructed account of this animal's extraordinary life. Winner of numerous awards, including an Academy Award for Best Documentary Feature, it reflects an increased awareness of and appreciation for the environment that is manifest in such documentaries as *An Inconvenient Truth* (2006) and *The 11th Hour* (2007) but also present in recent nature films as well. Where in *Winged Migration* (2001), miniature cameras attached to the birds allow us to fly along with different migrating species, and *Microcosmos* (2003) brings the world of insects alive through stunning microscopic photography, *March of the Penguins* uses long lenses, cameras suspended by balloon above the penguins' breeding ground and impressive underwater photography evocative of Jacques Cousteau's *The Silent World* (1956) to dramatise the story of 'these stalwart souls' who annually embark on a 'remarkable journey' of procreation and endurance.

As the film explains, the penguins leave the ocean in March every year, all at about the same time, to tramp across the icy Antarctic terrain for up to 70 miles, walking continuously day and night until they reach their ancestral breeding ground. We watch as they silently trudge across the frozen, inhospitable landscape, both in intimate close-ups and extreme long shots that emphasise the staggering scale of their trek. The film goes on to observe their unique mating rituals, particularly after the birth of the egg when the mothers pass them to the fathers for safekeeping and trek back to the ocean to feed; meanwhile, the fathers care for the eggs for two more months without eating until they hatch and the mothers return. Over the course of rearing their chicks, both parents will make several trips between the breeding ground and the ocean until they return to the sea, leaving the chicks on their own for weeks until they are ready to make the plunge for the first time.

Every phase of this remarkable cycle is presented in a well-crafted narrative, making it seem as if we are there, huddling in the cold with the penguins, and it is not until the end credits that we see the camera crew walking among the animals to set up their shots. In any good story, we identify with the protagonists, especially when they triumph over extreme adversity, and this is certainly true with the penguins, both because of their astonishing life cycle and because their human-like mannerisms make them easy to anthropomorphise, a tendency that the film encourages. The original French version contains overdubbed dialogue as if it were the penguins speaking, but in the English-language version American actor Morgan Freeman provides an earnest narration, telling us from the outset that 'this is a story about love'. The mating is presented as tender and romantic, the animals quietly and gently touching each other and standing together, a dance as harmonious as any by Fred Astaire and Ginger Rogers. Director Luc Jacquet has cautioned against viewing the penguins as metaphors of human behaviour, but in either version we cannot help but admire their indomitable spirit, collective co-operation and embrace of family values, selflessly going hungry for the sake of their children when necessary and remaining monogamous (for one season, at least). For these reasons, the film became a point of reference for conservative viewers, who saw the penguins' breeding cycle as natural evidence in support of their own traditional views about marriage. BKG

Dir: Luc Jacquet; **Prod**: Ilann Girard, Yves Darondeau, Christophe Lioud, Emmanuel Priou; **Scr**: Luc Jacquet, Michel Fessler, Jordan Roberts (narration, US version); **Phot**: Laurent Chalet, Jérôme Maison (colour); **Ed**: Sabine Emiliani; **Music**: Emile Simon, Alex Wurman (US version); **Sound**: Laurent Quaglio (sound design), Scott A. Jennings (supervising sound editor, US version); **Prod Co**: Bonne Pioche/National Geographic Films.

A Married Couple
Canada, 1969 – 112 mins
Allan King

Canadian film-maker Allan King had been making documentaries since
Skid Row (1956), which preceded Lionel Rogosin's more well-known *On
the Bowery* by a year, before creating several powerful direct cinema
documentaries beginning with *Warrendale* (1970), about a treatment
centre for emotionally disturbed children. King's follow-up film,
A Married Couple, is equally disturbing even though its setting is the
more banal bourgeois home. The film focuses on a Toronto couple, Billy
and Antoinette Edwards, along with their son, Bogart. Married seven
years, their relationship is foundering and they are teetering on the edge
of separation. In the film, while Billy and Antoinette do exchange a few
tender moments, mostly they argue, whether about furniture, money or
where to put the kitchen oven.

    The film was shot over a ten-week period, with the film-makers
shooting over seventy hours of footage as they spent as much time with
the Edwardses as they were able. The camera seems to be with the
couple constantly, from when they wake up in the morning in bed to
when they go to sleep at night. The film raises similar ethical questions to
those surrounding other documentaries such as GREY GARDENS (1975),
namely King's questionable choice of profilmic subjects. Standing for a
presumably representative bourgeois couple, the Edwards's marriage
already had serious problems before King began filming; and Billy and
Antoinette both had previous acting experience, and at times it is clear
that each is playing to the camera. Nevertheless, the film does offer a
revealing portrait of a couple locked in a cycle of mutual self-destruction
that is more convincing than any Ingmar Bergman film because it is
unscripted.

    In his career, King has alternated between documentary and
fiction film-making, both for cinema and for television, and like a
number of his other films, *A Married Couple* mixes fictional elements

with a fly-on-the-wall documentary aesthetic to create what the director referred to as 'actuality dramas'. While the events are unscripted, the film makes use of several techniques associated with fiction film-making. For example, after Billy and Antoinette go to bed for the night, there is a fadeout (an ironic touch, given that Antoinette steadfastly refuses to have sex with Billy), followed by an establishing shot in the morning as the camera cranes down a tree outside the Edwards's home before cutting inside to the bedroom as they wake up. As King freely acknowledges, sequences are not presented in chronological order; instead, the film has a classic narrative structure, with rising dramatic tension building to a climax followed by a denouement. The drama reaches a climax when, after an argument, Billy's anger boils over and he grabs Antoinette by the neck and pushes her through the doorway and out of the house, locking her out. Later, back home after a weekend trip to their cottage in Maine, they begin to discuss leading separate lives but sharing the house, as if tentatively acknowledging that their marriage is ending. In the final scene, there is a moment of tenderness as they tentatively touch, then silently embrace, rocking and sobbing, leaving the spectator to wonder whether they are accepting the end of their marriage or merely prolonging their mutual unhappiness. This ambiguity is heightened by a tone that is at once comic and horrifying, as these two articulate people engage in marital warfare with withering wit.

A Married Couple should be seen as a precursor to the multi-episode reality television shows, Alan and Susan Raymond's *An American Family* (1973) and Paul Watson's UK BBC TV spin-off, *The Family* (1974). BKG

Dir/Prod: Allan King; **Phot**: Richard Leiterman (colour); **Ed**: Arla Saare; **Music**: Zal Yanovsky, Douglas Bush; **Sound**: Christian Wangler; **Prod Co**: Allan King Associates.

Minamata (aka *Minamata: The Victims and Their World*) (*Minamata – Kanja santo sono sekai*)
Japan, 1971 – 155 mins
Tsuchimoto Noriaki

Post-war Japan has an honourable history of campaigning documentary films – often made over long periods of time, with extended running times and with few obvious parallels in Western documentary film-making. Tsuchimoto's *Minamata* is one such campaign film: it was finished some twenty years after the start of the sequence of events with which it is concerned, and climaxes – and appeared – at the moment of a new phase in its campaign. The year 1953 marked the first occurrence of 'Minamata disease' in the fishing community of Minamata in southern Japan. The source was traced to the Chisso chemical plant that in the early 1950s began using inorganic mercury compounds to increase production. Waste deposited in the sea resulted in mercury poisoning, affecting both adults and children born with the disease congenitally.

Tsuchimoto's team began to document the effects of the disease on both individuals and the community in 1953, recording on film and magnetic sound tape; much of the film consists of intimate documentation of the disease's effects, both physical – lack of motor neurone control, blindness, and so on – and emotional – the pain of the loss of parents and children to the disease, social ostracism, as well as the efforts of family members, doctors and care workers to undertake rehabilitation. The film achieves its powerful effects by a slow, sometimes apparently shapeless, accumulation of emotionally affecting documentation of personal experiences – though oddly distanced, too, by the lack of synch sound and frequent shots of microphones – rather than by a tight expository structure.

Also documented is the essential resilience but slowly evolving change in consciousness of the individuals affected, from an angry desire to break into the factory to splits in the community when some accept limited but absolute compensation while others seek legal confrontation

with the company, along with the gathering of support and consciousness-raising in cities throughout Japan – a process during which modest, humble people decide to question and confront the sacrosanct institutions of state and commerce. Thus, the astonishing, chaotic scenes of the climax when the victims, having become Chisso shareholders and won the right to attend its AGM, demand the right to speak and to hear what the chairman has to say about the company's guilt, a confrontation that inevitably leaves everything hanging – the futures of the victims as well as the roles and responsibilities of the corporation and the state.

While this may mark its climax, the film ends where it began – and where it returns at intervals throughout (including a long, marvellous sequence in which an old fisherman shows how he catches and kills octopus) – with the sea and fishing boats, sources of both livelihood and death. In the final poetic yet paradoxical shots, myriad small fishing boats manoeuvre a silvery sea under dark, low clouds, a reminder of unchanging yet fragile nature.

Post-war Japan, perhaps looking back to the radical newsreels of the leftist Prokino group – formed in 1929, declared illegal in the mid-1930s – produced a number of striking independent documentaries similar to *Minamata*, including the collective Ogawa Productions' series of films, made over a ten-year period, sharing and documenting the long campaign by peasant farmers in the Narita valley outside Tokyo against the construction of a new airport (including *Summer in Narita*, 1968, and *Narita: Peasants of the Second Fortress*, 1971). Tsuchimoto's involvement with the Minamata story continued with *The Shiranui Sea* (1975). A very different kind of Japanese campaigning documentary can be seen in THE EMPEROR'S NAKED ARMY MARCHES ON (1987). JH

Dir/Scr: Tsuchimoto Noriaki; **Prod**: Takagi Ryutaro; **Phot**: Otsu Koshiro (b/w); **Technical Collaborators**: Kubota Yukio, Ichinosu Masafumi, Hori Suguru, Sekizawa Takako, Asanuma Koichi, Shioda Takeshi; **Prod Co**: Higashi Productions.

My Winnipeg
Canada, 2007 – 80 mins
Guy Maddin

Canadian post-modern film-maker Guy Maddin is, paradoxically, so avant-garde that his movies look like they were made almost a hundred years ago, whether in the style of German Expressionism (*Careful*, 1992), Soviet montage (*Heart of the World*, 2000) or the brooding Nordic dramas of Carl Theodor Dreyer (*Brand upon the Brain*, 2006). Maddin's fiction films are typically hotbeds of emotion, highly stylised, roiling cauldrons of Freudian neuroses, family trauma and repressed desires. Thus, while it may strike one as an unlikely alliance, when the Documentary Channel invited Maddin to make a documentary film about his home town of Winnipeg, Manitoba, it was no surprise that the result, what he called a 'docu-fantasia', is a black-and-white work that stretches the definition of documentary to its limits by combining elements of psychodrama, autobiographical recollection and surreal dream film.

Admittedly, *My Winnipeg* does contain occasional documentary material, as periodically there is relatively straightforward documentary exposition and archival footage (though some of the scenes are portrayed by shadow puppets reminiscent of Lotte Reiniger) of major events in the history (real? imagined?) of Winnipeg, including the Winnipeg General Strike, the rash of ectoplasmic seances in the 1920s, the departure of the NHL's Winnipeg Jets from the city, and the astonishingly surreal tragedy in which panicked racehorses fled a stable fire and ran into the Red River, where they froze to death, encased in ice until they thawed in the spring. But despite the local historical interest of these events, more memorable are the scenes of the director's personal history, in which he has actors – including the cult actress Ann Savage, star of the classic film noir *Detour* (Edgar G. Ulmer, 1945), who plays the part of Guy's mother – enact traumatic scenes from his childhood. Considerable animus is heaped on the figure of Guy's mother, who owned the Ellice Ave beauty shop, above which he grew up.

Connecting both levels of documentation are recurrent images of people on a train, trying to escape Winnipeg, drowsily jostling in the railway car and falling asleep despite themselves as a kielbasa sausage hovers above, weaving its spell. Sometimes the historical and personal Winnipegs merge, as when narrator Maddin informs us that the city has the highest statistical rate of sleepwalkers of any city in the world or that it has unique electrical forces running through it because of its location at a fork of the river. Maddin spends time on mundane details that, for whatever reason, caught his attention as a youth, like the orange jello at the Paddlewheel Restaurant. Ultimately, Guy Maddin's Winnipeg is a thick soup of personal memory, distorted imaginings and factoids about the city, which is probably closer to the way most people relate to their environment than the urban celebrations depicted in city symphony films like BERLIN: SYMPHONY OF A GREAT CITY (1927) or MAN WITH A MOVIE CAMERA (1929).

The train with the floating kielbasa loops around Winnipeg, never leaving, reflecting Guy's psychic stasis ('I must leave it. I must leave it now,' the narrator declares), the adamant refusal (or inability) of this world-famous film-maker to depart the Canadian prairie for the likely more rewarding environs of Toronto or Hollywood. Yet, as Maddin hopes to film his way out of Winnipeg, paradoxically it is his continued residence there that has provided much of his creative inspiration. BKG

Dir: Guy Maddin; **Prod**: Michael Burns; **Scr**: Guy Maddin, George Toles; **Phot**: John Gurdebeke (colour); **Ed**: Jody Shapiro; **Prod Des**: Réjean Labrie; **Prod Co**: Documentary Channel/Buffalo Gal Pictures.

Nanook of the North
US, 1922 – 70 mins
Robert Flaherty

The first feature-length documentary, *Nanook of the North* was made by Robert Flaherty, an explorer and mining engineer who had spent much time in the Arctic and was familiar with the Inuit people's way of life. Although Flaherty had only minimal training in film-making, with *Nanook* he went beyond most travelogues of the period, such as *Grass* (dirs. Ernest B. Schoedsack, Merian C. Cooper, 1925), to create a compelling story of the harsh life of the Inuit of Hudson's Bay by focusing on individual characters, the hunter Nanook and his family. Made with financial backing from Revillon Frères, a fur company that operated trading posts in Canada, *Nanook of the North* received theatrical distribution by Paramount and was shown in theatres across North America.

Flaherty imported techniques from fiction film into *Nanook*, with the result that viewers are able to identify with Nanook's harsh struggle for survival rather than regard him simply as an exoticised, alien Other. The film begins by introducing Nanook and the members of his family as they disembark from their kayak. We then follow them through several adventures, including travelling across the ice, seal and walrus hunting, building an igloo and enjoying family playtime. In these scenes, Flaherty emphasises his subjects' resourcefulness for surviving in their harsh environment, a theme that would continue in his subsequent films, particularly MAN OF ARAN (1934). When Nanook builds his igloo, for example, he carves a window out of a block of ice, and even incorporates a reflector shield through which to concentrate the precious rays of the sun. In the final scene, Flaherty employs dramatic cross-cutting in the manner of D. W. Griffith between the family settling down to sleep in their igloo during a fierce night-time storm and the sled dogs outside; the wind and snow whip the animals, who must endure nature's onslaught, in contrast to the people inside their shelter, who have the unique ability to exploit nature even as it challenges their very existence.

Nanook of the North is sometimes claimed as an early example of ethnographic film-making in the tradition of such films as DEAD BIRDS (1965), but Flaherty did not hesitate to manipulate events for the purpose of dramatisation. For example, at one point Nanook discovers the breathing hole of a fox hiding in the snow and then captures it. However, it is clear that Nanook had prior knowledge of the fox's presence, as the camera is already set up at the location before Nanook approaches it. Similarly, on the day that Flaherty filmed the seal hunting episode, Nanook was unable to catch one, so a dead seal was tied onto his fishing line, and as he seems to fight mightily with the creature, Nanook's friends pulled on the line out of view of the camera. More problematically, at the time Flaherty made the film, modern technology and culture had already infiltrated Inuit life so that the use of rifles rather than harpoons and motorboats instead of kayaks was not uncommon. However, at Flaherty's insistence, Nanook divested himself of any such equipment in order to be presented as a noble primitive who hunts and survives in the traditional way. Flaherty was keenly aware of the irreversible impact that contact with more technologically 'advanced' cultures wrought upon the Inuit, as the scene where Nanook visits the white man's trading post reveals. One of the few documentary film-makers granted auteur status, Flaherty thus projected his romantic vision onto his subjects in order to celebrate their already disappearing heritage. BKG

Dir/Scr/Phot: Robert J. Flaherty (b/w); **Prod**: Robert J. Flaherty, John Revillon; **Ed**: Robert J. Flaherty, Charles Gelb; **Prod Co**: Les Frères Revillon/Pathé Exchange.

Native Land
US, 1942 – 80 mins
Leo Hurwitz, Paul Strand

Native Land represented the summit of US 1930s left documentary film-making, as the Film and Photo League morphed into Nykino in 1935 and Frontier Films in 1937: Leo Hurwitz had contributed to League films, co-founded Frontier Films and had worked on *Heart of Spain* (1937) with Paul Strand, the photographer who had co-directed MANHATTA (1921). By the late 1930s, Popular Front politics, the left-leaning New Deal and a growing awareness of European fascism allowed left film-making to move from the margins to the mainstream centre (making government films like Joris Ivens's *Power and the Land*, 1940).

Made over several years, *Native Land* bases itself on incidents recorded by the LaFollette Civil Liberties Senate Committee (1936–41). Though mainly dramatic re-enactment of civil rights abuses uncovered by the committee, it also uses newsreel footage and stills to root its re-enactments in actuality. Formally, its lyrical introduction, laying claim to historic, mainstream American values, is strongly reminiscent of Pare Lorentz's THE PLOW THAT BROKE THE PLAINS (1936) and *The River* (1937): imposing images, dramatic music and a sonorous voiceover often based, like *The River*, on repetition and alliteration ('We the plain people, plowman and pioneer') – hardly surprising, as Hurwitz and Strand were co-photographers, and Hurwitz co-scriptwriter, on *The Plow*. But here, Lorentz's emphasis on natural forces gives way to a focus on liberty and individual rights as enshrined in Jefferson's Bill of Rights, with industrialisation imagined as their consecration – 'democracy fought for and built into the steel girders of America' – and a wonderfully idealistic optimism in the film's evocation of both rural and city life and ordinary people working to create 'abundance'.

In a series of superb dramatic re-enactments, the film demonstrates the threats to citizens' rights to speak freely and organise: in Michigan, 1934, a farmer is badly beaten by thugs for speaking up at a meeting;

in Arkansas, 1936, black and white sharecroppers who spoke up to demand more for their cotton are chased down and shot dead; in Tampa, 1935, Klansmen torture and lynch liberal politicians. 'People never heard of it . . . Nothing in the newspapers. Wasn't on the radio. Don't understand it.' The longest re-enactment – a third of the film – concerns the 'security' and intimidation business, a story about a union spy, with later Hollywood (and blacklisted) actors like Art Smith and Howard Da Silva. This now looks like the weakest section, though one can easily understand the desire for an engaging narrative: it unbalances the film, and is less effective than the more impressionistic shorter incidents, held together by the commentary and the powerful speaking voice of Paul Robeson (icon of both social activism and racial equality). The film ends with a restatement of the threat of tyranny, with powerful news footage and stills of strike-breaking, intercutting the re-enacted funeral of a murdered union man with a return to images of Jefferson, Adams, Lincoln, the flag and the Statue of Liberty.

Native Land, released in May 1942, was well received but its impact was blunted by Pearl Harbour (7 December 1941), which shifted national priorities: reviewing the film in *The New York Times* (12 May 1942), Bosley Crowther called it 'one of the most powerful and disturbing documentary films ever made', but also wondered 'whether a picture of this sort is not disturbing to national unity at this time'. JH

Dir/Prod: Leo Hurwitz, Paul Strand; **Scr**: Leo Hurwitz, Paul Strand, David Wolff (Ben Maddow); **Phot**: Paul Strand (b/w); **Ed**: Leo Hurwitz; **Music**: Marc Blitzstein; **Sound Rec**: Robert Stebbins, Ralph Avseev; **Commentary**: David Wolff; **Principal Cast**: Paul Robeson (narrator), Art Smith, Housely Stevenson, Howard Da Silva, John Marlieb (John Marley); **Prod Co**: Frontier Films.

Necrology
US, 1971 – 12 mins
Standish Lawder

By their very nature – as well as by economic necessity – the majority of avant-garde or experimental films are rooted in documentary observation of real world events. What determines the films' classification as avant-garde rather than as documentary is determined less by the nature of what has been shot than by *the way in which* it has been shot and/or by *what is then done to* this documentary base material. Standish Lawder's own *Corridor* (1970), for example, manipulates shots of an office building corridor to kinetic effect, and other film-makers like Stan Brakhage (see THE ACT OF SEEING WITH ONE'S OWN EYES, 1971), Bruce Baillie (in, for example, *Castro Street* and *All My Life*, both 1966) and Michael Snow (in, for example, *Wavelength*, 1967, and *La Région centrale*, 1971) all base most of their work on what could be called documentary material.

Also, many avant-garde films have made extensive use of found footage, manipulated in experimental ways, as in the case of Bruce Conner's *A Movie* (1958) and *Report* (1965), and Lawder's *Dangling Participle* (1970), a hilarious reassemblage of 1950s sex education films that foregrounds the era's ideological assumptions about gender and sexuality through ironic editing of both image and voiceover narration.

Lawder's *Necrology* combines documentary observation with image manipulation and a playful sense of humour to comment on contemporary society. The film's title refers to a list of the dead, signalling its ironic attitude. Lawder uses the style of observational cinema, albeit with subsequent manipulation, simply training his camera on a seemingly random group of commuters. It consists of one long take of people descending on an escalator in Manhattan's Grand Central Station. The camera does not move and shows only part of the escalator, omitting both the top and bottom. The shot was processed backwards, so that the commuters appear instead to be ascending. Riding the escalator, the people captured by the camera appear transfixed in their gazes, looking off to nowhere in particular and somewhat awkward in their few movements (the result of reverse projection). The shot, which otherwise might be regarded as banal, tends to take on grander metaphysical connotations, suggesting another meaning of ascension as the people rise out of view at the top of the frame. Accompanied by dour cello music on the soundtrack, they appear out of the blackness below the bottom edge of the frame, rise upwards from shadow, are illuminated by a brief moment of light and then pass into shadow again before disappearing – a succinct yet effective visualisation of the way of all flesh.

But *Necrology* is not entirely as sombre as this description suggests. The shot lasts slightly over 8 minutes, and is then followed by lengthy bogus cast credits ('in order of appearance'), accompanied by a suitably rousing martial fanfare, which lasts approximately half as long. In these credits, Lawder projects identities onto the anonymous profilmic subjects shown in the shot, extrapolating information from their body language and style of dress. Some are merely descriptive ('man picking his nose', 'yawning girl'), others more obviously subjective ('man who looks very tired', 'girl who looks like Joan Baez'), and still others wildly interpretive ('man whose wife doesn't understand him', 'manufacturer of plastic novelties'). The credit joke addresses the kind of judgments we commonly make about people based on their appearance and mannerisms, often rooted in stereotypes, but also suggests the power of the observational camera to invest profilmic events with significance simply by capturing them on film – a fact that Lawder demonstrates so well in the long take that precedes the credit roll. BKG

Dir/Scr/Phot/Ed: Standish Lawder (b/w).

New Earth (*Nieuwe gronden*)
Netherlands, 1934 – 30 mins
Joris Ivens

No film-maker can have worked in more parts of the world than Joris Ivens, but he established his reputation in his native Netherlands, first with more or less experimental films like *The Bridge* (1928) and *Rain* (1929) and then with more radical films about work. Part of *We Are Building* (1929) dealt with the draining and reclamation of the Zuiderzee, which became the central focus of *Zuiderzee* (1930) and, eventually, *New Earth* Ivens's early creative expertise with montage drew the attention of Pudovkin, and Ivens was invited to the Soviet Union to work and lecture, directing *Komsomol* (*Song of Heroes*, 1931, about a steel plant) there (as well co-directing with Henri Storck, clandestinely, *Misère au Borinage*, 1933, about the bitter Belgian miners' strike).

New Earth is fascinating both in itself and in its history. The film includes footage from both *We Are Building* and *Zuiderzee* and remains the fullest account of the planning and execution of an extraordinary feat of engineering, using diagrams as well as extensive shots of the work itself, and especially the construction of the main dyke across the Zuiderzee. The original version moves from a first section about the building of the main polder, to a second section on the draining and reclamation of the land for food production. The final section – not the originally planned ending – which is characterised by a marked change of tone, uses stock shots and re-enacted material no longer confined to the Netherlands, moving to an angry conclusion protesting about the economic crisis – Dutch as well as global – and the world economic order, in which food commodities like wheat and milk were being dumped to maintain market prices while millions of people went hungry. Not surprisingly, the film was widely censored and the final reel containing this conclusion cut, for example in Britain.

Even now, the version generally available in Britain and North America is missing this crucial section. However, documentary material can be put to different uses at different historical conjunctures, and the version that *is* available in North America and Britain (about 8 minutes shorter than the original) employs the first two sections of Ivens's film in a distinct way, though one not necessarily at odds with many of the implications of the original first two sections. New material was added to the start of this version and the commentary rewritten – 'fighting the common foe as allies' and, later, 'this was our answer to a need for *lebensraum*' and 'we too know the meaning of blood, sweat and tears' – during World War II.

Despite these changes, much of the considerable power of the sequences concerning the closing of the Zuiderzee and reclamation of the land remains. Ivens and his collaborators make wonderful use of shots of sea and sky, machines and men, mud and rock, and almost unworldly images like the woven brushwood mattresses that were

floated out and sunk as a base for the dyke. Many are fast-moving handheld shots, or taken from boats or planes, the pace and vigour of the montage given added excitement by Hanns Eisler's reuse of the wonderful score he composed for Bertolt Brecht's and Slatan Dudow's *Kuhle Wampe* (1932). Even during the stirring and fast-moving montage of the climax of the battle against the sea as the dyke is closed – strongly reminiscent of, and doubtless influenced by, the Soviet TURKSIB (1929) – Ivens never loses sight of the centrality of human labour: cranes and dredgers work furiously, but the film's defining images are of the men, heroic but ordinary, and their labour. JH

Dir/Scr/Commentary: Joris Ivens; **Phot**: Joris Ivens, Joop Huisken, John Fernhout, Helen van Dongen, Eli Lotar (b/w); **Ed**: Helen van Dongen, Joris Ivens; **Music**: Hanns Eisler; **Prod Co**: CAPI-Amsterdam.

News from Home
France/Belgium/West Germany, 1976 – 85 mins
Chantal Akerman

Chantal Akerman left her native Belgium, on impulse, aged twenty, and went to live in New York City. After an extended stay, she returned to Belgium for three months, but back in New York decided to make a film about the city – and about the letters her mother wrote to her. *News from Home* is simply that – images and sounds of Manhattan, accompanied, intermittently, by Akerman reading her mother's letters. Is *News from Home* a 'documentary' or an avant-garde film? The overriding impulse behind the film is to *document*, but its *manner* is certainly experimental. Akerman regards her work as a whole as 'an adventure in perception' (a phrase also used by, and perhaps borrowed from, Stan Brakhage – see THE ACT OF SEEING WITH ONE'S OWN EYES, 1971).

Akerman's New York is nothing like the tourists' New York. Instead, as she says, it's 'what you see every day when you live there' – subway stations, streets, intersections, parking lots, shops, diners. Many of the film's fifty-eight shots use static camera positions, though many are from moving trains or cars; there is a random quality about them, in the sense that she doesn't, and can't, control what traffic – pedestrian or automobile – passes. When the camera does pan, its movement seems triggered by random events – the movement of a figure or vehicle.

No obvious system governs the use of voiceover. Akerman reads the letters in a brisk monotone, with no evident emotion. The letters tend to repetition, typically beginning 'my dearest little girl' and ending 'your mother who loves you' (in the 'original' version, Akerman reads the letters in French, but her French accent in the English version adds an effective further level of distance). The mother's letters tell of the conventional goings-on back home in the extended bourgeois family that Akerman has left behind – very different from the images and sounds of New York life that constitute the daughter's 'response'. We find out something of what Akerman is doing in New York from the mother's letters, though their specific content is frequently drowned out by subway or traffic noise. Despite the often wheedling tone and emotional blackmail of her largely unschooled mother's letters, Akerman insists they were 'love letters': 'she writes as she can, she formulates her feelings in an unsophisticated way'.

Though future researchers could do much worse than watch *News from Home* to see what New York looked like in the mid-1970s, Akerman's response to the city – as befits a film-maker who happily confesses to being influenced by both Jean-Luc Godard and Michael Snow – is at one level very formal. In one striking 10-minute sequence-shot, Akerman positions her (static) camera in a subway station, looking across several different platforms and train tracks, observing the way people saunter or hurry along, waiting, walking, in and out of frame, increasing as trains are due, emptying after their departure, the platforms and trains marking out different spatial planes. In another sequence, the camera looks statically out of a vehicle window moving up 11th Avenue, stopping and starting according to the vagaries of the traffic. The images vary from close-ups of double-parked vans to medium long shots of parked cars, sidewalks, parking lots, shop and garage fronts, plunging into the deep space of cross streets, when we see almost across town – a visual record, but also a riot of colours, spaces, planes, verging on abstraction at times, a movie version of a Richard Estes photo-realist painting like *Sloan's* (c.1970). Like Estes's street scenes, Akerman's realisation transforms the mundane and makes us see differently. As she says, 'it's a voluptuous film, because of the noise, because of the images, because of the colors. Sensual delight – there are a lot of people who don't know anymore what that is.' JH

Dir/Scr: Chantal Akerman; **Prod**: Alain Dahan; **Phot**: Babette Mangolte (colour); **Sound**: Dominique Dalmasso, Larry Haas; **Prod Co**: Institut National de l'Audiovisuel (INA)/Paradise Films/Unité Trois.

(*Next page*) *News from Home*

North Sea
UK, 1938 – 32 mins
Harry Watt

It is hard not to like *North Sea*, a GPO documentary about an Aberdeen
trawler, the *John Gillman*, that gets into difficulties and is helped out by
the Post Office radio station at Wick. It derives it tenor from the slightly
dour, no-nonsense Scottish lifestyles and often self-deprecating humour
of the skipper and his crew (as well as the women back in Aberdeen
and the radio operators in Wick) (Harry Watt was a Scot). It has a very
simple narrative structure: the crew assembles in early morning and
some home life is sketched in; they set out to fish, encounter difficulties
and have to call in Mayday; radio contact is lost but the crew are able to
overcome the difficulties themselves. It is, in effect, a 'docudrama'.
As the preface announces, 'the story of this film and all the names,
characters and places mentioned or shown are entirely authentic.
It reconstructs, as it actually happened, an incident in the life of deep
sea fishermen.' This was, of course, common 1930s documentary
practice: just as Watt's earlier, more celebrated *Night Mail* (1936) had
used a studio mock-up of the train sorting office, so *North Sea*
combined location shooting, on land and sea, with a studio mock-up of
the *John Gillman*'s main cabin, as did Watt's later wartime *Target for
Tonight* (1941). The studio shooting uses various fiction film
conventions, such as reverse angles, and the motif of the dangling
good-luck charm, seen in recurrent close-ups.

No doubt this more fictional approach, designed in part precisely to
attract a larger audience, contributed to those films' commercial success.
The detractors of *North Sea* argued that not enough attention was paid
to the processes involved. By contrast, in *100 British Documentaries*,
Patrick Russell notes in *Drifters* (1929) Grierson's significant 'lack of
interest in the fishermen's psychology' (p. 56), and this is what interested
Watt. The crew, amiable but becoming surly and fed up with the cold
and wet, need to be chivvied by the skipper and rallied by the promise of

a pot of tea. Back in Aberdeen, the skipper's sturdy wife doesn't forget to order a black pudding ('The skipper likes one when he comes in from the sea', and its delivery is a reminder that he is *not* safely back) and crewman Jimmy's almost blushing but robust girlfriend mends nets. There are some very effective scenes at sea – fishing, pumping water, dumping coal, repairing the broken radio aerial.

It is no denigration of the importance of the GPO's radio service for shipping to feel that the film's ending is a little deflating. The *real* ending is that the *John Gillman* is safe and homeward bound, rather than what we would now call the 'message from our sponsor' that 'All around our island shores the Post Office radio stations guard our ships' and, amid a montage of radio masts, 'Calling the ships of the world'. What with *Heroes of the North Sea* (1925), *Drifters*, *Granton Trawler* (1934, dirs. Edgar Anstey and John Grierson), MAN OF ARAN (1934),

North Sea and Michael Grigsby's later *Deckie Learner* (1965), the – almost always in crisis – fishing industry was a favourite British documentary subject. JH

Dir: Harry Watt; **Prod**: Alberto Cavalcanti; **Phot**: H. (E.) Fowle, Jonah Jones (b/w); **Ed**: R. Q. McNaughton (& Stewart McAllister, uncredited); **Music**: E. (Ernst Hermann) Meyer; **Sound**: George Diamond; **Prod Co**: GPO Film Unit.

Nuit et brouillard (*Night and Fog*)
France, 1955 – 31 mins
Alain Resnais

Nuit et brouillard, one of the earliest films about the Holocaust, has become a yardstick by which other documentaries on the subject – even SHOAH (1985) – have been judged. The organisers of a 1954 exhibition by the Comité de l'Histoire de la Deuxième Guerre Mondiale (Henri Michel and Olga Wormser) suggested the film to mark the tenth anniversary of the liberation of the concentration camps and served as historical advisers.

The film juxtaposes the overgrown state of the camps – not yet turned into museums and memorial sites – in the present with the recent past. The past is represented by monochrome propaganda, newsreel and stills material organised primarily through editing, and the present by colour material (newly shot at Auschwitz and Majdanek) relying primarily on camera movement. This produces some very striking transitions, such as the cut from the (black-and-white) transport arriving in 'night and fog' to the slow forward track over sunlit, overgrown rails in the present (colour). This contrast – strikingly reversed in Dariusz Jablonsky's 1998 Polish film *Fotoamator* (*Photographer*), which uses a German official's colour slides of Łodz and its ghetto and black-and-white contemporary footage – enables the film to document the horrors of the camps as well as address issues about the passage of time, memory, forgetfulness and vigilance. From the start, *Nuit et brouillard* emphasises the proximity of an ordinary world ('Even a quiet country scene . . .') as the camera pans slowly from blue skies and fields to barbed-wire fences and tracks slowly alongside camp buildings to 'another planet'. The commentary insists on the difficulty of imagining or summoning up images for a past of which 'only the husks and hues remain' – the Eastman colour stock emphasising green and blue, giving the material a slightly non-naturalistic cast – as if the constantly moving camera is searching for traces.

Resnais at first refused to make the film but was persuaded when Jean Cayrol, who had been deported to Mauthausen for Resistance activities (and whose poems about the experience – *Poèmes de la nuit et du brouillard* – were published in 1946), agreed to write the commentary. Michel Bouquet's delivery of Cayrol's text remains relatively neutral, even in ironic passages about camp design, and Hanns Eisler's score echoes relationships between past and present, the frequently brisk, more dissonant editing of newsreel material and the slower, more reflective pace of the colour material (very different from the pounding optimism of his score for NEW EARTH, 1934).

The covert German *Nacht und Nebel* operation, the rounding up of political opponents and Resistance figures in occupied countries, began before the systematic deportation and extermination of Jews, and *Nuit et brouillard* has been criticised for failing to focus on the Jewish question. The film does show the transportation of Jews, and this central aspect of the Holocaust would probably have been more widely known about than the treatment of other categories of victim. In any case, the film shifts away from the historical specificity of the camps and World War II towards the need for vigilance about any and all similar events and our complicity in them (Resnais has admitted that the Algerian war was much in his mind at the time).

Nuit et brouillard encountered French censorship problems over French complicity in German deportations. It won the 1956 Prix Jean Vigo but was not shown in competition at the Cannes Film Festival because of German objections, despite French government promises that it would be (though, ironically, it was immediately invited to the Berlin Film Festival and West Germany became the first country to buy the film). JH

Dir: Alain Resnais; **Prod**: Philippe Lifchitz, Anatole Dauman, Samy Halfon; **Phot**: Ghislain Cloquet, Sacha Vierny (b/w & colour); **Ed**: Henri Colpi, Jasmine Chasney; **Music**: Hanns Eisler, Georges Delerue (musical director); **Commentary**: Jean Cayrol (spoken by Michel Bouquet); **Prod Co**: Argos Films/Como Films.

Not a Love Story: A Film about Pornography
Canada, 1981 – 69 mins
Bonnie Sherr Klein

Perhaps the most controversial film ever released by the National Film
Board of Canada, *Not a Love Story* was produced by Studio D, the
women's studio that was created at the Board in 1974. The film follows
the film-maker, Bonnie Sherr Klein, as she sets out, along with a
professional stripper, Linda Lee Tracey ('Fonda Peters'), who had been
questioning her own role in the sex trade, to expose the patriarchal evils
of pornography in an attempt to understand what it means for her as a
woman. Included in the film are interviews with people involved in the
porn industry, both producers and consumers, activists in a number of
protest and support groups, and several well-known feminists including
Kate Millett, as well as examples of various forms of pornography
(magazines, films, live sex shows) that include explicit sexual imagery of
both male and female genitalia. Released at a time when most viewers,
at least in Canada, did not have easy access to such pornographic
images, the film's explicit content shocked many, and, ironically, it was
banned in two provinces, Ontario and Saskatchewan.

The interviews and vérité sequences about the porn industry are
grafted onto a journey narrative infused with spiritual and mythic
connotations. The two women descend into the netherworld of
pornography, reaching its heart of darkness on 42nd Street in New York
City, where they come face to face with its horrors, and then re-emerge,
renewed, into the daylight world once again. Most of the scenes inside
the porn theatres are dark, their spaces seeming dank and enclosed;
by contrast, the interviews with the feminists take place in more
wholesome domestic surroundings: author Susan Griffith, for example,
is presented by a window, through which the sun floods in and gives
her halo lighting, while the abundant garden visible through it suggests
more 'natural' values. Delightfully engaging and articulate, Tracey,
who went on to a new career as a journalist and film-maker herself,

acts as the viewer's surrogate, accompanying the film-maker on her quest. Like many spectators, she begins as blithely indifferent about pornography but then becomes enlightened about its pernicious effects – a representation that she regarded as reductive of her own actual views. In the film's emotionally charged final scene, both women sit in the pure air of a sunny beach, their souls cleansed of pornographic filth, as they share their feelings and embrace.

Not a Love Story takes an unambiguous and unwavering anti-porn position, regarding it as a perversion wherein women are degraded and men's misogynistic behaviour is reinforced. The film assumes an unproblematic definition of pornography, and tends to call upon the most egregious sado-masochistic examples it can find in order to demonstrate Robin Morgan's comment, paraphrasing James Baldwin in a powerful scene in which she shares tears with Klein, that 'to be female and conscious anywhere on the planet is to be in a constant state of rage'. The interviews with the theatre proprietors and the Canadian porn publisher David Wells, who is cornered by Klein into defending pornography as sex education, seem uncomfortably close (given the film-maker's leading questions) to the kind of ambush tactics employed by Michael Moore in ROGER AND ME (1989) and BOWLING FOR COLUMBINE (2002). However, the film is careful not to succumb to male-bashing, making the point in several of the interviews that men, too, are victims of pornography, as it teaches them to treat women as sexual objects and to deny their own emotions. And in seeking to empower women through knowledge with which to channel their rage, *Not a Love Story* is an extremely effective instance of documentary as agitprop, eliciting in an army of motivated soldiers a moral and political outrage as successfully as Frank Capra's WHY WE FIGHT 1: PRELUDE TO WAR (1943). BKG

Dir: Bonnie Sherr Klein; **Prod**: Dorothy Todd; **Scr**: Andrée Klein, Bonnie Sherr Klein, Irene Lilienheim Angelico, Rose-Aimée Todd; **Phot**: Pierre Letarte (colour); **Ed**: Anne Henderson; **Music**: Ginette Bellavance, Sylvia Moscovitz; **Prod Co**: National Film Board of Canada.

One Man's War (La Guerre d'un seul homme)
France, 1982 – 104 mins
Edgardo Cozarinsky

At one level, *One Man's War* is a compilation film in the tradition of THE FALL OF THE ROMANOV DYNASTY (1927) and IN THE YEAR OF THE PIG (1968), an account of life in France under German occupation and Pétain's Vichy regime (1940–4) as seen in the cinema newsreels Actualités Mondiales (1940–2) and France Actualités (1942–4). In those pre-television days, the newsreels – their content strictly controlled – were the only source of moving-image information for people, who went to the cinema in huge numbers. Some of the newsreels had already been used in LE CHAGRIN ET LA PITIÉ (1969), and Claude Chabrol revisited them expertly in *L'Oeil de Vichy* (*The Eye of Vichy*, 1993).

Edgardo Cozarinsky (an Argentine exile resident in Paris) added a wholly new dimension to the newsreels by introducing extracts from the journals of German writer Ernst Jünger, a cultivated, cosmopolitan figure who, despite his own totalitarian ideas, detested Hitler and the Nazis. Jünger spent most of the war years in Paris as an officer with the occupying forces. His reflections (read in French voiceover), detached and philosophical, heightened perceptions largely removed from personal feeling, punctuate the newsreel footage. Given the distasteful task of overseeing an execution, he recalls a fly buzzing around his head and landing on his cheek, and watches while 'five dark holes appear on the target like dewdrops'. Jünger's reflections link obliquely rather than directly to the screen images: his account of the execution, for example, is accompanied by images of Hitler meeting Mussolini and Franco, and crowds cheering Pétain.

Jünger saw Paris as an 'opportunity' that offered 'gifts'. While recalling dining with Sacha Guitry and Jean Cocteau, and meeting Picasso, he comments on Nazi ideas about race and notes that dining at the best Parisian restaurants 'gives a sensation of power'. Try as he might to have a 'civilised' war, he cannot help feeling like a cultured man among savage beasts. Reality asserts itself: the first yellow stars on passers-by in the Rue Royale make him ashamed of his uniform and he is shocked by the intense hatred on a shop assistant's face; sent to the Russian front, he is disgusted by his uniform and modern warfare, while we watch newsreels of the German 'liberation' of the Ukraine – alongside news items on *vélo-taxis*, Maurice Chevalier's breezy performances, Parisian fashions, and so on. Back in Paris, as the Allies invade and the German occupation enters its end game, Jünger watches bombs explode in St Germain as 'pure spectacle', while drinking 'burgundy with strawberries in it'. As he bids farewell to Paris, 'waiting for new embraces from history', the newsreels offer extraordinary images of the chaotic street resistance of August 1944, so different from the endless, disciplined German columns parading down the Champs-Élysées in 1940 that begin the film.

Cozarinsky gives the film a four-part musical structure ('Andante con moto' to 'Finale') and uses to excellent effect both 'Aryan' music (Hans Pfitzer and Richard Strauss) and 'degenerate' music (Arnold Schönberg and Franz Schreker). *One Man's War* was produced by INA (L'Institut National de l'Audiovisuel), France's radio and television archive, charged with the exploitation of its holdings, but also, particularly in the 1970s and 1980s, an innovative producer (for example, NEWS FROM HOME, 1976). JH

Dir: Edgardo Cozarinsky; **Prod**: Alain Dahan, Jean-Marc Henchoz; **Scr**: Edgardo Cozarinsky, from Ernst Jünger's 'Journaux parisiens'; **Ed**: Christine Aya; **Music**: Hans Pfitzer, Richard Strauss ('Aryan music'), Arnold Schönberg, Franz Schreker ('Degenerate music'); **Narrator**: Niels Arestrup; **Prod Co**: Marion's Films/L'Institut National de l'Audiovisuel/Zweites Deutsches Fernsehen (ZDF).

Paris Is Burning
US, 1990 – 71 mins
Jennie Livingston

Filmed over a two-year period between 1987 and 1989, *Paris Is Burning* chronicles the ball culture and street life of the black and Latino gay male and transgendered subculture in New York City. The Paris of the title refers to the world of high fashion, glamour and fame to which those who participate in the balls aspire. Conventional in terms of style – it is nothing like Marlon Riggs's formally more ambitious TONGUES UNTIED (1990), for example, which also is about the difficulties of being black and gay – and structured by alternating scenes of the balls and interviews with children and prominent 'house mothers', the film's exploration of the ball subculture nevertheless touches on central issues of race, class and gender in American culture.

The subculture's social organisation, in which performers belong to a 'house' with a 'mother', and private codes (for example, 'reading') are explained by the interviewees, and Livingston is clearly sympathetic towards them, emphasising how the houses serve as alternative families providing love and support for many gays and transsexuals who were ostracised from their own families and considered social outcasts. This social structure mirrors the ball subculture's appropriation of straight style for its own purposes. Individuals representing houses parade in the same way models walk runways in fashion shows, competing for trophies in specific categories of masquerade that consist of mimicking ('realness') through gesture and costume social roles in the real world such as 'schoolgirl' and 'executive', exaggerated and enhanced through 'vogueing', a dance composed of a series – a kind of montage – of striking poses imitative of fashion advertising and exaggerated gender performance. As one participant describes it, going to a drag ball is like passing through a looking glass to a space wherein fantasies may be acted out.

The ball walkers' imitations of straight white America bespeak the acceptance by mainstream culture they so desperately seek. As one house mother says, many want to be successful at passing, to get by as a straight person of the opposite gender in the world outside the balls, and to get home safely without being bloodied. Many tell Livingston that they aspire to fame and fortune, such as Venus Xtravaganza, who wants to become a white woman, get married and live happily ever after, but the reality is that they have to survive in the big city, often by turning tricks or shoplifting. In a sobering moment, we discover that Venus has been murdered in a hotel room during the shooting of the film, but more triumphantly, Willi Ninja, the only participant to gain some degree of recognition beyond the balls, beams with pride when he reveals, as a measure of his success, that he *bought* (rather than stole) the gold designer earring he is wearing.

Lest straight viewers assume a superior attitude to these poor (in both senses) drag queens who are so confused about their sexual identities that they are enslaved by the appearances of ideal heteronormativity, Livingston challenges dominant values and perceptions through the inclusion of seemingly random shots, images of what Dziga Vertov would call 'life caught unawares', of people on the street simply going about their business. One cannot help but wonder for a moment whether these are straight people merely being themselves, enacting their everyday roles, or voguers imitating their type – a speculation that puts us in mind of post-modern theorists such as Judith Butler, who, in her book *Gender Trouble*, argued that all gender roles are performative. *Paris Is Burning* ultimately suggests, with Butler, that there are no gender norms, and that the only gender reality is realness. BKG

Dir/Scr: Jennie Livingston; **Prod**: Jennie Livingston, Barry Swimar; **Phot**: Paul Gibson (colour); **Ed**: Jonathan Oppenheim; **Sound**: Pawel Wdowczak; **Prod Co**: Off White Productions.

People on Sunday (*Menschen am Sonntag*)
Germany, 1930 – 74 mins
Robert Siodmak, Edgar G. Ulmer

People on Sunday, a more or less experimental independent feature, was made by a group of untested film-makers (except for cinematographer Eugen Schüfftan) destined for important careers outside Germany, mainly in Hollywood – Robert and Kurt Siodmak, Billy Wilder, Edgar G. Ulmer and Fred Zinnemann (camera assistant). (The credits provided are taken largely from the film, but this was clearly an essentially collaborative project.) Only Zinnemann subsequently made anything remotely similar (the documentary feature *Redes/The Wave*, made in Mexico with Paul Strand, 1935).

This 'film without actors' features five young people, 'appearing before a camera for the first time in their lives', who, we are told, are now 'back in their own jobs'. Having introduced the taxi driver, shopgirl, womanising jack-of-all-trades, aspiring film actress and model in short sequences, a further title announces 'Berlin' and 'One Sunday', as if they were also 'characters'. *People on Sunday* is often described as 'part fiction, part documentary' or 'semi-documentary' – but that depends on always contentious definitions of 'documentary'. The characters here essentially play themselves in the narrative elements of a script based on observation and reportage. Does this make the film significantly different from, say, NANOOK (1922), NORTH SEA (1938) or FARREBIQUE (1946), all scripted films in which people play themselves, all accepted as valid documentaries? The difference may be that these characters seem intended as representative types rather than unique individuals (though, of course, their individuality necessarily emerges). Or is the difference that these are not more or less 'noble' seal hunters, fishermen or farmers, but rather ordinary people engaged in more or less mundane activities?

Focusing on the characters and what there is of their 'story' – more a series of observations, either in the city or out at a lake, of (strikingly modern) sexual mores and the gender dynamics of friendship and dating – is to miss the point. The film never stays too long on its characters and happily abandons them to look instead at Berlin's myriad city activities and people on a quiet sunny Sunday or a back-to-work Monday, as often as not 'life caught unawares' (in Dziga Vertov's phrase). Despite the film's title, Berlin, wonderfully photographed, is the film's real subject, rather than these characters and their inconsequential stories, ultimately just microcosmic manifestations of the city, their stories emerging from and fading back into unscripted city life. A characteristic early strategy is to introduce characters as if they were passers-by, part of the city's fabric, obscured by traffic, only gradually to isolate and focus on them.

Part city symphony, *People on Sunday* is a product of the prevailing German *Neue Sachlichkeit* (*New Objectivity*) spirit of the time and a not too distant cousin of BERLIN: SYMPHONY OF A GREAT CITY (1927) – though the city environment here is benevolent – and MAN WITH A MOVIE CAMERA (1929), albeit without their more argumentative structures. The film's look is often reminiscent of contemporaneous photographers like Alexander Rodchenko or André Kertész, and evokes several other films. At about the same time, Marcel Carné made his debut short documentary *Nogent – Eldorado du dimanche* (1929), about Parisians taking leave of the city on Sundays. A few years later, but in very different political circumstances, Slatan Dudow and Bertolt Brecht mixed documentary and fiction in another story about work, gender and sexual mores, *Kuhle Wampe* (1932), where Berlin has become a jobless, hostile environment, its country retreat taken over by the homeless, its young people actively political, its S-Bahn the setting for a scorching critique of capitalism. JH

Dir: Robert Siodmak, Edgar G. Ulmer; **Prod**: Edgar G. Ulmer; **Scr**: Billy Wilder, from a report by Kurt Siodmak; **Phot**: Eugen Schüfftan (b/w); **Music**: Otto Stenzeel (original score), Elena Kats-Chernin (modern score); **Prod Co**: Film Studio 1929.

The Plow that Broke the Plains
US, 1936 – 25 mins
Pare Lorentz

It took the nation's entry into World War II for the US federal government to co-ordinate its use of the mass media, including cinema, for political purposes, as with the case of the War Department's sponsorship of Frank Capra's WHY WE FIGHT series (1941–5). Before then, Pare Lorentz's *The Plow that Broke the Plains* was the first government-sponsored documentary aimed at a wide general audience. Taking as its subject the Dust Bowl that ravaged the Great Plains in the American Midwest in the 1930s, *Plow* implicitly supported the work of Franklin Delano Roosevelt's New Deal administration without referring to its programmes specifically.

Espousing a Griersonian view regarding the social utility of documentary film-making, Lorentz began his career as a film critic for a number of magazines. As a syndicated columnist, he praised Roosevelt's democratic values, and expressed his support for the New Deal's farm programme. The Resettlement Administration, a New Deal agency with a mandate to provide relief from poverty in the farm belt, had formed a photo unit with Walker Evans, Dorothea Lange and others to document its work, and Lorentz convinced the RA's director, Rexford Tugwell, to finance the film as well. Made on a minimal budget of under $20,000, *The Plow that Broke the Plains* offers a concise, even if simplified, lesson about how the Dust Bowl developed due to over-planting and the absence of planned crop rotation stimulated by the outbreak of World War I, the post-war land boom and the stock-market collapse that brought it to a resounding halt in 1929.

Lorentz had an instinctive sense of bold imagery, as seen in the shots of rows of threshing machines harvesting wheat to represent flush times, and in the images of tractors and tanks moving across the frame in opposite directions to represent the coming of war. He finds elegantly simple ways to depict historical events, as with the ticker-tape machine that falls to the floor to represent the stock-market crash. Working as his own editor, Lorentz collaborated closely with famed American composer Virgil Thomson to create the effective score as he was assembling the footage. Cinematographers Paul Strand (who made MANHATTA with painter Charles Sheeler in 1921), Ralph Steiner and Leo Hurwitz all had been involved in the Film and Photo League, Nykino Films and Frontier Films, leftist film collectives (see NATIVE LAND, 1942), and they provided the film with haunting images of impoverished farm families.

Thomas Chalmers (who also supplied the poetic voiceover for Lorentz's next film, *The River*, 1938) provides a suitably stentorian narration that matches *Plow*'s tone of strident urgency.

   Plow was released during an intense re-election campaign, and was in part the victim of political debate. The Hollywood studios had been unco-operative in providing stock footage for use in the film and also refused to distribute it when completed. But the manager of New York's Rialto Theater, Arthur Mayer, agreed to show the film and cannily promoted it as 'The Picture They Dared Us to Show'. Audience response was sufficiently favourable for *Plow* to be booked into an impressive 3,000 theatres in other cities across the country, providing leverage for Lorentz to become head of the short-lived United States Film Service (1938–40) and to produce *The River*, about the problems of erosion and the need for land reclamation projects along the Mississippi River, which Paramount agreed to distribute. BKG

Dir/Scr: Pare Lorentz; **Phot**: Leo Hurwitz, Ralph Steiner, Paul Strand, Paul Ivano (b/w); **Ed**: Leo Zochling; **Music**: Virgil Thomson; **Prod Co**: Resettlement Administration, US government.

Portrait of Jason
US, 1967 – 105 mins
Shirley Clarke

With *Portrait of Jason*, Shirley Clarke, a New York-based experimental film-maker, mounted a deliberate attack on direct cinema and the claims of truth and objectivity being expounded for it by her contemporaries Richard Leacock and others with such films as PRIMARY (1960) and CRISIS (1963). She trains her camera mercilessly on a frustrated and failed actor, Jason Holliday (the stage name of Aaron Payne), a close friend of her partner and collaborator, Carl Lee, who appears in Clarke's earlier fiction films *The Connection* (1962) as Cowboy and as the gangster Priest in *The Cool World* (1964), about Harlem gang life. Unseen behind the camera, Clarke and Lee spend an evening with Jason, filming as they ask him leading questions, invoking vérité's search for the privileged moment when the camera will penetrate the social persona of its profilmic subject in order to reveal his real self.

   The film consists of several long takes recorded over the course of the evening in Clarke's own living room and then edited. Shot almost entirely in close-up, Jason talks incessantly to the camera, discussing his life and his acting ambitions. He begins in an upbeat mood but, fuelled by alcohol and marijuana, becomes increasingly vulnerable and open as the evening progresses. Cracks begin to appear in Jason's sense of identity, and his psychological defences and social mask begin to crumble before the camera until he openly cries and confesses his underlying pain and insecurities. Clarke uses frequent shifts in focus, moving the image in and out of sharpness as a transitional device to disguise cuts, but also to express the tenuous clarity of Jason's sense of self.

   Clarke's work was consistently informed by a documentary approach. She had worked on a number of short films with Pennebaker, frequently as editor (*Brussels Film Loops*, 1958), sometimes as camera operator (*Breaking It up at the Museum*, 1960). Some of her own early shorts, *Bridges-Go-Round* (1958) and *Skyscraper* (1959, on which Willard Van

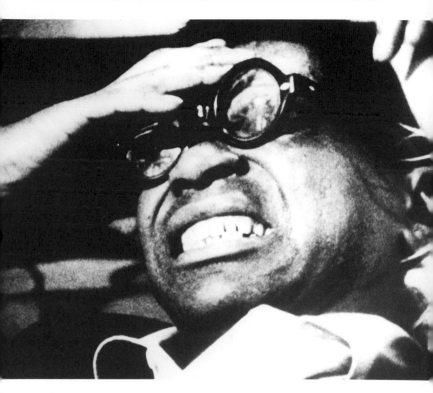

Dyke and Irving Jacoby, as well as Pennebaker, also worked), are short city symphony films. Both *The Connection* and *The Cool World*, which was produced by Frederick Wiseman, employ a mock direct cinema style, the former even including among its characters a documentary film crew supposedly filming the action but who inevitably become involved in trying heroin when the dealer arrives, a wry comment on direct cinema's imagined objectivity. *Portrait of Jason* certainly provides the kind of penetrating privileged moment that vérité and direct cinema film-makers aspired to, but not without raising several crucial ethical questions regarding documentary film practice. Like some of the people featured in the Maysles Brothers' films, Clarke's chosen subject is questionable: as an actor, Jason relishes performing for the camera, and because he is a failed actor, his true self-doubt, if not loathing, is fairly evident from the start. Invoking the interventionist strategies of vérité film-makers such as Jean Rouch and Edgar Morin (see CHRONIQUE D'UN ÉTÉ, 1961), the prodding questions ('Jason, did you hate your mother?') reveal how the film-makers' presence affects the 'truth' of the profilmic event, even if it is usually less overt. The questions border on being cruel, underscoring direct cinema's necessarily detached relation to the reality it documents. Late in the film, Jason reveals his sexual attraction to Lee, which further complicates the relation of film-maker to profilmic subject, just as the film crew become entangled with their subjects in *The Connection*. BKG

Dir/Prod/Scr/Ed: Shirley Clarke; **Phot**: Jeri Sapenen (b/w).

Primary
US, 1960 – 60 mins
Robert Drew

The first film by the Drew Associates, produced for Time, Inc., *Primary* follows two Democratic presidential candidates, Senators John F. Kennedy from Massachusetts and Hubert Humphrey from Minnesota, during their heated 1960 primary campaign in Wisconsin. As narrator Joseph Julian informs us at the beginning, in *Primary*, for the first time, people could watch politicians in more intimate moments beyond the staged public appearances that had presented them before. Such moments as Humphrey happily watching *The Red Skelton Show* (his 'favourite') on television or Kennedy pacing in his hotel suite anxiously awaiting the election returns were indeed glimpses of public figures in more informal circumstances than had been commonly shown in the past.

Photographed by Richard Leacock and Albert Maysles, edited by, among others, D. A. Pennebaker and produced by Robert Drew, the film was pioneering in its use of the handheld camera and synch-sound equipment. In its most celebrated scene, Kennedy arrives at a hall to give a speech to a group of Polish Americans, the camera following his entrance as he works his way through the friendly crowd, along a passageway and onto the stage accompanied by a burst of applause. The camera is able to record the event, despite the bustle and stark changes in ambient lighting, through deft adjustments of the lens aperture and focal length even while following Kennedy through the throng. Both candidates are seen manipulating their media images (Humphrey giving directions for a television phone-in show, and Kennedy sitting for a photographic portrait that is carefully composed to take into account such details as the length of shirt cuff visible beneath his suit jacket), suggesting that the candid images of direct cinema are less contrived, more authentic in what they show than these other mass-media images.

The film follows the two candidates as they stump their way across the state, meeting with crowds of voters, organising media events and travelling from one venue to the next. Generally, the film is structured by alternating between scenes of the two senators, often suggesting inevitable comparisons, and then building to a climax in which both camps nervously await the polling results on primary day. The differences between the two politicians are suggested by the candidates' respective theme songs, each of which we hear several times in the film: Humphrey's jingle is sung to the tune of the 'The Ballad of Davy Crockett', the theme of Walt Disney's TV show and movie about the legendary American pioneer that was wildly popular in the previous decade, while Kennedy's theme is adapted from 'High Hopes', a more contemporary song sung by Frank Sinatra in the film *A Hole in the Head* released just the year before. Humphrey throughout is associated with rural and agrarian values (the final image shows an old Model-T Ford with a campaign poster featuring his smiling face on the back), while Kennedy is associated with the more urban and sophisticated lifestyle (the cultural cachet of Sinatra's rat pack is alluded to directly when Bobby Kennedy speaks to the Polish crowd and mentions his brother-in-law, actor Peter Lawford).

Primary was shown on only a few television stations; it was not carried by the major networks because of their policy of using only their own staff for news and documentaries. However, the film did allow producer Robert Drew to secure a contract with Time, Inc., enabling the Drew Associates to make further documentaries for ABC-TV, beginning with *Yanki, No!* (1960) and continuing to CRISIS (1963). BKG

Dir/Prod/Scr: Robert Drew; **Phot**: Richard Leacock, D. A. Pennebaker, Al Maysles, Terence Macartney Filgate (b/w); **Ed**: Richard Leacock, D. A. Pennebaker, Terence Macartney Filgate, Robert Farron; **Sound**: Robert Drew, D. A. Pennebaker; **Prod Co**: Drew Associates.

Primate
US, 1974 – 167 mins
Frederick Wiseman

Shot at the Yerkes Primate Research Center in Atlanta, Georgia, Frederick Wiseman's *Primate* shows us in graphic detail a variety of scientific experiments on different species of simians, many involving behaviour modification with potential military application. Squarely focusing on the hot-button issue of animal research, the film is made in the director's characteristic direct cinema style (compare PRIMARY, 1960, CRISIS, 1963), with no voiceover narration or insert titles to contextualise the various experiments. Thus, the experiments (with one exception) are never described, thereby making them seem inexplicable and more likely to arouse the anger and outrage of viewers. But as the ambiguity of the film's title suggests, *Primate* is as much about people as it is about apes and monkeys, for it also addresses the arrogance of our science in its tinkering with nature.

Wiseman explores this theme by frequently encouraging an anthropomorphic view of the apes, thereby encouraging viewers to identify with the animals as victims rather than with the scientists in their quest for knowledge. There are approximately as many close-ups of the animals' faces in the film as there are of the scientists, and they seem to show them in fear, pain and incomprehension. Wiseman often cuts to them in the manner of reaction shots in classic narrative films. Also, baby chimps are dressed in nappies and fed with bottles and even cups. The film also offers several visual comparisons between the researchers (who are almost exclusively male) and the animals. Many of the scientists have beards, moustaches and long hair, and shown in profile their hirsute appearance looks remarkably ape-like. At one point, the scientist working on the divergent muscular evolution of humans and the higher primates swings from a trapeze, trying to coax the monkeys to imitate his behaviour.

But for all their similarities, the scientists seem less emotional, more callous, than the animals they unhesitatingly subject to questionable experimentation. During the experiments, the scientists wear prophylactic masks and gloves, transforming them into impersonal, unindividuated tormenters. In one experiment that takes up more than 23 minutes of screen time (almost one-quarter of the film), a squirrel monkey's brain is removed and sectioned for the ultimate goal of brain mapping. The ominous potential of the experiments for humans is suggested by the fact that the animals are under continuous surveillance by the researchers, who observe their every action. The animals are reduced to puppets, their behaviour and movement controlled by various wires, implants and electrical impulses. In the eerie final sequence, the zero-gravity experiment aboard a climbing and diving Air Force C-130 jet, no one in the airplane, including Wiseman's cameraman William Brayne, can keep his feet on the ground, suggesting that nature has been violated to the extent that we have lost our footing. Wiseman subverts the scientists' defence of pure research by concentrating on the Air Force logo on the plane as the camera approaches it on the runway. The film features many close-ups of machinery and technology in action, displacing the human element and suggesting the inhumanity of such work. Ultimately, *Primate* is one of Wiseman's bleakest, most disturbing views of American institutional life.

Primate was Wiseman's most controversial film after TITICUT FOLLIES (1967). After its completion, the Yerkes Center complained that the film wildly distorted its work and threatened legal action. Only approximately one-third of the stations that comprised the PBS network showed the film in December 1974; New York's WNET-TV (the station that produced it) received numerous complaints from viewers angry about the film's graphic imagery and the apparent cruelty to animals, as well as a bomb scare and a threat to Wiseman's life following its broadcast. BKG

Dir/Prod/Ed/Sound: Frederick Wiseman; **Phot**: William Brayne (b/w); **Prod Co**: Zipporah Films.

Les Raquetteurs (*The Snowshoers*)
Canada, 1958 – 15 mins
Michel Brault, Gilles Groulx

As French Canadian film critics have noted, *cinéma direct* allowed film-makers to capture and reveal aspects of Quebec society as never before. *Les Raquetteurs*, one of the most important documentaries within the Canadian *cinéma direct* movement, was instrumental in helping to give the people of Quebec a sense of their own distinct culture during the Quiet Revolution in the 1960s, when the province experienced rapid social and political change featuring significant secularisation and the rise of separatist sentiment. Ostensibly an unassuming account of the annual snowshoe convention in the city of Sherbrooke, the film observes aspects of communal life and ritual without explanation (apart from the opening text that provides Larousse's definition of a *raquet*, or snowshoe). Produced by the French unit of the National Film Board of Canada, the film in its original form featured no voiceover dialogue, though the version released in English-speaking Canada included narration by Stanley Jackson that helped 'explain' the event to Anglophone viewers.

Les Raquetteurs begins with the annual parade of snowshoe clubs marching through the city centre with band accompaniment, then shows the end of the distance race and a few of the sprint competitions, followed by the evening celebration where everyone gathers for food, drink and visibly effusive good cheer as the convention Queen makes her entrance and is crowned, after which an enthusiastic combo of local musicians get people up and dancing. The film ends as it cuts away from the party in progress to a long shot of the night-time city streets, where the parade had taken place earlier, now almost empty. Co-director Michel Brault used handheld, wide-angle shooting to show events close up and from within, walking with the showshoers and weaving through the dancers at the party. Anticipating the Czech New Wave films of Ivan Passer and Milos Forman, *Les Raquetteurs* shows group activities but focuses on the humorous idiosyncrasies and vivid uniqueness of participating individuals, such as the obviously drunk revellers, the racer who fails to get a good start, gives up and gestures helplessly, and the musician in the marching band who cannot manage to strap on his bass drum.

Brault and Gilles Groulx were central figures in Quebec's *cinéma direct* movement. Groulx made a few other socially committed documentaries for the NFB and adapted his style to fiction film-making, most notably with *Le Chat dans le sac* (1964), about a journalist who struggles to come to terms with Quebec society, before suffering severe brain damage in an automobile accident that abruptly ended his career. Brault began by working with the NFB's Unit B, which was making pioneering observational documentaries such as LONELY BOY (1962), and went on to direct several important documentaries, including *L'Acadie, l'Acadie* (with Pierre Perrault, 1971), about a strike by French-speaking students at the University of Moncton in New Brunswick, and the docudrama *Les Ordres* (*The Orders*, 1974), about the imposition of the War Measures Act by Prime Minister Pierre Trudeau during the hostage crisis of October 1970, for which Brault won the Best Director award at Cannes in 1975. Brault also photographed Claude Jutra's feature *Mon oncle Antoine* (1971), often cited as the greatest Canadian film of all time. Jean Rouch, impressed with Brault's camerawork on *Les Raquetteurs*, invited him to France, where he participated in the shooting of Rouch and Edgar Morin's landmark cinéma vérité film CHRONIQUE D'UN ÉTÉ (1961). BKG

Dir: Michel Brault, Gilles Groulx; **Prod**: Louis Portugais; **Phot**: Michel Brault (b/w);
Ed: Gilles Groulx; **Sound**: Marcel Carrière; **Prod Co**: National Film Board of Canada.

Roger and Me
US, 1989 – 91 mins
Michael Moore

Michael Moore's first feature-length documentary, about the closing of several General Motors (GM) plants in the film-maker's home town of Flint, Michigan (birthplace of the United Auto Workers union), the subsequent loss of 30,000 jobs and the devastation of the town's economy, was the most commercially successful documentary of all time (until it was topped by Moore's subsequent *Fahrenheit 911*, 1994, and BOWLING FOR COLUMBINE, 2002, about the US's preoccupation with guns and violence, which also feature his muckraking persona). (Moore also made a short PBS television documentary, *Pigs or Meat: The Return to Flint*, 1992, about Rhonda Britton, a woman who appears in *Roger and Me* bludgeoning and skinning a rabbit.) In *Roger and Me*, as in his other documentaries, Moore inserts himself in his work as a vérité catalyst, more aggressively than either the self-effacing Ross McElwee (see TIME INDEFINITE, 1993) or earnest investigator Nick Broomfield (see HEIDI FLEISS: HOLLYWOOD MADAM, 1995). The film first established Moore's homespun radical activist persona, fully evident here as he tries to chase down and meet with GM's CEO Roger Smith, including, for example, an attempt to enter Smith's office at GM headquarters in Detroit without an appointment and with only his Chuck E. Cheese restaurant membership card as identification.

The film begins with Moore introducing himself and his family to us with the aid of 8mm home movies and archival footage. He admits to being 'kind of a strange child', the son of a GM worker who assembles AC spark plugs. Moore explains the importance of GM to the economic and social life of Flint while trying to find Smith at places like the Detroit Athletic Club, but he is never successful and his attempts often end in his being escorted out by security. Various celebrities visit Flint for purposes of boosterism, including Pat Boone, Anita Bryant and TV personality Bob Eubanks, a Flint native whom the camera captures telling an unfortunate racist joke. But the joke here is at the expense of Eubanks, and the film is filled with Moore's typical brand of black humour, an uncomfortable mixture of comedy and pathos. In one memorable scene, for example, poignant irony is provided in the sequence showing the urban decay affecting Flint accompanied by the Beach Boys singing 'Wouldn't It Be Nice?'. In keeping with his comic persona, Moore distributed lint rollers (one of the hare-brained schemes proposed in the film to lift Flint into economic recovery) to everyone at the end of the film's premiere screening at the Toronto International Film Festival.

As with his later films, Moore was accused of manipulating the facts by several critics, most prominently Pauline Kael. Harlan Jacobson also raised questions about the film's handling of facts (for example, Ronald Reagan wasn't president but a candidate when he visited Flint in 1980, and Moore in fact did speak at the GM shareholders' meeting but did not include this footage in the final film), as well as the chronology and causal relationships of some of the events depicted (failed commercial developments like Autoworld were built and closed *before* the big GM layoffs, not after), and pressed Moore on these points in a testy interview in *Film Comment*. More recently, *Roger and Me* received its share of criticism in *Manufacturing Dissent* (dirs. Rick Caine and Debbie Melnyk, 2007), a film that turns the tables by seeking to discredit Moore for playing fast and loose with facts, and where co-director Melnyk attempts to confront him on the matter by chasing after him just as Moore had chased after Roger Smith. Regardless of Moore's seemingly loose approach to facts, audiences found *Roger and Me* both entertaining and enlightening in showing one blue-collar kind of guy tilting at the windmills of America's large corporations. BKG

Dir/Prod/Scr: Michael Moore; **Phot**: Chris Beaver, John Prusak, Kevin Rafferty, Bruce Schermer (colour); **Ed**: Jennifer Beman, Wendey Stanzler; **Sound**: Jennifer Beman, Judy Irving; **Prod Co**: Dog Eat Dog Films/Warner Bros.

Salesman
US, 1968 – 85 mins
Albert Maysles, David Maysles, Charlotte Zwerin

Following the lives of four salesmen for the Mid-American Bible Company – Paul Brennan, Raymond 'The Bull' Martos, Charlie 'The Gipper' McDevitt and James 'The Rabbit' Baker – *Salesman* combines a direct cinema approach with aspects of fiction film to provide a revealing account of their working lives that also offers an incisive examination of American material culture. The salesmen are shown making their sales pitches in the homes of potential customers and relaxing and strategising in their motel rooms at night, the Maysles capturing not only extraordinary moments of salesmanship but also raising important questions about the fraught relation between consumer and spiritual values that inform the American way of life. The customers are all working class, and most seem unable to afford the purchase, but the salesmen are shown to be adept at their pitches, employing a number of well-honed gambits and focusing on the desires, insecurities and religious faith of their customers in order to make the sale. The Maysles's interest in performance and its relation to truth (a central issue in observational documentary), which surfaces in *Meet Marlon Brando* (1966), *Gimme Shelter* (1970), GREY GARDENS (1975) and the films about the environmental artist Christo (*Christo's Valley Curtain*, 1974, *Running Fence*, 1978), in which the works of art are not simply the objects he constructs on the landscape but the process of meeting with and securing permissions from landowners and civic officials, is also key to *Salesman*.

Each of the four salesmen is introduced in his own shot as if he were a fictional character (which, of course, inevitably such subjects are, no matter how 'pure' the documentary), with his name and nickname superimposed in a title reminiscent of the credits of a classic Hollywood movie. While driving from one potential customer to another, Paul talks to the camera and explains the personality traits of his fellow salesmen that inspired their nicknames. Shortly after, the film cross-cuts between the sales meeting in Chicago and Paul's train journey from Boston to the meeting, with the motivational speeches at the meeting carrying over into the shots of Paul looking out of the train window as if they formed his inner monologue. These fictional techniques focus around Paul, who has had a run of bad luck and is clearly struggling to recapture his self-confidence and former success, and shows the Maysles Brothers, in their first feature-length documentary, adapting the crisis structure favoured by the Drew Associates (see PRIMARY, 1960, CRISIS, 1963), of which they had been members.

The Maysles cleverly tease out metaphors and meaning in the profilmic events they capture. Much of the film follows the four salesmen on a six-week sales trip to Opa Loca, Florida, near Miami – the city itself, a place built around an Ali Baba theme, is a prefab community, bereft of the spiritual roots the salesmen claim to be peddling. Paul gets lost there, driving in circles, a mirror of his own self-doubt. Critics were quick to interpret the bible salesmen as metaphors for the consumerism of American culture, many noting the film's unavoidable allusion to Arthur Miller's 1958 play *Death of a Salesman* and seeing the salesmen as four Willy Lomans. Miller himself said of the film that it is 'an adventure into the American dream where hope is a sale and a sale is confirmation of existence itself'. BKG

Dir/Scr: Albert Maysles, David Maysles, Charlotte Zwerin; **Prod**: Albert Maysles, David Maysles; **Phot**: Albert Maysles (b/w); **Ed**: David Maysles, Charlotte Zwerin; **Sound**: Dick Vorisek (sound mixer); **Prod Co**: Maysles Films.

Le Sang des bêtes (Blood of Beasts)
France, 1949 – 22 mins
Georges Franju

In many parts of post-war Europe, cinema programming favoured short films, very often documentaries, rather than feature double bills, allowing short films to be part of mainstream distribution and exhibition and carry some prestige. In France, short films were eligible for *primes de qualité* (financial awards), making them an ideal training ground for future feature film directors. Georges Franju directed a significant body of short documentaries – arguably, his best work – before his first feature in 1959 (as did Alain Resnais, including NUIT ET BROUILLARD, 1955).

Le Sang des bêtes owes its notoriety to the explicit scenes of animal slaughter, but these occupy roughly half the film and are deployed in a quite particular context. Superbly evoking a sense of place, the film opens with the semi-industrial *terrains vagues* (vacant lots) on the outskirts of Paris – wintry sunshine, a cloudless sky, a landscape 'empty' except for a leafless tree and distant apartment blocks, with gently lyrical music (by Jean Renoir's favourite composer, Joseph Kosma, reminiscent of his *Une partie de campagne* score). Here, a woman's voiceover tells us, children play and bric-a-brac is displayed for sale, artfully arranged for the camera in random juxtapositions beloved of the Surrealists – a shop mannequin, a wicker basket, an old-fashioned gramophone speaker, for example.

But here also is the Porte de Vanves horsemeat abattoir, at the very edges of the city proper, as if such places needed to be sited beyond the daily vision of Parisian consumers. In a brusque change of tone, a business-like male voice introduces the tools for killing animals. In quick succession, a horse is led in, shot in the head, keels over and is cut open, its blood drained and skin removed; we are told the uses of the different animal parts and the skills and dangers involved in the job. The everyday reality of the abattoirs is filmed and narrated not to horrify but 'neutrally', as one might film a bottling assembly line, as matter-of-factly

as the brutish lives of the villagers in LAS HURDES (1933) (reminding us
of Franju's surrealist kinship with Luis Buñuel). Later, at La Villette
abattoir, the graphic, often grotesque, images of slaughtered oxen, calves
and sheep exert a strange fascination – even beauty and absurdity.

The film's final section observes that the men work 'without anger,
without hate, and with the simple cheerfulness of killers who whistle or
sing as they cut throats, for they must earn their own daily bread'.
But Franju illustrates the words of Charles Trenet's popular 'La Mer', sung
by a worker, ironically accompanied by a montage of images of sheep,
instruments of slaughter, nuns' bonnets, etc. The woman's voice resumes

over shots of agitated, waiting sheep, who won't hear the sound of the Paris–Villette train 'off to gather the next victims'. The final shots – dark images of abattoirs, industrial buildings and smoking locomotives under evening skies – also return us to the *terrain vague* and the passage across the screen, as if from nowhere, of a barge (a homage to Jean Vigo and *L'Atalante*?).

Whereas Franju's equally celebrated *Hôtel des Invalides* (1951) is explicitly anti-militarist, *Le Sang des bêtes* has proved problematic to read. The film was made shortly after World War II, and it is difficult while watching not to reflect upon civilians being led to war, and Jews being transported to slaughter of a different kind. This is not to suggest that Franju intends such a metaphor, only that he must have been aware of the likelihood of provoking such reflection. *Le Sang des bêtes* was precisely the kind of personal, poetic but socially relevant film Lindsay Anderson and Karel Reisz wanted to make in Britain; it was included in the second (all non-British) Free Cinema programme at London's National Film Theatre in 1956. JH

Dir/Scr: Georges Franju; **Prod**: Paul Legros; **Phot**: Marcel Fradetal (b/w); **Ed**: André Joseph; **Music**: Joseph Kosma; **Sound**: Raymond Verchère; **Commentary**: Jean Painlevé, spoken by Georges Hubert, Nicole Ladmiral; **Prod Co**: Forces et Voix de la France.

Sans soleil (*Sunless*)
France, 1983 – 100 mins
Chris Marker

Chris Marker has been making a style of essay-travelogue film since the 1950s, despite more political work in the 1960s and 1970s. As he says in *Lettre de Sibérie* (1958), 'I am writing to you from a far country', though he might also be a visitor from another planet. As David Thomson writes, 'His films see nothing exceptional in an inquisitive traveller sending back films about the lands he has seen and the thoughts he has had while there.' Like his *nouvelle vague* 'Left Bank' colleague Agnès Varda (LES GLÂNEURS ET LA GLÂNEUSE, 2000), he is a 'gleaner'.

Letters from Sandor Krasna – an exiled, wandering Hungarian cameraman – read by an unseen, unidentified woman form the main structure of *Sans soleil*. The film begins with the woman's voice over black leader: 'The first image he told me about was of three children on a road in Iceland, in 1965', introducing a seven-second shot of three children, camera shy, blond hair blowing in the wind, green fields beyond. Over more black leader, 'He said that for him it was the image of happiness. Also that he had tried several times to link it with other images' (cutaway to a shot of US airplanes on a carrier), 'but it never worked. He wrote me, "One day I'll have to put it all alone at the beginning of a film with a long piece of black leader. If they don't see happiness in the picture, at least they'll see the black."' As this is just what Marker has done, and as 'Chris Marker' is not Marker's real name and he has studiously avoided publicising his identity, we can presume that Krasna stands in for Marker, though perhaps at some distance. And as this Iceland footage – fragile 'moments suspended in time' – is brought back, and supplemented, near the end, the film might be read as searching for a structure that *can* accommodate that first image, and for images with which it *can* be linked.

The film is held together by its overarching concern with the ways time, memory and images work: 'He wrote me, "I will have spent my life trying to understand the function of remembering . . . We do not remember. We re-write memory, much as history is re-written" '; he remembers not Tokyo in January, but 'the images I filmed in the month of January in Tokyo'. Although focused mainly on Japan and Japanese culture, the film shifts readily to Guinea-Bissau, the Cape Verde islands, the San Francisco of Hitchcock's *Vertigo*, and the Île de France. Marker does not hesitate to 'digress': a Tokyo sequence is followed by one in Guinea and then – 'By the way, did you know that there are emus in the Île de France?' Why Japan? Marker is attracted by its apparent 'otherness', and by its rituals, religious and secular, its attitudes to spirituality and death.

Sans soleil has a beginning and an end, but Marker's CD-Rom *Immemory* (1998) allows spectators to navigate different routes, and *Sans soleil* suggests this is how Marker would like the film to work, encouraging new ways for spectators to think about their *own* memory stock, and their own list of 'things that quicken the heart'. As an editor at Éditions du Seuil in the 1950s, Marker helped edit the Petite Planète cultural travel books whose quirky interest in national histories, cultures and myths marked them out as special. Each book's cover featured an alluring young woman, and Marker's films, including *Sans soleil*, are not averse to this 'weakness' that 'quickens the heart', of evoking a culture through the mysterious feminine. JH

Dir/Scr/Phot/Ed: Chris Marker (colour); **Prod**: Anatole Dauman; **Music**: Michel Krasna; **Sound Mix**: Antoine Bonfanti, Paul Bertault; **Narrator**: Florence Delay (French version), Alexandra Stewart (English version); **Prod Co**: Argos Films.

(*Next page*) *Sans soleil*

79 Primaveras (79 Springs, aka *79 Springtimes/79 Springtimes of Ho Chi Minh)*
Cuba, 1969 – 22 mins
Santiago Alvarez

The 1960s saw the worldwide rebirth of political cinema. The Instituto Cubano del Arte y Industria Cinematográficos was established a few months after the Cuban revolution, and cinema became – as it had been after the Russian Revolution – the most important of the arts in Cuba. Many Cuban fiction features travelled abroad but short films were just as important in Cuba for information and propaganda. Santiago Alvarez headed newsreel and documentary production at ICAIC. Short of funds and equipment and cut off from new material by the US blockade, Alvarez developed a documentary style that eschewed commentary and pillaged archive film and other found material, stills and captions, in films like *Now* (1965) and *LBJ* (1968). Alvarez's films relate to compilations like THE FALL OF THE ROMANOV DYNASTY (1927) and IN THE YEAR OF THE PIG (1968), but are more radically agitprop, closer to the spirit of the Soviet agit-trains and THE HOUR OF THE FURNACES (1968). However, Alvarez goes much further, exploiting negative/positive images, stop-motion animation/time-lapse, slow motion, re-photography, frame slippage/step-printing, etc.: barely an image in the film fails to remind us of its status *as* image.

79 Springs is at once the 'official' Cuban obituary film for Ho Chi Minh (who died in 1969 aged seventy-nine – hence the title), an impassioned plea for socialist unity and an experimental work assembling heterogeneous materials. The pre-title sequence sets the style: found footage of a time-lapse flower opening comes into focus, then dissolves into 'lazy dog' cluster bombs tumbling through the sky and bursting below like flowers; a black screen, accompanied by singing, gives way to the credits and negative footage of a young Ho Chi Minh dissolves into positive, grainy close-ups of an older Ho and back to negative.

The bulk of the film cuts between Ho Chi Minh's political and military struggles (participation in founding the French and Vietnamese communist parties, military struggles against the Japanese and French, etc.) at different stages of his life and Alvarez's contemporary footage of his funeral. Some funeral footage is presented 'straight', but most is manipulated via slow motion, superimposition and step-printing, to very powerful effect – slow-motion footage of young women weeping 'echoes' earlier footage of children singing and clapping happily with Ho, for example. The film shifts gear for a passage about the US in Vietnam, with disturbing stills of child victims of napalm, a Vietnamese being repeatedly kicked and rifle-butted, US soldiers unloading bullets into bodies and posing for photos, and Western demonstrations against the war (perhaps the film's only false notes).

The film's audacious final 2 minutes subject found footage of armed struggle to effects that make the celluloid appear to split and crack, foregrounding sprocket holes and edge lettering, and finally 'burn'. The image reassembles with titles urging an end to socialist disunity and building a better future; as at the start, time-lapse flowers open and armed struggle continues, with rockets launching accompanied by serene Bach music, ending with a freeze-frame of an open flower. It's a sequence worthy of avant-garde structuralist film-makers, but Alvarez has no interest in purely formal experimentation: the deconstruction of *79 Springs* is tied firmly to its politics and – more than Godard's BRITISH SOUNDS, also 1969 – remains entirely accessible. Few films make us more aware of watching a film while using their reflexivity to such emotional effect. The documentary tradition Alvarez helped establish long survived him: the equally astonishing *Oración* (*Prayer*, dir. Marisol Trujillo, 1984), for example, brings together the death of Marilyn Monroe, third world hunger and exploitation, and Blake's New Jerusalem. JH

Dir: Santiago Alvarez; **Phot**: Iván Nápoles (b/w); **Effects**: Jorge Pucheux, Pedro Luis Hernández, Pepín Rodríguez, Santiago Penate; **Ed**: Norma Torrado; **Sound**: Raúl Pérez Ureta (location recording), Isalberto Gálvez (sound/music editing); **Prod Co**: ICAIC (Instituto Cubano del Arte y Industria Cinematográficos).

Shipyard
UK, 1935 – 24 mins
Paul Rotha

Paul Rotha has often been the forgotten figure of British documentary, his films barely known, partly because they were made outside Grierson's Empire Marketing Board and GPO Film Units, lacked the status of the GPO films and did not remain in circulation. In the 1930s and 1940s, however, Rotha's films and his critical writing (notably *The Film till Now*, 1930, and *Documentary Film*, 1935) were justly recognised as important. He was a key British inheritor of the 1920s Soviet approach to cinema, emphasising a formal style centred on editing and a content focused on social and political purpose.

Shipyard looks at the process by which 'Job 697' becomes the Orient Lines luxury liner *Orion* at the Vickers Armstrong yard in Barrow-in-Furness. A modest but compelling film, it determinedly keeps the social and economic context in view – making it clear, for example, how dependent Barrow is on the yard and each job. In a striking opening sequence, individual workers and the streets they live in are named as they leave for work in early morning, but the names are dropped as they are joined in long shots by others, becoming a crowd, a collectivity. Throughout the film, collaboration, joint work towards a single goal is emphasised. Later on, individuals are picked out, identified by their supposed thoughts, but only as 'typical' of the others. Strikingly, too, the voiceover commentary is spoken in a soft Lancashire working-class accent, and the voiced thoughts of workers – about the ship, about the evenings or weekends ahead – put us in touch with their lives (rather like the end of HOUSING PROBLEMS, 1935). The film also incorporates a sympathetic sequence of men racing their whippets, almost experimental in its use of slow motion, and as unpatronising as Humphrey Jennings's look at working-class leisure in *Spare Time* (1939).

Looked at alongside other films about industry – Flaherty's *Industrial Britain* (1931) or Cavalcanti's COAL FACE (1935), say – the qualities of

Shipyard are very clear: it lacks the obfuscatory emphasis on beauty and craftsmanship amid smoke and dirt suggested by Flaherty or the combination of bluntness and experimentalism adopted by Cavalcanti, opting instead for thoughtful and clear exposition. Some – including Rotha himself – have claimed a greater political awareness on his part. Certainly, a worker muses on the inequalities inherent in the shipbuilders' labour at the service of a luxury liner destined for the wealthy, and the contrast between the dignitaries present at the launch of the ship and the working men watching – in their Sunday best, expressing pride but also anxiety about their futures – the product of their labour slide away from them, is very clear. Rotha later remembered his film as more radical than it was, suggesting it commented on the spectre of unemployment, but Brian Winston is surely right that though the film shows how 'the social irrelevance of *Industrial Britain* could be extended to encompass negative aspects of contemporary life', it joins other Grierson-inspired 1930s documentaries in an essentially 'depoliticised discourse'. It could hardly be otherwise given the state or corporate sponsorship that made the films possible and the resulting actual or self-imposed censorship: the sponsors of *Shipyard* objected to Rotha's local-accented commentary and re-edited the film with a more 'standard' voiceover, along with other changes. All the 1930s documentarists had to tread the fine line between what they would have liked to say and what they were (or felt) allowed to say, but as Rotha recognised in his 1936 book *Documentary Film*, a film-maker in a democracy like Britain's was allowed to project his beliefs 'only so long as they do not seriously oppose powerful vested interests, which most often happen to be the forces controlling production'. JH

Dir/Prod/Scr: Paul Rotha; **Phot**: George Pocknall, Frank Bundy, Frank Goodliffe, Harry Rignold (b/w); **Music**: Jack Beaver; **Sound**: W. Elliott; **Prod Co**: Gaumont-British Instructional for Orient Shipping Line/Vickers Armstrong.

Shoah
France/US, 1985 – 503 mins (US)/566 mins (UK)
Claude Lanzmann

Although *Shoah* (the term 'Shoah' or 'Ha Shoah' is the Hebrew word for 'destruction') is widely regarded as the most powerful documentary about the Nazi extermination of more than 6 million European Jews, it shows nothing of the 'Final Solution' itself. Rather than attempt to understand the atrocities of the Holocaust through archival footage as in, for example, Alain Resnais's NUIT ET BROUILLARD (1955), the film eschews re-enactments or archival footage and photographs, choosing instead interviews with Jewish survivors, Poles who lived on farms near the camps or drove the trains containing Jews to them, and German guards. Shot over a ten-year period and assembled from more than 350 hours of footage, *Shoah* confronts the memory of the Holocaust by focusing on people who lived through it. Taking the approach that the horrors of the Holocaust are unimaginable, hence unrepresentable (Simon Srebnik, one of two survivors of the 400,000 people killed at Chelmno, says 'It was terrible. No one can describe it'), director Claude Lanzmann, a French Jew who also served as editor of the journal *Les Temps Modernes*, creates a detailed oral history that ultimately shows how its legacy remains very much present. Loosely structured, the film focuses on Chelmno, where gas was first used to kill Jews; the death camps of Treblinka and Auschwitz-Birkenau; and the Warsaw Ghetto. No one story predominates, though the polyphony of voices overall provides a chilling narrative of the extermination procedures.

The film's lengthy running time (more than 9 hours) allows Lanzmann to delve deeply into the painful memories of the people he interviews, including Srebnik; Mordechai Podchiebnick, the other survivor of Chelmno; Franz Schalling, a guard who describes in dispassionate detail the unloading of the trains' human cargo and delivery to the gas chamber; and Franz Suchomel, a former SS officer who discusses the operation of the chambers. Disturbingly, the film shows how the Holocaust was enacted by common folk, whether Germans doing their duty or Polish farming people who looked the other way. A few of the interviewees speak in English, but most involve a translator who, appearing on screen along with Lanzmann and his subjects, speaks both Polish and French. Through the translator, Lanzmann persists with his questions, asking for elaboration of a particular point, to repeat something already said, or to clarify what is intended by a specific word, his prodding forcing the speaker's true feelings to emerge. Podchlebnick, for instance, recalls events with a smiling countenance, about which Lanzmann questions him, but as the interview continues, the smile is replaced by barely repressed anguish. Throughout the film, Lanzmann interweaves languid tracking and panning shots of the places where the terrible events, recollected by the interviewees in voiceover, occurred, the sites' present natural beauty or picturesque quaintness contrasting sharply with the horrors being described, thus rendering them even more incomprehensible.

Though *Shoah* has received much praise, some Poles criticised Lanzmann, claiming that he mistranslated some dialogue and that he

edited the film to create the impression that Poles willingly co-operated with the Nazis. Nevertheless, the inclusion of shots showing cheerful townsfolk surrounding Srebnik and others as they speak do suggest, at best, their continuing denial of the Holocaust's brutality, at worst a lingering anti-Semitism. Lanzmann continued to explore the history of the Holocaust in *Hotel Terminus: The Life and Times of Klaus Barbie* (1988) and *Sobibor, Oct. 14, 1943, 4 P.M.* (2001), about the only revolt of Jews in a Nazi concentration camp. BKG

Dir/Scr: Claude Lanzmann; **Phot**: Dominique Chapuis, Jimmy Glasberg, William Lubtchansky (colour); **Ed**: Ziva Poster, Anna Ruiz; **Prod Co**: Les Films Aleph/Historia Films/Ministère de la Culture de la République Française.

El sol del membrillo (aka *The Quince Tree Sun/ The Dream of Light*)
Spain, 1992 – 137 mins
Victor Erice

Among its several awards (including the 1992 Cannes Jury Prize), *El sol del membrillo* won the 'fiction film' prize at Chicago, so the old question 'is it a documentary?' immediately poses itself. It could not be unproblematically so, including as it does, for example, a dream sequence in which the main 'character' dreams or imagines his youth. And if it raises questions about blurring the fiction/documentary distinction, it does so in very different ways from, for example, THIS IS SPINAL TAP (1984), DAVID HOLZMAN'S DIARY (1967) or THE WAR GAME (1965), though it shares some qualities with CLOSE UP (1990).

At the film's core – in a real sense, its heart – is a documentary subject: Madrid painter Antonio López Garcia's attempt to paint, over two or three months, a quince tree growing in his backyard. From López preparing his canvas to the meticulous setting up of a grid for his painting and the marks he makes on the quinces and leaves, this is an extraordinary record and exploration of the creative act and process of painting (bringing to mind Henri-Georges Clouzot's 1956 *Le Mystère Picasso*). Like artists from Vermeer and Rembrandt to, in film, Stan Brakhage and Michael Snow, López is obsessed by light: he wants to capture his quinces in a certain autumnal morning sunlight (hence the film's alternative international title, *The Dream of Light*). However – and this may be part of director Victor Erice's 'fiction' – the weather is against him and, as he concedes to a Chinese visitor, the innate limitations of painting make the task impossible anyway. In fact, López eventually abandons the painting, consigns it to his cellar and begins drawing the subject instead. Meanwhile, the fruits continually grow, their weight pulling down branches and leaves (which explains the lines he painted on the fruit to measure their height against his grid). But this also means that López finds himself in a race against time, trying to capture things in still form while they constantly change (shades perhaps of Poe's 'Oval Portrait') – he even resorts to raising the branches manually, propping them up and arranging artificial illumination.

Around this central core are other 'events' and 'characters' (all apparently playing themselves) whose documentary status remains unclear and that may, to some degree, have been 'staged': López's partner, Marina Moreno, gets on with her own artwork; his children visit; painter and old art-school friend Enrique Gran drops round to reminisce and discuss art, as do other friends. Perhaps most intriguingly, three Polish labourers are rebuilding the house (and trying to learn Spanish): their final plastering – and their disappointment at tasting quince – is made to coincide with the final touches López makes to his drawing. The film is also clearly interested in evoking a certain rhythm of life and the rather nondescript quarter of the city, from López's scruffy garden to the mishmash of houses, train lines, etc., that surround it.

Of course, cinema *depends on* light, and Erice's highly regarded fiction features (*The Spirit of the Beehive*, 1973, and *The South/El sur*, 1983) were valued partly for their painterly qualities, particularly their use of light. Here, Erice's camera manages to capture some of the effects of light that López seeks in his painting. For almost the whole film, Erice's camera plays the role of invisible observer: López gets on with his work and we simply watch. However, some cuts on action and other devices begin to suggest that the film-makers stage, select and construct, just as López the painter does. Towards the end, strikingly, Erice's camera foregrounds itself fully and takes over the role of documenting the process of decay that the quinces undergo during the winter and the arrival of furry new fruit in spring. JH

Dir: Victor Erice; **Prod**: María Moreno; **Scr**: Victor Erice, Antonio López; **Phot**: Javier Aguirresarobe, Angel Luis Fernández (colour); **Ed**: Juan Ignacio San Mateo; **Music**: Pascal Gaigne; **Sound**: Ricardo Steinberg, Daniel Goldstein; **With**: Antonio López García, Marina Moreno, Enrique Gran, Maria López, Carmen López; **Prod Co**: María Moreno P.C.

The Spanish Earth
US, 1937 – 52 mins
Joris Ivens

The anti-fascist Popular Front period, from the mid- to late 1930s, with socialists striving to reach a wide audience, produced very interesting documentary work, not least in the US (such as Frontier Films' NATIVE LAND, 1942). After working in the Soviet Union and making NEW EARTH (1934) in his native Netherlands, Joris Ivens was invited by Contemporary Historians, Inc. (including Archibald MacLeish, Lillian Hellman, Dorothy Parker) to make a film about the Spanish Civil War to attract sympathy for the Republican cause and help raise money for ambulances. With a rough script, Ivens left for Spain to meet up with his old collaborator, photographer John Ferno, and work on *The Spanish Earth* (sometimes known as *This Spanish Earth*) began.

The film moves between two war fronts – the front-line war defending Madrid against the fascists, and the 'war' at home, in a rural village. Ivens places equal emphasis on both fronts; the film begins and ends in the village, albeit with the sound of war not far off. He returns to some of the concerns of *New Earth* – the centrality of the earth and its potential to feed the people, here reclaimed not from the sea but by irrigation being built by the villagers. The storyline strategy – what Ivens called 'personalisation', involving enacted or fictional elements – was to link village and front through Julian, a young soldier who returns to the village on leave. In the finished film, this link feels more tenuous than Ivens or editor Helen van Dongen would have liked, but the film material – often shot in dangerous situations at the front – simply wasn't available to make the link stronger.

The frequent chaos surrounding the front-line shooting (obviously, all from the Republican side) lends an appropriate sense of confusion, contrasting sharply with the controlled, composed sequences shot in the village. Equally impressive is the footage of besieged Madrid – citizens scurrying across eerily deserted streets, bombed houses and shops (very reminiscent of British World War II documentaries like Humphrey

Jennings's and Harry Watt's *London Can Take It*, 1940). Ivens and Van Dongen (who had earlier assembled *Spain in Flames*, 1936, from newsreel footage) skilfully incorporate highly dramatic newsreel footage. Starkly contrasting images, in both village and Madrid, evoke bright Spanish sunshine and dark shadow. Unsurprisingly, the film emphasises the Republicans' defence of democracy against fascist insurgents with German and Italian support, but it is hardly a polemic against the rebels; there is limited rancour towards Moorish mercenaries or Italian 'volunteers', or even German bombers. The focus here is on the devastating effects of war, and the spirit displayed by ordinary people. Similarly, Ivens includes little about party politics – only a sequence of impassioned speakers, including Dolores Ibarruri (La Pasionaria).

After completing the film with Ernest Hemingway's commentary spoken by Orson Welles, a definitive version used Hemingway speaking his own words, his delivery more muscular, matter-of-fact than Welles's richer voice. Shortly after completion, Ivens, Hemingway and Martha Gellhorn were invited to present the film at the White House to President and Eleanor Roosevelt. It was also shown at the League of Nations as evidence of German and Italian involvement in Spain – though the British censors excised all reference to it. The film found only very limited distribution. Soon after its US release, its sponsors financed Ivens's *The Four Hundred Million* (1938), about China's efforts to repel the Japanese invasion. Subsequently, Ivens made *Power and the Land* (1940) for the governmental United States Film Service. Barely a decade later, those involved in *The Spanish Earth* were condemned, in the House Un-American Activities Committee's absurd phrase, as 'premature anti-Fascists'. *The Spanish Earth* was not shown in Spain until 1977. JH

Dir: Joris Ivens; **Prod**: Herman Shumlin; **Scr**: Lillian Hellman, Joris Ivens, Archibald MacLeish; **Phot**: John Ferno (Fernhout), Joris Ivens (b/w); **Ed**: Helen van Dongen; **Music**: Marc Blitzstein, Rodolfo Halffter, Virgil Thomson; **Sound**: Irving Reis; **Commentary**: John Dos Passos, Ernest Hemingway (spoken by Ernest Hemingway/Orson Welles); **Prod Co**: Contemporary Historians, Inc.

Surname Viet Given Name Nam
US, 1989 – 108 mins
Trinh T. Minh-ha

Originally from Vietnam, Trinh is a film-maker, teacher and theorist who has been living in the US since 1970. In her films such as *Reassemblage* (1982) and *Naked Spaces: Living Is Round* (1985), Trinh's approach to documentary involves a deliberate attempt to resist the colonialist discourses of Western anthropology as found in such enthnographic documentaries as DEAD BIRDS (1965). Working with the theoretical assumption that all representations, including documentary, are ideologically determined, Trinh constructs *Surname Viet Given Name Nam* in a strikingly different manner in an attempt, as Jean-Luc Godard would say, to make a film politically rather than to make a political film (see BRITISH SOUNDS, 1969).

Trinh combines unorthodox interviews with five Vietnamese women now living in the US with contemporary documentary footage and archival material of traditional Vietnamese scenes and the mass exodus of South Vietnamese towards the end of the Vietnam War. The film emphasises the oppression Vietnamese women have experienced throughout their lives, whether in Vietnam, where they were subject to the decisions of their fathers, husbands and sons (according to the rules of 'The Four Virtues' and 'The Three Submissions', which constitute a strict code of behaviour for female identity), or in the US, where they are subject to prejudice as women and members of a visible minority. Because Vietnamese women have been oppressed both in their home country and abroad, they have struggled to discover their identity, both as individuals and collectively, a struggle that Trinh seeks to translate into cinematic terms.

Trinh tells us in her voiceover narration that 'the problem of translation is a problem of reading and identity', and *Surname Viet Given Name Nam* foregrounds this difficulty by employing numerous stylistic devices to problematise its own processes of representation.

The interviews continually undermine the convention of the authoritative talking-head approach: the camera often seems to roam at random, zooming in or zooming out on a face, challenging the convention of the slow zoom in to the face of the speaker for mounting dramatic emphasis. One interviewee paces back and forth across the frame, on occasion leaving the image entirely while she speaks. The soundtrack is dense, featuring multiple voices, including, in addition to the interviews, songs, poetry and oral myths, sometimes in English and sometimes in Vietnamese. Periodically, subtitles are provided in English even though the interviewees are speaking in (heavily accented) English; appearing in different parts of the screen, sometimes they differ from what is being said, or are gone before the viewer can read all the text. All in all, this polyphony of voices stands in opposition to documentary's conventional voice-of-God narrator, celebrating the multiplicity that constitutes Vietnamese female identity. The five interviews were recorded in Vietnamese by Mai Thu Van in 1982, translated into French, and then re-enacted in the film by women who have emigrated to the US – a process we find out about only towards the end of the film, when the interviewees appear as themselves to talk about being in the film.

Throughout, the women's experience is seen as parallel to that of Vietnam itself: the country, like the women, has been subjected to oppression, and its colonial history is seen as analogous to the women's subjugation to family. Even after the nation's reunification following the war, the women say they were not treated as equals. As one of them remarks in a rare and powerful moment when her gaze meets that of the camera, 'True revolution is a task that belongs to the women.' BKG

Dir/Prod/Scr/Ed: Trinh T. Minh-ha; **Phot**: Kathleen Beeler (colour); **Art Dir**: Jean-Paul Bourdier; **Sound**: Linda Peckham.

Talking Heads (Gadające głowy)
Poland, 1980 – 14 mins
Krzysztof Kieślowski

Krzysztof Kieślowski was a noted documentary film-maker – in a country noted for its documentarists – before he turned to fiction. Reflecting on the ethical problems of documentary film-makers' responsibility for the lives of their subjects – and wanting to penetrate more deeply the psychology of his characters – Kieślowski in the 1970s began to doubt the documentary form, abandoning subjects like *Bricklayer* (1973), *First Love* (1974) and *From a Night Porter's Point of View* (1977) in favour of more fictional forms – a transition fascinatingly explored in his fiction *Amator* (*Camera Buff*, 1979). *Talking Heads*, made around the same time as *Amator*, was one of his last documentaries.

The simplest film-making ideas are often the most powerful. 'Talking heads' are regarded as uninteresting cinematically, but Kieślowski – somewhat like Claude Lanzmann in SHOAH (1985) – turns this precept on its head here by (as the title implies) *only* shooting talking heads, largely avoiding the problems of involvement with his subjects by filming forty-four in 15 minutes (an average of 20 seconds per 'interview'), though this does not diminish the film's enormous emotional impact. Kieślowski's off-screen voice asks each subject the same questions: When were you born? Who are you? What is most important to you? What would you like from life? The first subject is only a few months old, born in 1979; the last was born in 1880. Needless to say, the baby has nothing to say but – like Tim in A DIARY FOR TIMOTHY (1945) – is full of unspoken promise and expectation. The 100-year-old woman, hard of hearing, announces, laughing, that she wants to live longer. In between, the subjects trace the desires, confusions, dilemmas and disappointments of the various stages of life, generally showing familiar patterns of experience – the carefree promise (and eloquence) of youth, the relative disillusionment of middle age, and so on. The film is shot in black and white, with faces often only half-lit, giving what they have to say a

slightly secretive, confessional quality (appropriately enough for a deeply moral Catholic society); backgrounds – home, work, street – remain blurred, though often intriguing (aurally as well as visually). We are also invited to contemplate the subjects' *physical* appearance, as if watching the process of human ageing.

The year of the film's release (1980) also marked the formation of the Solidarity movement, and we cannot help reading subjects' comments in the context of a hundred years of Polish history and that particular historical moment – a fascinating snapshot of the way Poles were thinking about themselves and their society when Poland, like the film's newborn baby, could not know what the future promised.

Though very little is said that relates *explicitly* to Poland's situation, the film stages a commentary on living through that history. Many subjects, for example, voice their discomfort at living in a society in which people fear, dislike and lie to each other, and many touch on issues about individual and collective freedom. A strong sense of socially imposed limitations, and the gap between desires and opportunities, emerges: several subjects speak of being happier as electricians or taxi drivers than as white-collar workers; a self-confessed alcoholic 46-year-old engineer wants 'Nothing. Everything's in perfect order.' As Kieślowski put it, the Communist world 'had been presented the way it should look, and not the way it really looked. There were many of us trying to describe it.' JH

Dir: Krzysztof Kieślowski; **Prod**: Lech Grabiński; **Phot**: Jacek Petrycki, Piotr Kwiatkowski (b/w); **Ed**: Alina Siemińska; **Sound**: Michał Żarnecki; **Prod Co**: WFD (Wytwórnia Filmów Dokumentalnych).

The Thin Blue Line
US, 1988 – 103 mins
Errol Morris

The breakthrough film for Errol Morris, *The Thin Blue Line* is regarded as a quintessential post-modern documentary, in that it reveals truth as composed of multiple truths filtered through subjective perception rather than a monolithic and objective Truth. The film focuses on a 1976 fatal shooting of police officer Robert Wood in Dallas, Texas, who had stopped a car for a routine violation. The police investigation identified two suspects: David Harris, a sixteen-year-old teenager from nearby Vidor, and a 28-year-old drifter named Randall Adams. The two men met by chance and spent part of an evening together, but it is unclear who was driving the car and shot the police officer. Combining interviews with the two men, participating attorneys, law officers and witnesses with stylised reconstructions of the murder from the perspective of each interviewee, the film examines the evidence and the handling of the case to suggest that the police altered and suppressed evidence in order to get a conviction. In the film's startling conclusion, the camera focuses on an audio cassette recorder playing back a taped interview conducted by Morris with Harris, then in jail on another murder charge (for which he was eventually executed in 2004), in which he all but explicitly confesses to the murder of Officer Wood and cryptically suggests that he let Adams take the rap.

Interviewing each of the three apparent eyewitnesses who placed Adams as the driver and shooter, Morris is patient enough to let them talk, to the point that they reveal possible ulterior motives for their testimony and thus call into question the veracity of their statements. In a sense, his camera functions to cross-examine them as they undermine themselves, an approach Morris has taken in other documentaries, such as *Mr Death: The Rise and Fall of Fred A. Leuchter, Jr* (1989). A dramatisation of each interviewee's account along with the official police version is provided, each one slightly different than the others depending upon what is being said. Because they are representations of what they claim to have seen or how

they believe the murder occurred, rather than objective fact, Morris is adamant in refusing to call these scenes re-enactments. In a seeming digression that he refers to as 'trivia', Don Metcalfe, the presiding judge in the case, recalls how his father, who had been an FBI agent in the 1930s and was involved in the killing of infamous gangster John Dillinger outside a movie theatre in Chicago, told him that though the woman who helped lure him into the ambush was known as 'the lady in red', her dress was in fact orange but only looked red in the glow of the theatre marquee's lights. The remark is crucial to *The Thin Blue Line* because it reveals the extent to which what we regard as truth is a matter of subjective perception. Philip Glass's score accentuates the film's concern with the polyvalence of truth, for as with the dramatisations, its serial quality is characterised by repetition with slight variation.

The Thin Blue Line was entered as evidence in Adams's appeal, which was successful, and after a retrial he was released. The title of the film derives from prosecuting attorney Doug Mulder's comment in his closing argument, paraphrasing Rudyard Kipling, that the police are the 'thin blue line' that separates orderly society from crime and chaos. *The Thin Blue Line* shows that line to be the thin edge of the wedge, for if circumstances can conspire to place Randall Adams on death row, then it may well happen to anyone. BKG

Dir/Scr: Errol Morris; **Prod**: Mark Lipson; **Phot**: Robert Chappell, Stefan Czapsky (colour); **Ed**: Paul Barnes; **Art Dir/Prod Des**: Ted Bafaloukos, Lester Cohen; **Music**: Philip Glass; **Sound**: Brad Fullert; **Prod Co**: Third Floor Productions/Channel 4 Television/American Playhouse.

This Is Spinal Tap
US, 1984 – 82 mins
Rob Reiner

Among the several mock rock docs, *This Is Spinal Tap* ranks with Eric Idle's
parody of the Beatles, *All You Need Is Cash – The Rutles* (1978), as the
funniest. Focusing on a fictional heavy metal band named Spinal Tap, the
film brilliantly parodies real-life heavy metal music as well as the
rockumentaries about them. Director Marty DiBergi (a joking reference to
Martin Scorsese, who directed *The Last Waltz*, 1978, and worked as an
editor on WOODSTOCK, 1970), played by director and co-writer Rob
Reiner, follows the group, making a documentary about them, as they
embark on an ill-fated American tour to promote the release of their
album *Smell the Glove*. The film's satire was so sharp, and its style so much
like that of actual rockumentaries, that *This Is Spinal Tap* was taken as real
by many viewers upon its initial release, and has since attained cult status.

Spinal Tap is comprised of David St Hubbins (Michael McKean), Nigel
Tufnel (Christopher Guest) and Derek Smalls (Harry Shearer). There is no
permanent drummer because the band has had a succession of them die
under strange circumstances, including one who, like Jimi Hendrix and
John Bonham, the drummer of prototype metal band Led Zeppelin,
choked on vomit (though in this case, it is unclear whose vomit it was),
another who died in a mysterious gardening accident, and a third who
was the victim of spontaneous combustion. The trio, who reappear as the
pop folk group The Folksmen in *A Mighty Wind* (2003), actually play their
instruments, adding to the film's documentary realism. Further enhancing
this sense of realism is the improvised nature of much of the dialogue, an
approach Guest has maintained in his subsequent films *Waiting for
Guffman* (1996), *Best in Show* (2000) and *A Mighty Wind*.

While the target of much of the film's humour is the excessive
machismo of the heavy metal style, many of the jokes, such as the band's
problems with stage props, including the mistakenly miniature
Stonehenge monument that is trampled on by dwarves, refer to specific

experiences of bands in the hallowed annals of rock history. The tour seems doomed from the beginning, like the fated Rolling Stones tour that ended in the murder of a fan at the Altamont Speedway concert (captured in the Maysles Brothers' *Gimme Shelter*, 1970), with their manager resigning in anger along the way, their LP cover being changed to all black by Polymer Records, and receiving second billing to a puppet show at one gig. Nigel quits in disgust after they are booked into a military base (the commanding officer greets them as Spinal Tarp), but at film's end, Spinal Tap, like Kiss and Deep Purple before them, manage to find a new audience in Japan, and Nigel is reunited with the band, happily blasting power chords with David again.

The film alternates between backstage scenes, using a handheld camera, and concert footage, as is typical of rockumentaries. Ironically, *This Is Spinal Tap* attained such popularity that the band has given actual concerts and released two albums and two singles. Over the years, Christopher Guest has appeared in role as Nigel Tufnel on TV shows and in commercials, further giving the band an actual presence and history. *This Is Spinal Tap* was Reiner's first feature film as director, and though he co-wrote the script and the music with McKean, Shearer and Guest, it has little in common with his subsequent features, which are more conventional fictional narratives, but is stylistically consistent with Guest's other films. BKG

Dir: Rob Reiner; **Prod**: Karen Murphy; **Scr**: Christopher Guest, Michael McKean, Harry Shearer, Rob Reiner; **Phot**: Peter Smokler (colour); **Ed**: Kent Beyda, Kim Secrist; **Art Dir**: Bryan Jones; **Music**: Christopher Guest, Michael McKean, Harry Shearer, Rob Reiner; **Prod Co**: Spinal Tap Productions.

Time Indefinite
US, 1993 – 117 mins
Ross McElwee

Ross McElwee has devoted himself, for over twenty years, to filming his
own life, notably with *Sherman's March* (1985). *Time Indefinite* continues
McElwee's life story into the early 1990s, meeting and marrying his
assistant Marilyn, who becomes pregnant but miscarries, and being
troubled by the deaths of his grandmother and father; as the film ends,
Marilyn, pregnant again, gives birth.

   Are McElwee's films subjective, autobiographical, diary films, in a
tradition essayed by Ed Pincus (*Diaries*, US, 1971–6) and David Perlov
(*Yoman/Diary*, Israel, 1983), and even LOST LOST LOST (1976) and DAVID
HOLZMAN'S DIARY (1967)? Yes, but they would not have the success
and resonance they do if that was all they were. McElwee took the
technology and observational methods of direct cinema pioneered by
Richard Leacock (McElwee's teacher and friend who appears in this film),
D. A. Pennebaker and others twenty-five years earlier (see PRIMARY,
1960, CRISIS, 1963) but diverging from – perhaps turning on their head
– both their typical subject matter and their professed 'simply observers'
ethic. McElwee applies their methods to a subject – the film-maker
himself – that would have been anathema to them, at least in the early
1960s. He records, as he puts it, 'the objective data of the world with a
very subjective, very interior consciousness', registered via voiceover and
on-camera appearance. The camera is certainly very visible; as McElwee
says – echoing Jean Rouch and Edgar Morin's CHRONIQUE D'UN ÉTÉ
(1961) more than Leacock and Pennebaker – the camera acts as a
catalyst, makes things happen – 'it does intensify and force things'.
McElwee's method here is also increasingly self-reflexive, whether
reflecting upon shimmering old family home movies or on an earlier
direct-to-camera monologue.

   As in *Sherman's March*, McElwee appears to live out his often
mundane life with a camera and sound equipment on his shoulder

almost as if it wasn't there; people don't respond particularly oddly to it. However, *Time Indefinite* is punctuated by periods in which, significantly, McElwee stops shooting: filming his father, the camera battery runs out, or the film jams (which McElwee, typically, puts down to his father's 'Freudian force-field'); he loses the urge to film around the time of Marilyn's miscarriage and his father's death; and he professes himself too amazed and exhausted to film much during his son's first six months.

McElwee's voiceover, recorded in post-production and adding distance to the immediacy of the shot footage ('I labour for hundreds of hours over the narration, revising endlessly'), is crucial: here, McElwee develops his wry, self-deprecatory view of himself and the world and elaborates metaphors for his 'metaphysical angst'. Increasingly, the film focuses on the pull of family and dealing with death and what, if anything, comes after it, explaining in part the film's wide appeal, as it deals with personal tragedies and epiphanies that we all share. The film's title is drawn from his encounter with a Jehovah's Witness who quotes the Bible about life after Judgment Day in 'time indefinite'. McElwee's gloom eventually lifts when his parental family's black housekeepers ask him to film their fiftieth wedding anniversary, and when his son is born, affirmations underlined in the end credits gospel rendition of 'Bye and Bye' – another version of 'time indefinite'.

Is the film's McElwee the 'real' McElwee? Undoubtedly, yes, in many respects, but he has certainly developed a 'persona', a character (though, as he insists, don't we all?). McElwee has continued to engage with his life and his persona in later works such as *Six O'Clock News* (1996) and *Bright Leaves* (2003). JH

Dir/Prod/Scr/Phot/Ed/Sound: Ross McElwee (colour); **Sound Mix**: Richard Bock; **Prod Co**: Home Made Movies, with Channel 4 & ZDF (Zweiten Deutschen Fernsehen).

Titicut Follies
US, 1967 – 83 mins
Frederick Wiseman

Titicut Follies is a powerful exposé of the appalling conditions at Bridgewater, a state institution for the criminally insane in Bridgewater, Massachusetts, which is shown as impersonal, its staff for the most part indifferent and abusive. A lawyer and teacher before he was a film-maker, Frederick Wiseman got the idea for the film while visiting the facility with a class of law students. The first in his series of documentaries about institutional life in America, it also has been his most controversial. Reviled in the press during its short theatrical run in the New York Film Festival as ghoulish and voyeuristic, devoid of redeeming social value, it engendered lengthy litigation based on the state's contention that the inmates were not mentally competent to grant permission to be filmed. Apart from the legal arguments, Wiseman's contention was that the public has a right to know about the institutions it funds.

The film contains some shocking scenes of inmates being taunted and abused, both physically and psychologically. In one example, a former schoolteacher is harshly scolded and slapped in the face for not keeping his room clean. He is taken for a shave, where the barber cuts the man's face while roughly scraping at his whiskers. But such unconscionable conditions are balanced with scenes that have wider implications. As with Wiseman's other films, *Titicut Follies* uses its subject to explore broad social issues, in this case by treating Bridgewater as a provocative metaphor for the insanity of contemporary America, similar to Sam Fuller's *Shock Corridor* (1962) or Ken Kesey's novel *One Flew over the Cuckoo's Nest*. Filmed during the Vietnam War era, *Titicut Follies* contains a courtyard debate between two inmates about American intervention in South-east Asia, a crazy mirror of the 'hawks and doves' arguments that at the time were dividing Americans everywhere. Diagnosing the cause of the war, another inmate delivers a delirious monologue that explicitly makes an analogy between Bridgewater and America.

As in all of Wiseman's documentaries, there is no voiceover narrator, and sequences are connected thematically rather than chronologically. He combines detached observation and subtle manipulation, merging observational cinema's fly-on-the-wall approach with an expressive use of *mise en scène* and montage (compare other US direct cinema films such as PRIMARY, 1960, CRISIS, 1963). The film's most pointed moment – a series of cross-cuts between images of an inmate being force-fed through a tube and shots taken at a later date of the same inmate's body being prepped for his funeral – is its most blatant manipulation of its observational footage. *Titicut Follies* begins and ends with a performance of the institution's annual variety show by inmates and guards, suggesting the timelessness, the infinite sense of alienation that, for Wiseman, characterises Bridgewater. Near the film's end, one inmate is shown standing on his head in the yard, singing, ironically, of sacred glory – the upside-down close-up of the man's face conveying Wiseman's view that the mad world of *Titicut Follies*, perhaps like the nation itself, is topsy-turvy. The film ends with a question, as one of the guards, acting as emcee of the variety show, asks the audience, as well as the film's viewer, 'Weren't they terrific?' These haunting last words prod us to think about the conditions that exist in publicly funded institutions like Bridgewater and our own responsibility as citizens. BKG

Dir/Prod/Ed/Sound: Frederick Wiseman; **Phot**: John Marshall (b/w); **Prod Co**: Bridgewater Film Co, Inc.

Tongues Untied
US, 1990 – 55 mins
Marlon Riggs

Openly celebrating black gay life, Marlon Riggs's *Tongues Untied* addresses the double stigma of racism and homophobia that exist for gay black men, examining the relation of that community to the black community generally and American society at large. A gay activist, poet and film-maker, Riggs made a handful of other documentary films on black culture and representation before dying of AIDS-related illnesses at thirty-seven in 1995, including *Ethnic Notions* (1986), about black stereotypes, and *Color Adjustment* (1992), which looks at the history of black representation on television. *Tongues Untied*, by comparison, is a more ambitious work formally, in that it seeks not just to be about black gay life but also to embody and express a black gay aesthetic in its stylistic mix of poetry, rap and performance. Working towards a unique style of personal, semi-autobiographical documentary, *Tongues Untied* also draws upon and documents Riggs's own experience as a black gay man coming to terms with his own sexual identity even as he locates his own experience within the wider cultural context.

Shot on video, *Tongues Untied* celebrates black gay culture in its performative aspects, featuring 'Snap! divas' and vogue dancers along with documentary footage of the civil rights movement. A clip from a stand-up comedy routine by Eddie Murphy shows, in the context of the film, how homophobia divides African-American men – in direct opposition to the call of 'brother to brother' that opens the documentary. Riggs provides the reflexive, poetic voiceover, in which he moves from shame and dealing with the death of friends from AIDS to acceptance and embrace of his sexuality. His stylised dancing suggests both the delicate cultural negotiations that black gay men must continually undergo, as well as his eventual joyful acceptance of himself. Riggs's voice, along with that of poet Essex Hemphill and others, creates a polyphony of voices and suggests a sense of black gay masculinity as multifaceted. Several young men speak to the camera in talking-head shots, as if granting them the subjectivity of which both dominant white culture and patriarchal black culture has deprived them. If black gay identity has been silenced until now by a culture that is predominately white, patriarchal and heterosexist, then the exuberance of Riggs's documentary will untie those tongues to speak out against the torrent of taunts that we hear emanating from black mouths calling him 'faggot' and 'freak' and, from a white mouth, 'mother-fuckin' coon'. At the same time, Riggs contextualises the personal experiences of individual black men when, for example, a zoom into a close-up of a photograph of one black man is intercut with titles referencing 'Howard Beach', 'Crack', 'AIDs', 'Black Men' and 'Endangered Species'. Making its intentions clear, the documentary ends with a quote from Joseph Beam, 'Black men loving Black men is *the* revolutionary act'.

Tongues Untied marked a new direction for gay documentary film-making, moving beyond more conventionally structured films such as Rob Epstein's *Word Is Out* (1978) and *The Times of Harvey Milk* (1984). It first appeared on the Public Broadcasting System television series *P.O.V.* before going on to win documentary awards at a number of film festivals. But its unabashed depiction of gay sexuality became a flashpoint for attacks by conservative politicians on public funding for PBS and the National Endowment for the Arts; among them, presidential hopeful Pat Buchanan decried the film's images of male buttocks as pornographic. Riggs's response was that such a reaction was a demonstration of the patriarchal and heterosexist ideology that defines 'community standards'. BKG

Dir/Scr/Phot/Ed: Marlon Riggs (colour); **Prod**: Brian Freeman; **Prod Co**: MTR Productions.

Triumph of the Will (*Triumph des Willens*)
Germany, 1935 – 114 mins
Leni Riefenstahl

One of the most notorious documentaries ever made, *Triumph of the Will* chronicles the sixth national rally of the National Socialist or Nazi Party in Nuremberg in September 1934. Director and editor Leni Riefenstahl, who began her career as a dancer, was an actress and star of several popular German film melodramas known as mountain films, including *Das Blaue Licht* (*The Blue Light*, 1930), which she produced, co-wrote, edited and directed. A friend of Adolph Hitler, she was personally assigned by him to make *Triumph of the Will*. Since its release, the film has been regarded as a frighteningly persuasive fascist document (even though Riefenstahl herself always claimed to have been apolitical), and with the outbreak of the war, Allied film-makers, including Frank Capra in his WHY WE FIGHT series, were quick to use footage from Riefenstahl's film to show the evils of Nazism.

The planning of the Nuremberg rally happened with the filming of the event in mind. The film was financed by the film studio UFA, then owned by Nazi sympathiser Alfred Hugenberg, and Riefenstahl had eighteen cameras at her disposal. Several of them can be seen in the film moving up and down elevators specially constructed for the event. Though a number of high-ranking Party officials, including Hitler himself, give speeches, there is no voiceover, Riefenstahl preferring instead to let viewers be swept up by the grandeur of the event.

The famous opening of the film depicts Hitler, god-like, descending silently through the clouds in an airplane and landing in Nuremberg to the thunderous applause of the rapturously waiting crowd. Following this, he and his entourage proceed through the streets of the city to adoring throngs of people eager to catch a glimpse of the mighty and mystical

(*Opposite page*) Leni Riefenstahl (centre right, in light-coloured dress, back to camera) directing a shot while filming *Triumph of the Will*

Führer. Workers and soldiers set up tents and prepare the rally site, happily united in their shared national purpose, and Hitler watches a parade emphasising Bavarian folk traditions. When the Party Congress begins, Riefenstahl presents clips of speeches by various Nazi Party officials, concluding with Propaganda Minister Joseph Goebbels, who declaims on 'the creative art of modern political propaganda', of which *Triumph of the Will* is itself a prime example. The rally goes on late into the evening, and Riefenstahl presents numerous images of uniformed marchers filling the frame, carrying flags and banners. Shot with a telephoto lens, these images present the crowd of participants as endless waves that build upon one another. As critics such as Susan Sontag have noted, the sheer spectacle and scale of the demonstration, enhanced by Herbert Windt's appropriately grand Wagnerian score, perfectly express the fascist ideal of the individual submerged within the consciousness of the mass, willing to sacrifice all for the leader and the state.

With the defeat of Germany in World War II, Riefenstahl was brought before both American and French tribunals, but was ultimately released. Never a member of the Nazi Party, she claimed to have been naive about the brutal realities of Nazism, which she overlooked for the sake of art. If her defence seems somewhat disingenuous, certainly *Triumph of the Will* shares with *Olympia* (1938), her follow-up film about the 1936 Berlin Olympics, as well as with her later post-war photographs of African tribesmen, a celebration of masculine physical discipline. BKG

Dir/Prod/Ed: Leni Riefenstahl; **Scr**: Leni Riefenstahl, Walter Ruttmann; **Phot**: Sepp Allgeier, Karl Attenberger (and seventeen other credited cinematographers) (b/w); **Music**: Herbert Windt; **Prod Co**: Leni Riefenstahl-Produktion/Reichspropagandaleitung der NSDAP.

Truth or Dare (aka *In Bed with Madonna/ Madonna: Truth or Dare*)
US, 1991 – 114 mins
Alek Keshishian

Truth or Dare, one of the most high-profile and widely released music documentaries ever made, documents Madonna's 1990 Blond Ambition world tour – her pointy breast period and probably the height of her popularity – combining performance footage (in colour) and 'candid' backstage footage (in black and white). DONT LOOK BACK (1967), the original 'rockumentary', with much the same approach, though far from 'innocent', offered some degree of presumption that Bob Dylan and others did not significantly adapt their behaviour for the camera and that film-maker D. A. Pennebaker did not significantly orchestrate or re-enact events – that he was, in Leacock's phrase, 'simply an observer' – and that he was largely free to film and edit as he wanted. No such contract can be presumed for *Truth or Dare*. Here, Madonna and others interact with the camera and though the handheld backstage camera adopts some of the stylistic tics of 'direct cinema', everything implies that what we see is happening *for* it. Near the beginning, for example, in an 'intimate' scene played entirely for the camera, Madonna goes to bed, closes her door, and the camera creeps in after her and films her 'asleep'. In short, *Truth or Dare* (to risk a wordplay on the title) is 'embedded' in the Madonna project just as war reporters in Iraq were embedded with the military, a vehicle with which she can construct and project an image of power, authority, non-conformity and iconoclasm.

As executive producer and star, Madonna clearly had absolute control: what we see and hear must be what she wanted us to. This makes watching the 'candid' backstage footage a rather odd process. As well as taking in the action, the spectator has to ask why Madonna wants us to see this, and what part of the Madonna persona it is meant to help construct. And what *do* we see? Madonna with her then boyfriend Warren Beatty lurking in the background; Madonna joshing with her make-up artists; Madonna dealing with censorship problems in Toronto (on-stage masturbation) and Italy (crucifixes); Madonna holding (excruciatingly egotistical) pre-show prayer sessions with her back-up singers and dancers; Madonna holding (adolescent) sexual court, with titillating sex games, in bed with her dancers (providing the film with its various titles); Madonna meeting other celebrities, sometimes a little out of her depth; Madonna backstage with her father in Detroit; and so on. Madonna comes across as powerful and dedicated, certainly, but demanding, moody, often bored, with inflated ideas about herself as an 'artist' – though no doubt lonely and isolated too; there is no overt suggestion here of, say, the kinds of frailties Jane Fonda revealed in the Drew Associates' film *Jane* (1962), and not just because of the differences in their situations and personae.

The sequences with Beatty are very telling: Madonna 'parades' him for the cameras (until she dumps him), and he comments that for Madonna 'everything is on camera' – she cannot see the point in saying or doing anything off camera. A 'warts and all' candid portrait implies that we see things the subject would rather not have revealed; but the curious impression here is that what spectators might consider 'warts', Madonna seems to view as part of her 'liberated', 'powerful' persona. Given Madonna's self-absorption, the banality and pretension of her 'art' and her total control of the project, the film poses tantalising questions about exactly what persona she wanted to project. JH

Dir: Alek Keshishian (tour video dir.: Mark Aldo Miceli); **Prod**: Madonna, Sigurjón Sighvatsson, Jay Roewe, Tim Clawson, Steve Golin; **Phot**: Robert Leacock, Doug Nichol, Christophe Lanzenberg, Marc Reshovsky, Daniel Pearl, Toby Phillips (b/w & colour); **Ed**: Barry Alexander Brown; **Prod Co**: Boy Toy/Miramax Films/Propaganda Films.

Turksib
USSR, 1929 – 57 mins
Viktor A. Turin

Turksib takes its name from the railway constructed to join up two distant
and disparate parts of the new Soviet Union, the parched southern lands
of Turkmenistan (bordering Afghanistan and Iran) and the icy wastes of
Siberia. Echoing successful earlier 1920s documentaries on 'exotic'
cultures like Flaherty's NANOOK OF THE NORTH (1922) and Schoedsack
and Cooper's *Grass* (1925), the film sketches in Turkmenistan's nomadic
peoples, deserts and camels, before focusing on the problems of drought
and transportation. More abundant crops of Turkmenistan's cotton – and
more wool – would feed the recently developed Siberian cotton mills and
other factories, short of raw materials. From these linked problems
emerges the idea of building the 1,445km railway to join the two areas in
an exchange of goods and benefits – the classic structure of exposition
and elaboration of a problem followed by the solution.

The film seeks to give a living sense of the enormity of the Soviet
Union and the diversity of the landscapes and cultures that comprise it –
seen very clearly in the repeated contrast of desert-like Turkmenistan and
frozen Siberia. The building of the railway, which occupies the second
half of the film, *unifies* these distant and different parts of the Soviet
Union and also rationalises the country's economic and social problems:
the development that accompanies the railway brings irrigation,
increasing cotton and food crop production, which feeds productivity in
the Siberian cotton mills and other factories making clothes.
The montage style of the film also has a unifying function, contrasting
but bringing together and fusing disparate elements, particularly in the
lengthy, rapid – at times almost subliminal – combination of rail and
locomotive imagery, cotton spinning and caption titles like 'TURK', 'SIB',
'TURKSIB', '30/1930' (the railway had to be finished in 1930) at the film's
climax. At the same time, the building of the railway is seen as a *war*,
principally against nature and the elements – searing heat and extreme

cold (work stops when the temperature reaches –42 degrees) and the need to blast a path through mountains. But also a 'WAR ON THE PRIMITIVE', against the 'backwardness' of Turkmenistan (part of the Soviet Union only since 1926): the 'primitive' peoples have their first, curious contact with cars and trains, the titles talk of 'civilisation breaking through' and we see people learning to read.

Documentary film enjoyed significant status in 1920s Soviet cinema (see THE FALL OF THE ROMANOV DYNASTY, 1927) and *Turksib* was one of its most popular and influential films. Inside the Soviet Union, it was regarded as a montage film that, unlike Eisenstein's *October* (1928) and *The General Line* (1929) and Dziga Vertov's MAN WITH A MOVIE CAMERA (1929), was immediately intelligible to the masses. In the West, John Grierson singled the film out as the only Soviet production 'that takes us into the future', and Grierson himself was responsible for the English intertitled version. No doubt the widespread Western admiration was because, ideologically speaking, there was little that was obviously 'communistic' about the film: its overall progressive social and economic message, and its focus on a remarkable feat of engineering, intense human labour and the benefits of development – much like Joris Ivens's NEW EARTH (1934), which it surely influenced – were acceptable almost everywhere in the climate of the late 1920s/early 1930s. JH

Dir: Viktor A. Turin; **Scr**: Viktor A. Turin, Yakov Aron, Viktor Shklovsky; **Phot**: Evgeni Slavinsky, Boris Frantsisson (b/w); **Prod Co**: Vostok-kino.

Very Nice, Very Nice
Canada, 1961 – 7 mins
Arthur Lipsett

A film-maker working for the animation unit of the National Film Board of Canada, Arthur Lipsett was a singular talent whose films were at once documentary and experimental. They were composed entirely of found footage and recorded sound, combined in a dense associative montage to create new meaning about the materialism and spiritual emptiness of contemporary life. After beginning his career working on several films by animator Norman McLaren, *Very Nice, Very Nice* was the first in a series of short films, including *Free Fall* (1964) and *A Trip Down Memory Lane* (1965), that Lipsett made for the NFB that became increasingly metaphysical before he became inactive and then committed suicide in 1986. *Very Nice, Very Nice*, which was nominated for an Academy Award for Best Animated Short, perhaps stretched to the limit the NFB's mandate 'to interpret Canada to Canadians and the rest of the world', though the film certainly offers a perspective on contemporary society.

Depicting Western society as alienated and determined by mass culture, advertising, consumerism and militarism, the film is, appropriately, composed almost entirely of still imagery. Similarly, the soundtrack consists of snippets of talk and dialogue gleaned from the waste-baskets and files of other NFB film-makers. The film's critical tone is established from the outset: it begins with a voice saying 'In this city marches an army whose motto is—', accompanied by a shot of a sign with the word 'No' writ large on it and the blare of automobile horns in traffic; this is followed by a shot of a billboard saying only 'Buy', as if it doesn't matter what is being bought and sold, and an image of mannequins all dressed alike. Much of the film depicts contemporary life as crowds, and though some of them (the political rallies, for example) seem purposive, Lipsett isolates a skull displayed by a demonstrator at an anti-nuclear rally in close-up to emphasise the deathly road down which we are collectively travelling. When a voice says 'People who have made no attempt to educate themselves live in a kind of dissolving phantasmagoria of a world', Lipsett uses an anamorphic lens to distort some of the faces.

Several of the still images are given a dynamic quality through camera movement, and one sequence uses the technique of cut-out animation to mock consumer goods. Tellingly, the only images that are actual motion pictures are of a nuclear explosion and a missile blasting off. At one point, Lipsett cuts back and forth so rapidly between a left profile of Soviet leader Nikita Khrushchev and a right profile of American president Dwight D. Eisenhower that they seem to become one head turning or two sides of the same face – a comment on the military-industrial complex that exists on both sides of the Iron Curtain. Frequent drum rolls are accompanied by quick montages, the shots often flashing by too rapidly to be perceived individually but giving a sense of the film's bleak view: one series, for example, includes, among others, images of football players on the field, a political rally, a modern highway cloverleaf and Jewish children being rounded up by Nazis.

In one of the street rallies, someone holds aloft a sign that says 'The end is at hand', which certainly seems to reflect the film's dim view of the way the world is going. The film ends with the comment 'Bravo . . . very nice, very nice' on the soundtrack, its bland compliment a final ironic comment in this savage critique of contemporary culture. BKG

Dir/Ed: Arthur Lipsett (b/w); **Prod**: Colin Low, Tom Daly; **Prod Co**: National Film Board of Canada.

Waiting for Fidel
Canada, 1974 – 58 mins
Michael Rubbo

An Australian film-maker who found a niche at the National Film Board of
Canada with producer Tom Daly, Michael Rubbo made a series of highly
regarded documentaries including *Sad Song of Yellow Skin* (1970) and
Daisy: Story of a Facelift (1982). Before Michael Moore (ROGER AND ME,
1989, BOWLING FOR COLUMBINE, 2002), Nick Broomfield (HEIDI FLEISS:
HOLLYWOOD MADAM, 1995) and Ross McElwee (TIME INDEFINITE, 1993),
Rubbo situated himself within profilmic events, so that both he and his
relation to those events became part of his films' subject. In *Persistent and
Finagling* (1971), for example, he prods the group of middle-class proto-
feminists he is filming to mobilise by utilising the media. With *Waiting for
Fidel*, Rubbo finds the perfect context for his neoliberal persona:
accompanying Joey Smallwood, former Premier of Newfoundland, and
media tycoon Geoff Stirling, 'the socialist and the capitalist', as he
describes them, on a trip to Cuba to interview President Fidel Castro in a
film for the NFB. As is suggested by the title's reference to Samuel Beckett's
quintessential absurdist play *Waiting for Godot*, they never do get to meet
Castro: pre-empted by a state visit from East German leader Erich
Honecker, the closest they get is to film him from the street as he waves
from the motorcade taking Honecker to his plane at the Havana airport –
but Rubbo manages nonetheless to find his real subject in the divergent
opinions of his two fellow travellers towards Cuban society.

While the trio, along with the rest of their film crew, wait for the call
from Fidel, they are taken on government-organised tours of various
aspects of Cuban society, including an urban building project, a school, a
university, a farm, a hospital and the Bay of Pigs invasion site. In their
accommodation at Protocol House 9, where they are served surprisingly
well-appointed meals that contrast sharply with the general poverty of
the country they encounter beyond their compound walls, they debate
the relative pros and cons of capitalist democracy and what one of the

university students happily calls 'the dictatorship of workers'. Smallwood is consistently appreciative of the social innovations and arrangements they discover (such as schools where students spend part of their time working in factories, or housing where rents are a fixed low percentage of the occupants' income), while Stirling is steadfastly sceptical, if not openly hostile, to them. Smallwood spends much of his time preparing thoughtful questions for Castro; Stirling reads books about covert CIA operations and does yoga. Throughout the film, Rubbo provides a retrospective narration, contextualising what we see from his vantage point as a quizzical, open-minded film-maker.

Smallwood is involved in the film because he has hopes of normalising political relations between Cuba and the US, but Stirling's primary concern is profit, as his aim is to sell the rights to the film to an American television network. As a producer working with the NFB, Stirling grows impatient over the delay in meeting with Castro and, according to Rubbo, becomes increasingly annoyed with his approach to directing. Their differences finally come to a head in a heated argument where Stirling insists that they shoot according to a ratio of 3:1 and Rubbo responds that he and the NFB commonly shoot 25:1. Stirling points to the camera and the tape recorder and verbally attacks Rubbo, declaring that professional film-makers would laugh at his approach to documentary. Rubbo responds that value can be measured in ways other than the bottom line, and in the end, Stirling's materialist philosophy seems only to prove Marxist critiques of capitalist fetishism correct, and gives the demure Rubbo the last laugh. BKG

Dir/Ed: Michael Rubbo; **Prod**: Tom Daly, Colin Low, Michael Rubbo; **Phot**: Douglas Kiefer (colour); **Sound**: Jacques Chevigny; **Prod Co**: National Film Board of Canada.

The War Game
UK, 1965 – 48 mins
Peter Watkins

A faux documentary – essentially what we would now call a 'docudrama' – about the results of a possible nuclear attack on Great Britain, *The War Game* was commissioned by the BBC but was considered so powerful that it was banned from television broadcast and not shown until July 1985, despite winning an Academy Award for Best Documentary Feature in 1966. The film's exposure of the superfluity of civil defence planning was a revelation that had the potential to create panic in a Cold War environment only three years after the Cuban Missile Crisis. Watkins's use of documentary techniques to depict a possible future event is so convincing that the BBC issued a public statement regarding its decision declaring that it deemed the film 'to be too horrifying for the medium of broadcasting' – a backhanded compliment that only confirmed Watkins's belief, which he has adamantly maintained throughout his career, that the media (which he ominously refers to as 'the monoform') are controlled by dominant interests that conspire to silence truly alternative perspectives. The banning of the film was controversial to the extent that it was discussed in the Prime Minister's Office and in Parliament. Eventually, *The War Game* was released as a film and got limited distribution in art cinemas and alternative venues such as church halls, as well as being later released on video.

The film begins by positing a flashpoint involving the Chinese invasion of South Vietnam followed by an escalation of tensions leading to NATO's use of tactical nuclear weapons in response to the Soviet invasion of West Germany; the Soviet Union in turn retaliates with a 'limited' nuclear strike against Britain. As events unfold, we see the wholly inadequate attempt by the authorities to evacuate the area in expectation of the attack, and what follows from just one nuclear airburst over the town of Rochester in Kent. A devastating firestorm follows, and then the inevitable breakdown of civilisation as rioting civilians are executed by police and the remaining survivors suffer from extreme trauma and radiation poisoning. In the chilling conclusion, some survivors gather for Christmas dressed in tattered clothing and with radiation burns on their faces, as a priest hand-cranks a turntable to play a recording of 'Silent Night' and traumatised children tell the camera they 'don't want to grow up to be nothin''.

The film combines psuedo-vérité footage of the events leading up to and following the attack, mock interviews with authorities and people on the street, and talking-head shots of actors quoting actual passages from actual official documents. Interspersed among this narrative are statistics and quotations from civil defence policies and government officials that cannot help but seem ludicrous in light of the scenario that Watkins so convincingly shows. As in his other films, Watkins employs non-professional actors and gets the maximum expressive effects from close-ups of their faces. Shot on grainy 16mm and in handheld style, the film melds science fiction and documentary, presenting the unthinkable as real.

By the time *The War Game* was shown on British television, several other docudramas about nuclear holocaust had been broadcast, including *The Day After* (1983) and *Threads* (1984), a BBC production that recalled Watkins's style. In the interim, he continued to explore speculative themes with documentary techniques in *Privilege* (1966), *The Gladiators* (1969) and *Punishment Park* (1971). Watkins has also essayed alternative methods of documentary film-making, as in the case of *The Journey* (1987), a Brechtian exploration of the international implications of nuclear war, more than 14 hours in length and shot in more than a dozen countries with volunteer cast and crew. BKG

Dir/Prod/Scr: Peter Watkins; **Phot**: Peter Bartlett, Peter Suschitsky (b/w); **Ed**: Michael Bradsell; **Sound**: Lou Hanks, Stanley Morcom, Derek Williams; **Prod Co**: BBC Television.

We Are the Lambeth Boys
UK, 1958 – 52 mins
Karel Reisz

We Are the Lambeth Boys, a very accomplished film documenting the activities of Alford House youth club, Lambeth, was the main film in the 'Last Free Cinema' programme shown at London's National Film Theatre in March 1959, and the second (and last) in the Ford-sponsored 'Look at Britain' series (Lindsay Anderson's 1957 *Every Day Except Christmas*, which Karel Reisz co-produced, being the first).

The few years between *Every Day Except Christmas* and *Lambeth Boys* (both shot by Walter Lassally and recorded and edited by John Fletcher) were marked by some important changes in technology. Anderson's film appears to have no direct sound – though there are efforts to fake it – while some sequences in *Lambeth Boys*, when the settings are relatively controllable, make important use of it. A discussion about the death penalty, for example (said to have influenced Jean Rouch's *La Pyramide humaine*, 1959), and a late-night chip shop sequence, rely on direct sound for their effect, while the very start of the film – boys in the cricket nets, girls chatting – seems to celebrate the ability to record direct sound on location. More commonly, though, sound is used – very successfully – in the same creative ways it was used in *Every Day Except Christmas* and most 1930s and wartime documentaries: after a lively club evening and late-night high jinks at the chip shop and a fade to black, the film fades up on early morning at a deserted block of council flats and one boy cycles off on his bike, a train whistle sounds atmospherically (though no train is visible); the narrator's voiceover informs us that 'Being young in the morning is different from being young at night . . .' and a sequence follows in which two boys arrive at school and join in a morning hymn ('The King of Love My Shepherd Is'), the sound (and sentiments) of which are carried over a series of shots of other youth club members at work (seamstress, office worker, butcher's apprentice, post office worker, etc.); the voiceover tells us they are learning a trade, waiting to get married, and so on, and purports to make us privy to their thoughts.

Although *Lambeth Boys* certainly offered fresh images of British society and youth culture, the working-class 'we' of the title is framed for us by the middle-class film-makers, particularly by the voiceover, which, after the capital punishment discussion, questions the adequacy of the teenagers' responses and asks who is helping them to think differently about such issues, before withdrawing with 'just talking about things like this is a beginning – and it's good for a giggle'. Similarly, though the teenagers dance to rock music, the *film's* music is jazz (Johnny

Dankworth), another subtle way in which the film-makers assert their own values in relation to their subjects'. Issues about social class run throughout the film, sometimes clearly intentionally – as in the sequence when the boys play a cricket match in the sumptuous grounds of Mill Hill public school – but at other times it is not always clear how consciously the film-makers have approached such uncomfortable questions. Reisz's debut fiction feature, *Saturday Night and Sunday Morning* (1960), the best film of the so-called 'British New Wave', extended his interest in working-class life and culture. JH

Dir: Karel Reisz; **Prod**: Leon Clore, Robert Adams; **Phot**: Walter Lassally (b/w); **Ed**/**Sound**: John Fletcher; **Music**: Johnny Dankworth; **Narrator**: Jon Rollason; **Prod Co**: Graphic Films/Ford Motor Company.

When the Levees Broke: A Requiem in Four Acts
US, 2006 – 256 mins
Spike Lee

To express his anger over the US government's handling of Hurricane Katrina and the breaching of the levees that flooded New Orleans in August 2005, Spike Lee turned to documentary. He had channelled righteous anger through the documentary form, with the particular status it enjoys, before: *4 Little Girls* (1997) powerfully commemorates the deaths of four children attending Sunday school when an Alabama church was dynamited during the 1960s civil rights struggles. Home Box Office backed Lee's Katrina project – in which race is an important but not overriding issue – agreeing to double the length and budget as Lee began to realise the scale of what he wanted – and perhaps needed – to do.

The film eschews any unifying voiceover commentary, and is experienced primarily as an accumulation of heartbreaking personal testimonies, punctuated by often astonishing newsreel footage of Hurricane Katrina and its aftermath and newly shot material of devastated New Orleans neighbourhoods. Structurally, one disaster gives way to another: Act I looks at the gathering storm, the breaking of the levees and the flooding, ending with deteriorating conditions at the Superdome and the complete failure of the Federal Emergency Management Agency (FEMA); Acts II and III document the chaos of evacuation and dispersal and the beginnings of a return to New Orleans; Act IV explores signs of the city's revival, the continuing failure of FEMA and insurance companies, and the inadequacy of levee defences. Lee closes each act powerfully: Act II, for example, ends with a shocking montage of dead bodies floating in water; Act III concludes with a child's funeral, its inconsolably sobbing mother stumbling away; Act IV ends with the – for the moment calm – watery expanses of the Mississippi River and the Gulf.

Though Lee includes a historical dimension – the failure to secure proper flood defences after the 1927 floods and Hurricane Betsy in 1965

– what comes across forcefully is total disillusion with government agencies and the Bush administration's disregard for its people, black and white. People respond with palpable shock to 'something you'd never think would happen in America', frequently referring to the money spent on Iraq but not on its own citizens. Lee's interviews include political figures (Mayor Ray Nagin, Louisiana Governor Kathleen Blanco), journalists, historians, scientists and celebrities (Harry Belafonte, Kanye West, Wynton Marsalis), and ordinary people caught up in events. Tellingly, several interviewees are overcome with emotion and unable to continue. Perhaps inevitably, the film comes to somewhat contradictory conclusions. Lives are destroyed and the future remains uncertain, but New Orleans retains its soul: a funeral jazz band mournfully 'buries' Katrina, but then shifts, as is the custom, into celebratory mode.

Lee's 'film document' calls itself a 'remembrance' of all Katrina's victims in New Orleans and the Gulf states, all still struggling to 'rebuild, revive and renew in these United States of America'. As a 'requiem', it provides some closure for the dead, and music – not only jazz – is integral to its design. It is a monumental work, in that it addresses events and issues of great importance, at great length: it gives the impression that, in the future, anyone wanting to know what happened in that place, at that time, need look no further than Lee's film. JH

Dir: Spike Lee; **Prod**: Spike Lee, Sam Pollard; **Phot**: Cliff Charles (colour); **Ed**: Sam Pollard, Geeta Gandbhir, Nancy Novack; **Music**: Terence Blanchard; **Prod Co**: 40 Acres and A Mule Filmworks/Home Box Office.

Why We Fight 1: Prelude to War
US, 1943 – 53 mins
Frank Capra

When the US entered World War II, the government was aware that it had to overcome a pronounced isolationist sentiment that had prevailed during the 1930s. As part of its effort to mobilise Americans for the war, Frank Capra, one of the most popular Hollywood directors of the pre-war era, was given an officer's commission and charged with the task of making a series of documentary films that, as instructed by Chief of Staff General George C. Marshall, would explain to troops the reasons 'as to the causes, the events, leading up to our entry into the war and the principles for which we are fighting'. Major Capra went on to produce a number of war-related documentaries, including a series of seven films on *Why We Fight* (1941–5, several co-directed by another Hollywood director, Anatole Litvak). They were viewed as part of military training by millions of US and Allied military personnel, becoming some of the most influential and effective propaganda films ('information films', as the series describes itself in the opening credits) in the history of documentary.

Prelude to War, the first film in the series, cannily relies on the iconography of patriotism and righteous sentiment, setting the tone for the films to follow. Capra brought to *Prelude to War* his ability to touch his viewers' emotions by invoking American cultural myths, as demonstrated so successfully in his earlier Hollywood hits *It Happened One Night* (1934), *Mr Deeds Goes to Town* (1936) and *Mr Smith Goes to Washington* (1939). As in these films, Capra creates a folksy populist vision that in this case spoke effectively to the swelling ranks of inductees as the country geared up for war on several fronts. *Prelude to War* addresses the viewer as an American Everyman, a conceit literalised as the imaginary 'John Q. Public' in the voiceover narration spoken by Hollywood actor Walter Huston, whose image was already associated with American patriotism through his portrayal of the President of the

United States in two films, *Gabriel over the White House* (1933) and *The Tunnel* (1935), the former characterising him as a spiritually reborn New-Dealer fighting for social reform.

Prelude's use of Huston, who brings a perfect tone of common-sense righteous indignation to his narration, is indicative of the film's overall effective mix of exhortatory commentary with footage culled from newsreels, fiction films and documentaries from other nations. Capra relies heavily on shots from Leni Riefenstahl's pro-Nazi film TRIUMPH OF THE WILL (1935), but recontextualises the footage by contrasting it with potent images of Americana in which American children laugh and play in the sun instead of donning gasmasks and rehearsing trench warfare, to suggest that its depiction of what the commentary refers to as the 'inbred German love of regimentation' is ghastly rather than glorious. Original footage was shot by Robert Flaherty, whose approach to film-making was markedly different from that of the Hollywood director, but here they blend perfectly. The film offers a stark contrast between what it describes as a slave world and a free world ('it's us or them, the chips are down'), reinforced with graphic animated sequences created by the Walt Disney Studios that show maps of the Axis countries spreading inky darkness across the world. Such images effectively explained the war to all the John Qs who were now in uniform. *Prelude*'s self-righteousness builds to the point of referring to the Japanese as Hitler's 'buck-toothed pals' and concludes with an image of the Axis leaders, Hitler, Mussolini and Hirohito, as Huston exhorts us to 'Remember their faces . . . If you ever meet them, don't hesitate.' BKG

Dir/Scr: Frank Capra, Anatole Litvak; **Prod**: Julius J. Epstein, Philip G. Epstein, Robert Heller; **Phot**: Robert J. Flaherty (b/w); **Ed**: William Hornbeck; **Music**: Hugo Friedhofer, Leigh Harline, Arthur Lange, Cyril J. Mockridge, Alfred Newman, David Raksin; **Narrator**: Walter Huston; **Prod Co**: US War Department.

Woodstock
US, 1970 – 184 mins (Director's Cut, 1994, 228 mins)
Michael Wadleigh

The mother of all concert films and winner of the Academy Award for Best Documentary Feature, *Woodstock* chronicles the Woodstock Music and Art Fair ('three days of peace and music') held at Max Yasgur's 600-acre farm in the town of Bethel near Woodstock, New York, from 15–18 August 1969. Attended by an unexpectedly large crowd of close to half a million people, the festival proceeded peacefully despite inadequate toilet facilities, insufficient supplies and a rainstorm that turned the fields into muddy bogs. The event was regarded as the pinnacle of the hippie movement (immortalised in Joni Mitchell's song 'Woodstock'), an image of harmonious pastoral community that was shattered only four months later at another epic musical event in December, the Rolling Stones' free concert at Altamont Speedway in northern California, which culminated in violence and the murder of a fan in the crowd – captured in *Gimme Shelter* (1970) by Albert and David Maysles (SALESMAN, 1968, GREY GARDENS, 1975).

Woodstock includes sequences of the performances, interviews with the organisers and the response of local citizens, and montages of people listening to the music, dancing, bathing, smoking marijuana and swimming in the nude. Among the musical artists whose performances are captured in the film are Crosby, Stills and Nash, Richie Havens, Joan Baez, The Who, Joe Cocker and Country Joe and the Fish. (Artists who performed at Woodstock but do not appear in the film include The Grateful Dead, Creedence Clearwater Revival, Jefferson Airplane and Janis Joplin, though the latter two make it into the Director's Cut.) The five cameras that filmed the event combine shots of great intimacy and images of impressive scope: on the one hand, in close-ups taken from under Richie Havens's face as he sings, we can see the roof of his mouth and then, shown in profile after he finishes, sweat dripping from his nose; on the other, long shots from the stage show a sea of people stretching as far as the eye can see, and helicopter shots sweeping across the ground emphasise the enormity of the crowd. The film periodically employs a split screen, occasionally even becoming a triptych, as if to suggest the impossibility of capturing an event of such epic scale within one frame.

The film often emphasises the idea of the generation gap, casting the 'Woodstock nation' as an alternative to the bourgeois and outdated adult world. Often prodded by the film-makers, local residents and shopkeepers either express moral outrage about the behaviour of the young people, or see them as polite and merely having fun. Three nuns at the festival, one of whom flashes a peace sign at the camera, are shown in a brief freeze-frame, suggesting the ephemeral utopian potential signified by Woodstock. Similarly, much of the music included in the film protests the Vietnam War. Hendrix's riveting performance of 'The Star-Spangled Banner', its melodic beauty alternating with screaming electronic distortion, perfectly captured the social and political tensions of the era.

Shot on 16mm, *Woodstock* was edited from more than 1,210 hours of footage by Thelma Schoonmaker, who was nominated for an Academy Award (Schoonmaker also edited numerous Martin Scorsese films, including *The Last Waltz*, 1978, the acclaimed documentary about The Band). Documentary films have also been made about the follow-up Woodstock concerts in 1994 and 1999, the most interesting of which is *My Generation* (2000) by Barbara Kopple (see HARLAN COUNTY USA, 1976), which contrasts all three events and focuses on the changing values that informed them. BKG

Dir: Michael Wadleigh; **Prod**: Bob Maurice; **Phot**: Michael Wadleigh, David Myers, Richard Pearce, Donald Lenzer, Michael Margetts, Al Wertheimer (colour); **Ed**: Michael Wadleigh, Martin Scorsese, Stan Warnow, Jere Huggins, Yeu-Bun Yee, Thelma Schoonmaker; **Sound and Music Ed**: Larry Johnson (*et al.*); **Prod Co**: Wadleigh-Maurice Ltd.

Zidane: A 21st Century Portrait
(*Zidane: un portrait du 21ième siècle*)
France/Iceland, 2006 – 90 mins
Douglas Gordon, Philippe Parreno

Several films in this volume – see, for example, THE ACT OF SEEING WITH ONE'S OWN EYES (1971), LOST LOST LOST (1976), NEWS FROM HOME (1976) – blur the boundaries between 'documentary' and 'avant-garde' film, but *Zidane* pushes that blurring further: though distributed theatrically, it is easy to imagine it as a video installation. The film's co-directors are both best known as film/video gallery artists (Douglas Gordon being best known for *24 Hour Psycho* – Hitchcock's *Psycho* slowed down to two frames per second).

Zidane was filmed at a football match between Real Madrid and Villareal in Madrid on 23 April 2005; it used seventeen cameras and unfolds in real time. It is nothing like a conventional documentary about football or a football player: the cameras focus on one player, Zinédine Zidane, for the entire match. It may seem counter-intuitive to make a film about a team sport that systematically excludes all but one player, even one considered the world's greatest footballer – and, moreover, a determinedly reflexive film as fascinated by the fluid boundary between photographic representation and abstraction (are we looking at Zidane's feet, or at pixels?), and the differences between high- and low-definition images, as by football. Whether this is a film for football fans or not, it does provide what the title suggests, a portrait of Zidane that tries to capture the 'flow' of the player rather than the 'flow' of the game. The film gets 'inside' Zidane by closely observing his 'outside' – facial expression, body language, physical tics (for example, his characteristic toe-stubbing/dragging movement) and, of course, moments of sublime soccer action. The perception of Zidane's subjectivity is bolstered by intermittent subtitles that make us privy to his thoughts and impressions, such as his fragmentary memory of games or his selective perception of game noise (enhanced by the film's sound

design, which weaves music with different levels of crowd noise and grunts, sighs, intakes of breath).

To be precise, the film does occasionally cut to other material, such as the production's control room, empty areas of the stadium, a central montage of other world events, large and small, taking place the same day and bits of televised recording of the match (reminding us how single-mindedly television coverage follows the ball, with limited context, constantly describing and interpreting). There is none of that here: we rarely see how the ball comes to Zidane, or what happens after he passes it on. Even the fracas that results in Zidane being sent off – ending the film before the final whistle – is only glimpsed in his facial expressions and gestures. It is not quite true that we only see Zidane: the presence of his *galácticos* teammates and, indeed, the opposition, on screen or off, is readable in his spontaneous looks and reactions.

The film is intended – and works – as a paean to Zidane's rich talent, but the near-exclusive focus on him suggests some odd undercurrents. His grizzled, unshaven, tough looks and his fixed, undemonstrative expression (except for a revealing moment when he shares a joke with Roberto Carlos and breaks into a wide smile), plus his sweating, bald patch, age, his implied solitariness and the amount of time spent running around to no obvious purpose, generate a mood of fatuousness and fatigue: is this all there is, running about after a ball? Why go through all this nonsense? A year later, Zidane was sent off for another violent incident, in the World Cup, and retired. Perhaps Parreno was right when he called *Zidane* 'an exercise in solitude'. IH

Dir/Scr: Douglas Gordon, Philippe Parreno; **Prod**: Sigurjón Sighvatsson, Anna Vaney, Victorien Vaney; **Phot**: Darius Khondji (*et al.*) (colour); **Ed**: Hervé Schneid; **Music**: Mogwaï; **Prod Co**: Anna Lena Films (France)/Naflastrengir (Iceland), with Arte France Cinéma/Love Streams Productions Agnès B.

References

Bazin, André, 'Le Cinéma et l'exploration', in *Qu'est ce que le cinema 1: ontologie et langage* (Paris: Éditions du Cerf, 1958), translated in André Bazin, *What Is Cinema? Volume 1* (ed. and trans. Hugh Gray) (Berkeley: University of California Press, 1967).

—— , '*Farrebique*, or the Paradox of Realism', in André Bazin, *Bazin at Work: Major Essays and Reviews from the Forties and Fifties* (ed. Bert Cardullo) (New York and London: Routledge, 1997).

Brik, Osip *et al.*, 'The *Lef* Ring: Comrades! A Clash of Views!', in Richard Taylor and Ian Christie, *The Film Factory: Russian and Soviet Cinema in Documents 1896–1939* (London and New York: Routledge, 1988).

Butler, Judith, *Gender Trouble: Feminism and the Subversion of Identity* (London and New York: Routledge, 1990).

Citron, Michelle, 'Concerning *Daughter Rite*', *Journal of Film and Video* vol. 38 no. 3–4 (Summer/Autumn 1986).

Corner, John, *The Art of Record: A Critical Introduction to Documentary* (Manchester and New York: Manchester University Press, 1996).

Gorki, Maxim, Review of the Lumière programme. Appendix 2 in Jay Leyda, *Kino: A History of Russian and Soviet Film* (London: Allen & Unwin, 3rd edn. 1983).

Hall, Stuart, 'Songs of Handsworth praise', *Guardian*, 15 January 1987 (discussed in Corner, *Art of Record*).

Jacobson, Harlan, 'Michael and Me', *Film Comment* vol. 25 no. 6 (November–December 1989).

James, David E., 'Film Diary/Diary Film: Practice and Product in *Walden*', in David E. James (ed.), *To Free the Cinema: Jonas Mekas and the New York Underground* (Princeton, NJ: Princeton University Press, 1992).

Kael, Pauline, 'Melodrama/Cartoon/Mess', *New Yorker*, January 1990.

Leyda, Jay, *Kino: A History of the Russian and Soviet Film* (New York: Collier Books, 1973).

McElwee, Ross, 'When the Personal Becomes Political', an interview with Ross McElwee by Cynthia Lucia, *Cineaste* vol. 20 no. 2 (December 1993).

Mamber, Stephen, *Cinema Verite in America: Studies in Uncontrolled Documentary* (Cambridge, MA, and London: MIT Press, 1974).

Mekas, Jonas, 'The Diary Film', in P Adams Sitney (ed.), *The Avant-Garde Film* (New York: New York University Press, 1978).

Nichols, Bill, *Introduction to Documentary* (Bloomington and Indianapolis: Indiana University Press, 2001).

Rosenbaum, Jonathan, '*David Holzman's Diary*/*My Girlfriend's Wedding*: Historical Artifacts of the Past and Present' (booklet accompanying Second Run 2006 DVD edition of *David Holzman's Diary*/*My Girlfriend's Wedding*).

Rotha, Paul, *Documentary Film* (London: Faber & Faber, 1936).

—— , *The Film till Now* (London: Spring Books, rev. edn., 1967).

Rushdie, Salman, 'Songs doesn't know the score', *Guardian*, 12 January 1987 (discussed in Corner, *Art of Record*).

Russell, Patrick, *100 British Documentaries* (London: BFI, 2007).

Thomson, David, *The New Biographical Dictionary of Film* (London: Little, Brown, 4th edn. 2003).

Varda, Agnès, 'The Modest Gesture of the Filmmaker: An Interview with Agnès Varda', by Melissa Anderson, *Cineaste* vol. 26 no. 4 (2001).

Winston, Brian, *Claiming the Real* (London: BFI, 1995).

Wood, Jason, *100 American Independent Films* (London: BFI, 2004).

Select Bibliography

Aitken, Ian (ed.), *Encyclopedia of Documentary Film* (New York and London: Routledge, 2005).

Bakker, Kees (ed.), *Joris Ivens and the Documentary Context* (Amsterdam: Amsterdam University Press, 1999).

Barnouw, Eric, *Documentary: A History of the Non-Fiction Film* (Oxford: Oxford University Press, rev. edn. 1993).

Barsam, Richard Meran (ed.), *Nonfiction Film Theory and Criticism* (New York: E. P. Dutton, 1976).

—— , *Nonfiction Film: A Critical History* (Bloomington and Indiana: Indiana University Press, rev. edn. 1992).

Beattie, Keith, *Documentary Screens* (Basingstoke and New York: Palgrave Macmillan, 2004).

Bruzzi, Stella, *New Documentary* (London and New York: Routledge, 2000, 2nd edn. 2006).

Corner, John, *The Art of Record* (Manchester: Manchester University Press, 1996, 2nd edn. 2006).

Delmar, Rosalind, *Joris Ivens: 50 Years of Film-Making* (London: BFI, 1979).

Eaton, Mick (ed.), *Anthropology, Reality, Cinema: The Films of Jean Rouch* (London: BFI, 1979).

Ellis, Jack C., *The Documentary Idea: A Critical History of English-Language Documentary Film and Video* (Englewood Cliffs, NJ: Prentice-Hall, 1989).

Grant, Barry Keith, *Voyages of Discovery: The Films of Frederick Wiseman* (Urbana: University of Illinois Press, 1992).

Grant, Barry Keith, and Jeannette Sloniowski (eds), *Documenting the Documentary: Close Readings of Documentary Film and Video* (Detroit, MI: Wayne State University Press, 1998).

Grierson, John, *Grierson on Documentary* (ed. Forsyth Hardy) (Berkeley: University of California Press, 1966).

Heider, Karl, *Ethnographic Film* (Austin: University of Texas Press, 1973).

Jacobs, Lewis (ed.), *The Documentary Tradition* (New York: Norton, rev. edn. 1979).

Lane Jim, *The Autobiographical Documentary in America* (Madison: University of Wisconsin Press, 2002).

Levin, G. Roy, *Documentary Explorations: 15 Interviews with Film-Makers* (Garden City, NY: Anchor Doubleday, 1971).

Lovell, Alan, and Jim Hillier, *Studies in Documentary* (London: BFI/New York: Viking Press, 1972).

Macdonald, Kevin, and Mark Cousins (eds), *Imagining Reality: The Faber Book of Documentary* (London and Boston: Faber & Faber, 1996, 2nd edn. 2005).

Mamber, Stephen, *Cinema Verite in America: Studies in Uncontrolled Documentary* (Cambridge, MA, and London: MIT Press, 1974).

Marcorelles, Louis, *Living Cinema: New Directions in Contemporary Film-Making* (trans. Isabel Quigly) (London: George Allen & Unwin, 1973).

Nichols, Bill, *Representing Reality* (Bloomington and Indianapolis: Indiana University Press, 1991).

——, *Blurred Boundaries* (Bloomington and Indianapolis: Indiana University Press, 1994).

——, *Introduction to Documentary* (Bloomington and Indianapolis: Indiana University Press, 2001).

Paget, Derek, *True Stories? Documentary Drama on Radio, Screen and Stage* (Manchester: Manchester University Press, 1990).

——, *No Other Way to Tell It: Dramadoc/Docudrama on Television* (Manchester: Manchester University Press, 1998).

Plantinga, Carl, *Rhetoric and Representation in Nonfiction Film* (Cambridge: Cambridge University Press, 1997).

Rabinowitz, Paula, *They Must Be Represented: The Politics of Documentary* (New York and London: Verso, 1994).

Renov, Michael (ed.), *Theorising Documentary* (New York and London: Routledge, 1993).

——, *The Subject of Documentary* (Minneapolis: University of Minnesota Press, 2004).

Roscoe, Jane, and Craig Hight, *Faking It: Mock-Documentary and the Subversion of Factuality* (Manchester: Manchester University Press, 2001).

Rosenthal, Alan (ed.), *The New Documentary in Action* (Berkeley: University of California Press, 1971).

——, *The Documentary Conscience: A Casebook in Film Making* (Berkeley: University of California Press, 1980).

—— (ed.), *New Challenges for Documentary* (Berkeley: University of California Press, 1998).

Rotha, Paul, *Documentary Film* (London: Faber & Faber, 1936/New York: Norton, 1939).

——, *Documentary Diary: An Informal History of the British Documentary Film, 1928–1939* (London: Secker & Warburg, 1973).

Rothman, William, *Documentary Film Classics* (Cambridge and New York: Cambridge University Press, 1997).

Rouch, Jean, *Ciné-ethnography* (ed. and trans. Steven Feld) (Minneapolis and London: University of Minnesota Press, 2003).

Russell, Patrick, *100 British Documentaries* (London: BFI, 2007).

Vaughan, Dai, *For Documentary: Twelve Essays* (Berkeley: University of California Press, 1999).

Ward, Paul, *Documentary: The Margins of Reality* (London: Wallflower Press, 2005).

Warren, Charles (ed.), *Beyond Document: Essays on Nonfiction Film* (Hanover, NH, and London: Wesleyan University Press/University Press of New England, 1996).

Waugh, Thomas (ed.), *'Show Us Life': Toward a History and Aesthetics of the Committed Documentary* (Metuchen, NJ, and London: Scarecrow Press, 1984).

Winston, Brian, *Claiming the Real: The Documentary Film Revisited* (London: BFI, 1995).

——, *Lies, Damn Lies and Documentaries* (London: BFI, 2000).

Index

This Index aspires to be reasonably comprehensive as regards film titles, names of principal personnel involved in the making of particular films, organisations, companies, etc. referred to in the entries; it does not include names mentioned only in the credits. Non-film names (for example, Allende, Salvador) are included when crucial to a film's content or context. Additionally, but selectively, major motifs, conventions, currents, fashions and movements in the field of documentary film are included in the Index.

Page numbers in *italics* denote illustrations; those in **bold** indicate detailed analysis

4 Little Girls (1997) 239
11th Hour, The (2007) 110, 136
16mm 23, 29, 32, 107, 121, 235, 244
24 Hour Psycho (1993) 245
79 Primaveras (*79 Springs*) (1969) 60, 93, 103, **194–5**
79 Springs see *79 Primaveras*
100 American Independent Films 3
100 British Documentaries 3, 5, 158

ABC-TV 80, 178
À bout de souffle (1960) 44
À Propos de Nice (1930) **7–9**

abstract/abstraction 10, 16, 128, 155, 245
ACTT 78
Academy Award 20, 30, 84, 103, 107, 136, 230, 234, 243, 244
Acadie, l'Acadie, L' (1971) 182
Act of Seeing with One's Own Eyes, The (1971) **10–11**, 122, 149, 154, 245
Actualités Mondiales 165
Âge d'or, L' (1930) 97
agitprop 164, 194
Aguirre, The Wrath of God (1972) 75
Aitken, Ian 1
Akerman, Chantal 154–5
All My Life (1966) 149

All You Need Is Cash – The Rutles (1978) 214
Allende, Salvador 14–15
Alvarez, Santiago 60, 93, 194–5
Amator (1979) 208
America Is Hard to See (1970) 102
American Dream (1990) 84
An American Family (1973) 139
And Life Goes On (1992) 35
Anderson, Lindsay 51, 189, 236
Animalicious (1999) 27
animation 19, 194, 230, 242
Anka, Paul 118–20
Anstey, Edgar 96, 159

Anthology Film Archives 121

archival/archive 12, 19, 59, 102–3, 105–6, 116, 143, 166, 183, 194, 199, 206

Ashur, Geri 42

Atomic Café, The (1982) **12–13**, 60

Attille, Martina 78

Auden, W. H. 37

autobiographical film 35, 45, 122, 143, 216, 220

avant-garde film 5, 121, 122, 128, 143, 149, 154, 195, 245

Baez, Joan 51

Baillie, Bruce 149

Balcon, Michael 130

Baraka (1992) 110

Baray-e Azadi see *For Freedom*

Baseball (1994) 105

batalla de Chile, La see *The Battle of Chile*

Battle of Algiers, The (1965) 66

Battle of Chile, The (*La batalla de Chile*) (1975–9) **14–15**, 67

Battle of San Pietro, The (1945) 114

Bazin, André 61, 63, 109

BBC 12, 22, 49, 53, 100, 234, 235

Beale, Edith Bouvier ('Big Edie') 73–4

Beale, Edie ('Little Edie') 73–4

Beales of Grey Gardens, The (2006) 74

Beatty, Clyde 65

Beatty, Warren 225–6

Beckett, Samuel 232

Behind the Rent Strike (1974) 87

Bergman, Ingmar 138

Berlin: Die Sinfonie der Großstadt see *Berlin: Symphony of a Great City*

Berlin: Symphony of a Great City (*Berlin: Die Sinfonie der Großstadt*) (1927) 8, **16–18**, 110, 128, 129, 133, 144, 170

Best in Show (2000) 214

Biberman, Herbert 84

Biggie and Tupac (2002) 87

Biquefarre (1983) 63

Black Audio Film Collective 78

Blackwood, Maureen 78

Blake, William 79, 195

Blaue Licht, Das (*The Blue Light*) (1930) 222

Blood of the Beasts see *Le Sang des bêtes*

Botes, Costa 68

Bouquet, Michel 162

Bowling for Columbine (2002) **19–20**, 29, 54, 83, 86, 103, 164, 183, 232

Boyfriend, The (1971) 21

Brakhage, Stan 10–11, 122, 149, 154, 202

Brand upon the Brain (2006) 143

Brault, Michel 181–2

Brayne, William 180

Breaking It up at the Museum (1960) 174

Breathless (1983) 44

Brecht, Bertolt 153, 170

Brennan, Paul 185–6

Bricklayer (1973) 208

Bridge, The (1928) 151

Bridges-Go-Round (1958) 174

Brief History of Time, A (1991) 64

Brig, The (1964) 121

Bright Leaves (2003) 217

Brik, Osip 59

British Commercial Gas Association 96

British Picture: Portrait of an Enfant Terrible, A (1989) **21–2**

British Sounds (1969) **23–4**, 83, 195, 206

Britten, Benjamin 37

Broadway Boogie Woogie (Mondrian) (1943) 16

Broomfield, Nick 19, 87–8, 183, 232

Brussels Film Loops (1958) 174

Buñuel, Luis 97–8, 189

Burns, Ken 105–6

Bus 174 (2002) **25–6**

Butler, Judith 168

Caine, Rick 184

Camera Buff see *Amator*

Cane Toads: An Unnatural History (1988) **27–8**

Cannes Film Festival 20, 162, 202

Capra, Frank 114, 164, 170, 222, 241–2

Capturing the Friedmans (2003) 100

Careful (1992) 143

Carné, Marcel 170

Carson, L. M. Kit 44

Castro, Fidel 232

Castro Street (1966) 149

Cavalcanti, Alberto 16, 37, 128, 196, 197

Cayrol, Jean 162

CBS Reports: Harvest of Shame see *Harvest of Shame*

Chabrol, Claude 165

Chagrin et la pitié, Le (*The Sorrow and the Pity*) (1968) **29–31**, 165

Chalmers, Thomas 173

Channel 4 Television 78

Chat dans le sac, Le (1964) 182

Chelovek s kino-apparatom see *The Man with a Movie Camera*

Chevalier, Maurice 30, 166

Chopra, Joyce 80–1

Christo's Valley Curtain (1974) 185

Chronicle of a Summer see *Chronique d'un été*

Chronique d'un été (*Chronicle of a Summer*) (1961) 29, **32–4**, 55, 56, 87, 93, 176, 182, 216

Churchill, Joan 87

cinéma direct 181–2

cinéma vérité/vérité 19, 29, 32, 55, 56, 68, 87, 89, 93, 118, 126, 135, 163, 174, 175, 176, 182, 183

Cinématographe, La 124

City of God (2002) 25

City of Gold (1957) 106

city symphony film 7, 16, 110, 128–9, 133, 144, 170, 175

Civil War, The (1990) 105

Clarke, Shirley 174, 176

Cléo de 5 à 7 (1962) 70

Clooney, George 85

Close-Up (1990) **35–6**, 202

Clouzot, Henri-Georges 202

Coal Face (1935) **37–8**, 94, 196

Cocteau, Jean 165

Color Adjustment (1992) 220

Communist Manifesto, The 24

compilation film 59, 60, 102, 116, 165, 194

Connection, The (1962) 174

Connor, Bruce 10, 149

Contemporary Historians, Inc. 204

Cool World, The (1964) 174

Cooper, Merian C. 107, 145, 227

Corner, John 38

Corridor (1970) 149

Cousteau, Jacques 136

Coutant, André 32

Coutant camera 29, 32

Cozarinsky, Edgardo 165–6

Crisis: Behind a Presidential Commitment (1963) 23, 29, 32, **39–41**, 42, 55, 80, 83, 86, 93, 102, 174, 178, 179, 186, 216, 219

crisis structure 40, 186

Crowther, Bosley 148

Cyclist, The (1989) 35

Czech New Wave 181

Daisy: Story of a Facelift (1982) 232

Daly, Tom 118, 232

Dangling Participle (1970) 149

Dankworth, Johnny 238

Daughter Rite (1979) **42–3**, 100, 116

David Holzman's Diary (1967) **44–5**, 202, 216

Davis, Peter 103

Day After, The (1983) 235

de Antonio, Emile 29, 60, 102–4, 116

Dead Birds (1965) **46–7**, 126, 146, 206

Death of a Salesman
(play) (1958) 186
Deckie Learner (1965)
160
Demy, Jacques 63
Dengler, Dieter 76
Detour (1945) 143
Deux Ex (1971) 10
Diaries (1971–6) 216
*Diaries, Notes and
Sketches* (1969)
122
diary film 49, 107,
121–2, 216
Diary for Timothy, A
(1945) **48–50**, 61,
208
Dickson, W. K. L. 123
direct cinema 23, 39–41,
42–3, 44–5, 51, 55,
67, 83, 89, 93, 102,
122, 174, 175, 179,
216, 225 see also
cinéma direct; fly-
on-the-wall
documentary;
observational
cinema
Disney, Walt 27, 242
docudrama/documentary
drama/drama
documentary 2, 48,
182, 234–5
Documentary Film (1936)
196, 198
Dont Look Back (1967)
41, **51–3**, 225
Dovzhenko, Alexander
59
Dream of Light, The see
El sol del membrillo

Dreaming Rivers (1988)
78
Drew, Robert 32, 39, 86,
177–8
Drew Associates 39, 80,
177–8, 186, 226
Dreyer, Carl Theodor 143
Drifters (1929) 158, 159
Du côté de la côte (1958)
70
Dudow, Slatan 153, 170
Dugum Dani tribe 46–7
Dylan, Bob 51–3, 225
Dziga Vertov Group 23,
135

Ebert, Roger 89
Éclair camera 29, 32
Edison, Thomas Alva 123
Egli, Sam 75
Eisenstein, Sergei M. 17,
59, 67, 228
Eisler, Hanns 153, 162
Elephant Boy (1937)
132
Elton, Arthur 96
*Emperor's Naked Army
Marches On, The*
(1987) **54–5**, 142
Empire Marketing Board
130, 196
Empire Windrush 79
*Encyclopedia of
Documentary Film* 1
End of St Petersburg, The
(1927) 59
Epstein, Rob 221
Erice, Victor 202–3
Estes, Richard 155
Ethnic Notions (1986)
220

ethnographic film 46,
107, 126, 135, 146,
206
Être et avoir (2002) **56–8**
Evans, Walker 86, 171
*Every Day Except
Christmas* (1957)
236, 237
Every Little Thing see *La
Moindre des choses*
Eye of Vichy, The see
L'Oeil de Vichy
Eyes (1971) 10

Fahrenheit 9/11 (1994)
19, 183
*Fall of the Romanov
Dynasty, The* (1927)
29, 57, **59–60**, 93,
102, 133, 165, 194,
228
Fallen Champ (1993) 84
Family, The (1974) 139
Farm Security
Administration 86
*Farrebique, ou les
quatres saisons*
(1946) 33, **61–3**,
99, 169
*Fast, Cheap and Out of
Control* (1997)
64–5
Feed (1992) 13
Ferno, John 204
Fields, Gracie 95
Film and Photo League
147, 172
Film Culture 121
Film Society, The 37, 128
Film Till Now, The (1930)
196

Fires Were Started (1943) 48

First Love (1974) 208

Fitzcarraldo (1982) 75

Flaherty, Robert 38, 47, 130, 145–6, 196, 197, 227, 242

Fleiss, Heidi 87–8

Fletcher, John 237

fly-on-the-wall documentary 44, 58, 139, 219

Fog of War, The (2003) 64

Fonda, Jane 226

For Freedom (1979) 15, **66–7**

Ford, John 114

Forgotten Silver (1995) **68–9**

Forman, Milos 181

Formby, George 95

Forster, E. M. 49

Fotoamator (1998) 161

found footage 149, 194–5, 230

Four Hundred Million, The (1938) 205

France Actualités 165

Franju, Georges 187–9

Free Cinema 189, 236

Free Fall (1964) 230

Freeman, Morgan 137

French New Wave 44

Freud (1962) 115

Fricke, Ron 110

Friendly, Fred 85

From a Night Porter's Point of View (1977) 208

Frontier Films 102, 147, 172, 204

Fuller, Sam 218

Gabriel over the White House (1933) 242

Gadające głowy see *Talking Heads*

Gai savoir, Le (1968) 23

Gardner, Robert 46–7

Gates of Heaven, The (1980) 64

Gaumont British 130

Gellhorn, Martha 205

Gender Trouble 168

General Line, The (1929) 228

German Expressionism 143

Getino, Octavio 93

Gimme Shelter (1970) 73, 185, 215, 243

Ginsberg, Allen 53, 122

Gladiators, The (1969) 235

Glâneurs et la glâneuse, Les (*The Gleaners and I*) (2000) **70–2**, 190

Glass, Philip 110–11, 212

Glass Menagerie, The (1944) 73

Gleaners and I, The see *Les Glâneurs et la glâneuse*

Godard, Jean-Luc 23–4, 32, 44, 135, 155, 195, 206

Goodnight and Good Luck (2005) 85

Gorki, Maxim 125

Goskino 59

GPO Film Unit 37, 196

Granton Trawler (1934) 159

Grass (1925) 107, 145, 227

Gray, Lorraine 116

Great Road, The (1927) 59

Greater London Council 78

Grey Gardens (1975) **73–4**, 138, 165, 243

Grierson, John 2, 17, 69, 123, 130, 159, 196, 198, 228

Grierson, Ruby 94

Griffith, D. W. 68, 145

Grigsby, Michael 169

Grizzly Man (2005) **75–7**, 112

Groulx, Gilles 182

Guerre d'un seul homme, La see *One Man's War*

Guest, Christopher 214–15

Guevara, Che 93

Guitry, Sacha 165

Guns of the Trees (1964) 121

Guzmán, Patricio 14–15

Hall, Stuart 79

Hamptons, The (2002) 84

handheld camera 27, 32, 70, 153, 177, 181, 215, 225, 235

Handsworth Songs (1986) **78–9**

Happy Mother's Day, A
(1963) 32, 42,
80–1
Hara, Kazuo 55
Harlan County USA
(1976) **82–4**, 244
Harvest of Shame (1960)
39, **85–6**
Heart of Spain (1937) 147
Heart of the World
(2000) 143
Hearts and Minds (1974)
103
Hedouin, Pierre Edmond
70
Heider, Karl 46
*Heidi Fleiss: Hollywood
Madam* (1995) 19,
87–8, 183, 232
Hellman, Lillian 204
Hemingway, Ernest 205
Henricksen, Leonardo
14–15
Heroes of the North Sea
(1925) 159
Herzog, Werner 75–6,
112–13
Heston, Charlton 19–20,
54
Heyerdahl, Thor 107
*History of Postwar Japan
as Told by a Bar
Hostess, The* (1970)
55
Hitchcock, Alfred 44,
191
Hitler, Adolf 222–4
Hole in the Head, A
(1959) 178
Holliday, Jason 174
Home Box Office 239

home movies 21–2,
42–3, 64, 100, 101,
183, 216
*Homicide: Life on the
Street* (1997–9) 84
Hoop Dreams (1994)
89–91
Hoop Dreams Reunion
(1995) 91
Hora de los hornos, La
see *The Hour of the
Furnaces*
Hôtel des Invalides (1951)
189
Hôtel Terminus (1988)
31
*Hour of the Furnaces,
The* (*La hora de los
hornos*) (1968) 15,
92–3, 194
House Un-American
Activities
Committee 205
Housing Problems (1935)
37, **94–6**, 196
Hugenberg, Alfred 222
Humphrey, Hubert 177
Hurdes, Las (*Land
without Bread*)
(1933) **97–9**, 188
*Hurdes, Land of Legend,
Las* (1922) 97
Hurley, Frank 107
Hurwitz, Leo 147, 172
Huston, John 114–15
Huston, Walter 114,
241

I for India (2005) 43,
100–1

ICAIC (Instituto Cubano
del Arte y Industria
Cinematográficos)
15, 194
Idle, Eric 214
Imamura, Shohei 55
Immemory (CD-Rom)
(1998) 191
In Bed with Madonna
see *Truth or Dare*
*In Search of Unreturned
Soldiers* (1971) 55
In the Land of the Deaf
see *Le Pays des
sourds*
In the Year of the Pig
(1968) 15, 29, 60,
102–4, 116, 165,
194
INA (Institut National de
l'Audiovisuel) 166
Inconvenient Truth, An
(2006) 136
Industrial Britain (1931)
38, 130, 196, 198
interviews 56, 64, 68,
78, 85, 90, 102,
103, 105, 116, 163,
167, 199, 200, 206,
207, 211, 235
Intolerance (1916) 68
It Happened One Night
(1934) 241
Ivens, Joris 96, 128, 147,
151–3, 204–5, 229

Jablonsky, Dariusz 161
Jackson, Peter 68–9
Jacobs, Lewis 45
Jacobson, Harlan 184
James, David 121

Jane (1962) 226
Janie's Janie (1971) 42
Jarecki, Andrew 100
Jazz (2001) **105–6**
Jennings, Humphrey
   48–50, 196, 205
Jerusalem 79
Journey, The (1987)
   235
Julian, Joseph 177
Julien, Isaac 78
Jünger, Ernst 165
Jutra, Claude 182

Kael, Pauline 184
Katzenbach, Nicholas 41
Kaufman, Boris 8
Kaufman, Mikhail 8,
   134
Kennedy, John F. 39–41,
   86, 177–8
Kennedy, Robert F. 39–41
Kerensky, Alexander
   Fyodorovich 59
Kertész, André 170
Kiarostami, Abbas 35–6
Kieślowski, Krzystof 208,
   210
King, Allan 138–9
Kino-eye 135
Kino Pravda 135
Kinski, Klaus 76
Klein, Bonnie Sherr
   163–4
Koenig, Wolf 106
Komsomol (*Song of
   Heroes*) (1931) 151
Kon Tiki (1950) **107–9**
Kopple, Barbara 82–4,
   244
Kosma, Joseph 187

*Koyaanisqatsi: Life Out of
   Balance* (1982)
   110–11
Kozintsev, Grigori 59
Kracauer, Siegfried 17
Kroitor, Roman 120
Kuhle Wampe (1932)
   153, 170
Kuleshov, Lev 59
Kurt and Courtney (1998)
   87

LaFollette Civil Liberties
   Senate Committee
   147
Land without Bread see
   Las Hurdes
Lange, Dorothea 86,
   171
Lanzmann, Claude
   199–201, 208
Lassally, Walter 237
Last Waltz, The (1978)
   214, 244
Lawder, Standish 10,
   111, 149–50
LBJ (1968) 194
Leacock, Richard 32, 39,
   40, 44, 80–1, 83,
   124, 174, 177, 216,
   225
Leaves of Grass
   (Whitman) 128
Lee, Spike 91, 239–40
Lektionen in Finsternis
   see *Lessons in
   Darkness*
Lessons in Darkness
   (*Lektionen in
   Finsternis*) (1992)
   75, **112–13**

Let There Be Light (1946)
   114–15
Letter to Jane (1972) 23
Lettre de Sibérie (1958)
   190
Lévi-Strauss, Claude 47
Lewis, Mark 27–8
Library of Congress 12
*Life and Times of Rosie
   the Riveter, The*
   (1980) 84, **116–17**
Lipsett, Arthur 230–1
Listen to Britain (1942)
   48
Lisztomania (1975) 21
Little Dieter Needs to Fly
   (1997) 76
Litvak, Anatole 241
'Living Camera' 39
Living Theatre 121
Livingston, Jennie 167–8
London Can Take It
   (1940) 205
London Weekend
   Television 24
Lonely Boy (1962)
   118–20, 182
Looking for Langston
   (1989) 78
Lopez, Georges 56, 58
López Garcia, Antonio
   202–3
Lorentz, Pare 147, 171–2
Los Alamos Scientific
   Laboratories 12
Lost Lost Lost (1976)
   121–2, 216, 245
Lotte in Italia (1969) 23
Louisiana Story (1948)
   61, 132
Low, Colin 106

Lumière, Louis and
    Auguste 123–4
Lumière Programme
    (1895) 63, **123–5**

McBride, Jim 44–5
McElwee, Ross 19, 45,
    87, 183, 216–17,
    232
McLaren, Norman 230
MacLeish, Archibald 204
Mad Masters, The see
    Les Maîtres fous
Maddin, Guy 143–4
Madonna 225–6
Madonna: Truth or Dare
    see *Truth or Dare*
Mahler (1974) 22
Maîtres fous, Les (*The
    Manic Priests/The
    Mad Masters*)
    (1955) 32, 46,
    126–7
Makhmalbaf, Mohsen
    35–6
Maltin, Leonard 68
Mamber, Stephen 39
Man of Aran (1934) 61,
    99, **130–2**, 145
*Man with a Movie
    Camera* (1929) 8,
    16, 32, 59, 93,
    110, 128, 129,
    133–5, 144, 170,
    228
Manhatta (1921) 16,
    128–9, 147, 172
Manic Priests, The see
    Les Maîtres fous
Manufacturing Dissent
    (2007) 184

March of the Penguins
    (*La Marche de
    l'empereur*) (2005)
    136–7
Marche de l'empereur, La
    see *March of the
    Penguins*
Marey, Jules 72
Marker, Chris 15, 70,
    190
Married Couple, A (1969)
    138–9
Marshall, Gen. George C.
    241
Maysles, Albert 177
Maysles brothers 73–4,
    83, 176, 185–6,
    215, 243
Meet Marlon Brando
    (1966) 185
Mekas, Adolfas 121
Mekas, Jonas 121–2
Méliès, Georges 123
Melnyk, Debbie 184
Memory of Justice, The
    (1975) 31
Menschen am Sonntag
    see *People on
    Sunday*
Michael Moore 13,
    19–20, 83
Microcosmos (2003) 136
Mighty Wind, A (2003)
    214
Miller, Arthur 186
Millet, Jean-François
*Millhouse: A White
    Comedy* (1971) 102
*Minamata – kanja santo
    sono sekai* see
    Minamata

Minamata (*Minamata:
    The Victims and
    Their World*) (1971)
    140–2
Minh, Ho Chi 102,
    194
Misère au Borinage
    (1933) 96, 151
'mockumentary' 4, 44,
    214
Moi, un noir (*Me, a Black
    Man*) (1957) 32
Moindre des choses, La
    (1997) 57
Mon oncle Antoine
    (1971) 182
Mondrian, Piet 16
montage 16, 38, 48, 49,
    61, 67, 92, 93, 96,
    111, 116, 132, 143,
    153, 167, 219, 227,
    230, 231, 239, 240,
    246
Moore, Michael 19, 29,
    54, 86, 164, 183–4,
    232
Morin, Edgar 32–4, 55,
    87, 126, 176, 182,
    216
Morris, Errol 64–5, 87,
    211–12
Mourir à Madrid (1963)
    60
Movie, A (1958) 149
Movietone News 12
*Mr Death: The Rise and
    Fall of Fred A.
    Leuchter Jr* (1999)
    64, 87, 211
Mr Deeds Goes to Town
    (1936) 241

Mr Smith Goes to Washington (1939) 241

Murrow, Edward R. 85–6

Music Lovers, The (1970) 22

My Best Fiend (1999) 75

My Generation (2000) 84, 244

My Girlfriend's Wedding (1969) 45

My Winnipeg (2007) **143–4**

Mystère Picasso, Le (1956) 202

Nagra tape recorder 29, 32

Naked Spaces: Living Is Round (1985) 206

Nanook of the North (1922) 47, 130, **145–6**, 169, 227

Naqoyqatsi: Life as War (2002) 110

Narita: Peasants of the Second Fortress (1971) 142

National Endowment for the Arts 221

National Film Board of Canada 106, 118, 163, 181, 182, 230, 232–3

National Socialist Party 222

Native Land (1942) 102, **147–8**, 204

Natural History of the Chicken, The (2000) 27

Necrology (1971) 10, 111, **149–50**

Nema-ye nazdik see *Close-Up*

Neue Sachlichkeit 170

New Earth (*Nieuwe gronden*) (1934) **151–3**, 162, 204, 229

New Wave 70, 190

New York Film-Makers Co-operative 121

New York Newsreel 42

New York the Magnificent see *Manhatta*

news footage/newsreel 12, 25, 59, 64, 67, 78, 79, 100, 102, 103, 116, 117, 148, 165, 166, 194, 205, 239, 242

News from Home (1976) **154–7**, 245

Nichols, Bill 1, 5, 68

Nieuwe gronden see *New Earth*

Night and Fog see *Nuit et brouillard*

Night Mail (1936) 37, 158

No Direction Home (2005)

Nogent – Eldorado du dimanche (1929) 170

North Sea (1938) 37, 61, 99, **158–60**, 169

Not a Love Story: A Film about Pornography (1981) 116, **163–4**

nouvelle vague see French New Wave

Novyi Lef 59

Now (1965) 194

Nuit et brouillard (*Night and Fog*) (1955) **161–2**, 187, 199

Nykino 147, 172

O Lucky Man! (1973) 51

observational cinema/ documentary 56, 133, 149, 169, 185, 216, 219

October (1928) 59, 67, 228

Oeil de Vichy, L' (1993) 165

Ogawa Productions 142

Okuzaki, Kenzo 54

Olympia (1938) 224

On the Bowery (1957) 138

Onassis, Jacqueline Kennedy 73

One Flew over the Cuckoo's Nest (novel) (1962) 218

One Man's War (*La Guerre d'un seul homme*) (1982) **165–6**

One Plus One (*Sympathy for the Devil*) (1968) 23

Ônibus 174 see *Bus 174*

Ono, Yoko 122

Opéra Mouffe (1958) 70

Ophüls, Marcel 29–30

Oración (1984) 195

Ordres, Les (*The Orders*) (1974) 182

Padenie dinastii
  Romanovykh see
  The Fall of the
  Romanov Dynasty
Padilha, José 25–6
Paramount Studios 173
Paris Is Burning (1990)
  167–8
Parker, Dorothy 204
partie de campagne, Une
  (1936) 187
Passer, Ivan 181
Passion of Remembrance,
  The (1986) 78
Pays des sourds, Le
  (1992) 57
PBS *see* Public
  Broadcasting System
Peepshow (1956) 22
Pennebaker, D. A. 32,
  39, 41, 44, 51, 53,
  174–5, 177, 216,
  225
People on Sunday
  (*Menschen am*
  Sonntag) (1929)
  169–70
Perlov, David 216
Perrault, Pierre 182
Persistent and Finagling
  (1971) 232
Pétain, Maréchal 29, 165
Pett and Pott (1934) 37
Pfitzer, Hans 166
Philibert, Nicolas 56–8
Photographer see
  Fotoamator
Pigs or Meat: The Return
  to Flint (1992) 183
Pilger, John 86
Pincus, Ed 216

Pinochet, Augusto 14–15
Pittsburgh Trilogy 10
pixilation 64, 122, 134
Plow that Broke the
  Plains, The (1936)
  147, **171–3**
Point of Order (1963)
  29, 102
Pontecorvo, Gillo 66
Portrait of Jason (1967)
  174–6
post-modernism 3, 87,
  143, 168, 211
Powaqqatsi: Life in
  Transformation
  (1988) 110
Power and the Land
  (1940) 147, 205
Pravda (1969) 23
Prayer see *Oración*
Primary (1960) 23, 29,
  32, 39, 41, 42, 55,
  80, 83, 86, 93, 102,
  174, **177–8**, 179,
  186, 216, 219
Primate (1974) 57, 87,
  179–80
Privilege (1966) 235
Prokino 142
Psycho (1960) 28
Public Broadcasting
  System 89, 105
  106, 180, 183, 221
Pudovkin, Vsevolod 59,
  151
Punishment Park (1971)
  235
Pyramide humaine, La
  (*The Human*
  Pyramid) (1959) 32,
  237

Quince Tree Sun, The see
  El sol del membrillo
Quint City, USA (1963)
  80

Raquetteurs, Les (*The*
  Snowshoers) (1958)
  181–2
Rafferty, Kevin 13
Rafferty, Pierce 12
Rain (1929) 128, 151
Rainbow, The (1989) 22
Rat (1998) 27
Raymond, Alan and
  Susan 139
Rear Window (1954) 44
Reassemblage (1982)
  206
Red Badge of Courage,
  The (1951) 115
Red Skelton Show, The
  177
Redes (1935) 169
Redgrave, Michael 49
Reggio, Godfrey 111
Région centrale, La
  (1971) 149
Reichert, Julia 116
Reiner, Rob 214–15
Reisz, Karel 189, 236–8
Renoir, Jean 187
Report (1965) 149
Report from the
  Aleutians (1943)
  114
Rescue Dawn (2006) 76
Resnais, Alain 162, 187,
  199
Richardson, Robert 64
Riefenstahl, Leni 18,
  222–4, 242

Rien que les heures
   (1926) 16, 37, 128
Riggs, Marlon 167,
   220–1
River, The (1937) 147,
   172
Robeson, Paul 148
'rockumentary' 51,
   214–15, 225
Rodchenko, Alexander
   170
Roger and Me (1989)
   13, 19, 29, 83, 86,
   103, 164, **183–4**
Rogosin, Lionel 138
Rolling Stones 73, 215
Rosenbaum, Jonathan
   45
Rotha, Paul 196–8
Rouch, Jean 32–4, 55,
   61, 87, 126–7, 135,
   176, 182, 216, 237
Rouquier, Georges 57,
   61
Rubbo, Michael 232–3
Running Fence (1978)
   185
Rush to Judgment (1967)
   102
Rushdie, Salman 79
Russell, Ken 21–2
Russell, Patrick 3, 158
Russell, Shirley 21–2
*Russia of Nikolai II and
   Lev Tolstoy, The*
   (1928) 59
Ruttmann, Walter
   16–18, 110

*Sabotier du Val de Loire,
   Le* (1955) 63

Sad Song of Yellow Skin
   (1970) 232
Salesman (1969) 55, 83,
   185–6, 243
Salt of the Earth (1953)
   84
Sang des bêtes, Le (1949)
   187–9
Sankofa Film and Video
   Collective 78
Sans soleil (Sunless)
   (1983) 70, **190–3**
Sans toit ni loi (1985) 71
Saturday Evening Post 80
*Saturday Night and
   Sunday Morning*
   (1960) 238
Savage, Ann 143
Sayles, John 64
Schoedsack, Ernest B.
   107, 145, 227
Schönberg, Arnold 166
Schoonmaker, Thelma
   244
Schreker, Franz 166
Schüftan, Eugen 169
Scorsese, Martin 51, 64,
   214, 244
See It Now (CBS) 85
See You at Mao see
   British Sounds
Sense of Loss, A (1972)
   31
Shah Pahlevi 66–7
Sheeler, Charles 128–9,
   172
Sherman's March (1985)
   45, 216
Shipyard (1935) **196–8**
Shiranui Sea, The (1975)
   142

Shoah (1985) 29, 161,
   199–201, 208
Shock Corridor (1962)
   218
Shub, Esfir 29, 59–60,
   102
Shut Up & Sing (2006)
   84
Sicko (2007) 19
Sidran, Ben 89
Silent World, The (1956)
   136
Silva, Jorge Müller 15
Siodmak, Kurt 169
Siodmak, Robert 169
Six O'Clock News (1996)
   217
Skid Row (1956) 138
Skyscraper (1959) 174
Sloan's (c.1970) 155
Smallwood, Joey 232–3
Smith, Roger 183, 184
Snow, Michael 149, 155,
   202
Snowshoers, The see *Les
   Raquetteurs*
*Sobibor, Oct. 14, 1943,
   4 P.M.* (2001) 201
Socialist Realism 135
*sol del membrillo, El
   (The Quince Tree
   Sun/The Dream of
   Light)* (1992) 35,
   202–3
Solanas, Fernando
   Ezequiel 93
Soldier Girls (1981) 87
Solidarity 209
Song of Ceylon (1934)
   37
Sontag, Susan 224

Sorrow and the Pity, The
see *Le Chagrin et la
pitié*
South (1919) 107
South, The (1983) 203
Spain in Flames (1936)
205
Spanish Earth, The (1937)
99, 102, **204–5**
Spare Time (1939) 196
Spirit of the Beehive, The
(1973) 203
Spurlock, Morgan 83
*Standard Operating
Procedure* (2008)
64
Steiner, Ralph 172
Stirling, Geoff 232–3
Stone, Oliver 64
Storck, Henri 96, 151
Strand, Paul 128–9, 147,
169, 172
Strauss, Richard 166
Sucksdorff, Arne 27
Summer in Narita (1968)
142
Sunless see *Sans soleil*
Super Size Me (2004) 83
*Surname Viet Given
Name Nam* (1989)
206–7
Surrealism 8, 97, 143,
187, 188
Svilova, Yelizaveta 134
Sympathy for the Devil
see *One Plus One*
synch sound 32, 61,
132, 140, 177

talking heads 13, 221,
235

Talking Heads (1980)
208–10
Tarantino, Quentin 64
Target for Tonight (1941)
158
television news 12, 79
Thin Blue Line, The
(1988) 64, 87,
211–13
third cinema 92–3
This Is Spinal Tap (1984)
202, **214–15**
Thomson, David 190
Thomson, Virgil 172
Threads (1984) 235
Through the Olive Trees
(1994) 35
Time Indefinite (1994)
19, 43, 45, 87, 100,
183, **216–17**, 232
Time Inc. 39, 177
Time magazine 52
Times of Harvey Milk, The
(1984) 221
Titicut Follies (1967) 57,
87, 180, **218–19**
To Be and to Have see
Être et avoir
To Die in Madrid see
Mourir à Madrid
Tongues Untied (1990)
167, **220–1**
Torabi, Hossein 66–7
Tout va bien (1972) 23
Tracey, Linda Lee 163
Trauberg, Leonid 59
travelogue 97, 128, 145,
190
Treadwell, Timothy
75–7
Trinh T. Minh-ha 206

*Trip Down Memory Lane,
A* (1965) 230
Triumph des Willens see
Triumph of the Will
Triumph of the Will
(*Triumph des
Willens*) (1935) 18,
67, **222–4**, 242
Truth or Dare (1991)
225–6
Tsuchimoto, Noriaki 140
Tugwell, Rexford 171
Tunnel, The (1935) 242
Turin, Viktor 59
Turksib (1929) 59, 133,
153, **227–9**
TV Nation (1994) 19

UFA 222
Ulmer, Edgar G. 143,
169
Union Maids (1976) 116
United Mine Workers of
America 82, 83
United States Film Service
173, 205

Vagabonde see *Sans toit
ni loi*
Valentino (1977) 21
Van Dongen, Helen
204–5
Van Dyke, Willard 175
Varda, Agnès 70–2,
190
Vent d'est (1969) 23
Verdi, Giuseppe 113
vérité see cinéma vérité
Vernon, Florida (1982)
64
Vertigo (1958) 191

Vertov, Dziga 6, 16, 32, 34, 59, 110, 133–5, 168, 170, 228
Very Nice, Very Nice (1961) **230–1**
Vichy regime 29, 63, 165
Vigo, Jean 7–9
Vladimir et Rosa (1971) 23
voiceover (commentary) 42, 47, 61, 66, 81, 90, 105, 110, 112, 121, 126, 131, 147, 154, 173, 179, 181, 187, 190, 196, 198, 200, 206, 216–17, 219, 220, 237, 239, 241

Wagner, Richard 113
Waiting for Fidel (1974) **232–3**
Waiting for Godot (play) (1952) 232
Waiting for Guffman (1996) 214
Walden see *Diaries, Notes and Sketches*
War, The (2007) 105
War Game, The (1965) 13, 202, **234–5**
War of the Worlds (1938) 68
Warhol, Andy 118, 122
Warrendale (1970) 138
Watkins, Peter 13, 234–5

Watson, Paul 139
Watt, Harry 37, 158, 205
Wave, The see *Redes*
Wavelength (1967) 149
We Are Building (1929) 151
We Are the Lambeth Boys (1958) 32, **236–8**
Weinstein, Harvey 68
Welles, Orson 68, 205
When the Levees Broke (2006) **239–40**
Whitman, Walt 128, 129
Why We Fight: Prelude to War (1943) 114, 164, 171, 222, **241–2**
Wild Blue Yonder, The (2005) 112
Wild Man Blues (1997) 84
Wilder, Billy 169
Williams, Tennessee 73
Windt, Herbert 224
Winged Migration (2001) 136
Winston, Brian 198
Wiseman, Frederick 57, 87, 175, 179–80, 218–19
With Babies and Banners (1978) 116
women's movement 42, 116, 117

Wonder Ring, The (1955) 10
Wonderful World of Dogs, The (1990) 27
Wood, Jason 3
Woodstock (1970) 214, **243–4**
Word Is Out (1978) 221
Words for Battle (1941) 48
World at War (1974–5) 30
Wright, Basil 37
Wyler, William 114

Yanki, No! (1960) 178
Yoman (*Diary*) (1983) 216
Young Soul Rebels (1991) 78
Yuki yukite shingun see *The Emperor's Naked Army Marches On*

Zidane: A 21st Century Portrait (*Zidane: un portrait du 21ième siècle*) (2006) **245–7**
Zidane: un portrait du 21ième siècle see *Zidane: A 21st Century Portrait*
Zinnemann, Fred 169
Zuiderzee (1930) 151

List of Illustrations

While considerable effort has been made to correctly identify the copyright holders this has not been possible in all cases. We apologise for any apparent negligence and any omissions or corrections brought to our attention will be remedied in any future editions.

A Propos de Nice, Jean Vigo/Boris Kaufman; *Berlin: Symphony of a Great City*, Fox-Europa Film; *Chronique d'un été*, Argos-Films; *Crisis: Behind a Presidential Commitment*, Drew Associates; *A Diary for Timothy*, Crown Film Unit; *Dont Look Back*, © Leacock Pennebaker; *Être et avoir*, © Maïa Films/© Arte France Cinéma/ © Films d'Ici/© Centre National de Documentation Pédagogique; *Farrebique, ou les quatre saisons*, Écran Français; *Les Glâneurs et la glâneuse*, Ciné-Tamaris; *Grizzly Man*, © Lion Gate Films; *Harlan County USA*, Cabin Creek Films; *Hoop Dreams*, Kartemquin Films/KTCA-TV/Fine Line Features; *Housing Problems*, Arthur Elton/ E. H. Anstey; *Las Hurdes*, Luis Buñuel; *Kon-Tiki*, Ole Nordemar Artfilms; *Lonely Boy*, National Film Board of Canada; *Lumière programme: Demolition of a Wall*, Lumière; *Man with a Movie Camera*, VUFKU; *Man of Aran*, Gainsborough Pictures/ Gaumont-British Picture Corporation; *Minamata*, Higashi Productions; *New Earth*, CAPI; *News from Home*, Unité 3; *North Sea*, GPO Film Unit; *The Plow that Broke the Plains*, Resettlement Administration Film Unit; *Portrait of Jason*, Shirley Clarke/ Film-makers' Distribution Center; *Le Sang des bêtes*, Force et Voix de France/Fred Orain; *Sans soleil*, © Argos-Films; *Shipyard*, Gaumont-British Instructional/Orient Shipping Line/Vickers Armstrong; *Shoah*, Films Aleph/Historia Films; *Talking Heads*, Film Polski; *The Thin Blue Line*, © Third Floor Productions; *Triumph of the Will*, Nazionalsozialistische Deutsche Arbeiterpartei; *Turksib*, Vostok-Kino; *We Are the Lambeth Boys*, Graphic Films; *Zidane: A 21st Century Portrait*, © Anna Lena Films/ © Naflastrengir/© Love Streams Productions/© Arte France Cinéma.